MW01089394

ROMMEL
in Normandy

Field Marshal Rommel and the author.

ROMMEL
in Normandy

Reminiscences by Friedrich Ruge

Foreword by Lt. Gen. E. B. Roberts
Translated by Ursula R. Moessner

PRESIDIO PRESS
San Rafael, California & London, England

Published by Presidio Press
of San Rafael, California, and London, England,
with editorial offices
at 1114 Irwin Street, San Rafael, California

and simultaneously in England by Macdonald & Jane's

Originally published in Germany by
K. F. Koehler Verlag, Stuttgart

Library of Congress Cataloging in Publication Data

Ruge, Friedrich.
  Rommel in Normandy.

  Translation of Rommel und die Invasion.
  Includes index.
  1. World War, 1939–1945—Campaigns—France—Normandy.
2. Rommel, Erwin, 1891–1944. 3. World War,
1939–1945—Personal narratives, German. 4. Ruge,
Friedrich. 5. Normandy—History.
I. Title
D756.5.N6R813 1978   440.54'21   78-12928
ISBN: 0-89141-010-4

Printed in the United States of America

Contents

Foreword	ix
Preface	xiii
The Assignment	1
First Experiences in Denmark	11
Beginning in the West	25
The Work of the Staff	43
After Assuming Command	53
To the Mediterranean and to the Bay of Biscay	73
Working Out Details	85
At the New Headquarters	99
Progress and Opposition	113
Final Measures	145
The Landing	171
The Loss of Cherbourg	181
The Battle for Caen	199
The Breakthrough	217
Rommel's Death	245
Index	255

Illustrations

Maps

	following pg.
Inspection tours, Dec. 1943 to Jan. 1944	106
Inspection tours, Feb. to March 1944	106
Inspection tours, April to May 1944	168
Deployment of German divisions on D-day	168
German deployment in Normandy on D-day	168
Approach routes, landing areas, and potential airborne landings of Allies	179
Situation on evening of D-day	179
Situation until the breakthrough at Avranches	243
Situation after breakthrough at Avranches	243

Photographs

Rommel and the author	frontispiece
Obstacles and weapons	following page 51
Rommel and his troops	following page 197

Foreword

I have often been asked the question, "What does a general do in war and how is his day occupied in combat?" For those who would ask this question, Admiral Ruge's reminiscences on Rommel in Normandy give splendid insight into the multitude of details with which a top commander in combat is constantly confronted.

There is a long-established principle in military leadership which dictates that things will be done efficiently only when the leader visits units to ensure that plans, orders and instructions are understood by all and are being implemented in accordance with the commander's concept. So Rommel, day after day, spent long hours visiting the troops in whose hands rested the defense of Western Europe. One cannot read this book without being tremendously impressed with the meticulous effort Rommel made to "shore up" the flagging defenses in *Festung Europa*.

Admiral Ruge raises the issue of the conflict between the Wehrmacht High Command and Rommel on the strategy for defending against the impending Allied invasion on the coast of France. Rommel believed that the invasion forces would have to be defeated on the beaches. He was convinced, as later events were to prove, that if Allied troops were allowed to get ashore and establish a lodgment area, they would then be able to build up military strength of such magnitude that it would be impossible to thwart the invasion.

Conversely, the German High Command advocated a strategy based on defending the beaches primarily with fortress troops and holding back strong mobile reserves for a major counterattack after Allied invasion plans became known. This view probably came from the fact that German intelligence concerning Allied intentions was not clear. To be sure, they were certain that landings would occur somewhere on the coast of France and that at least some scale of effort would take place in Normandy; but because of skillful deception plans, the exact location of the main effort was unknown. Hitler was convinced that the main invasion would be in the Pas de Calais area; so believing, six divisions—three crack panzer divisions and three first-line mobile infantry divisions—were retained there. These troops were never released to Rommel, and they remained out of the battle during the crucial stages of the Normandy Invasion.

During this time, I was a battalion operations officer in the 501st Parachute Infantry Regiment of the 101st Airborne Division. This division, along with other U.S. and British airborne forces, was committed to land behind the coastal defenses in Normandy, to neutralize gun positions and strong points controlling the exits from the beach, and so to assist the invading forces coming over the beaches. During the critical time of the early landings, if the panzer units in the general reserve had been released to Rommel, as he so urgently requested, they most certainly would have had a profound effect on the Invasion.

Admiral Ruge also makes the point that Rommel's plans for coastal defenses had not been implemented completely. My observations on the ground in the early morning hours of fighting on D-day confirmed this fact. In many areas the defenses had not been constructed properly or were only partially completed. The anti-airborne obstacles in particular were less than effective.

Admiral Ruge's account conveys the impression that although Rommel had been given the task of thwarting the Allied invasion of the coast of France, he was not given the freedom of action or control of the forces needed to do the job. Unity of command was lacking. The German High Command did not seem to have sufficient confidence in Rommel. Although he was an early favorite of Hitler's and had moved up in rank rapidly after his successes in North Africa, Rommel probably was not fully accepted by the High Command. He may have been regarded as an "outsider," a somewhat unwelcome latecomer to the ranks of his contemporaries—the senior Junker generals in the Wehrmacht. This may explain the complicated command situation that was allowed to exist in France, and which contributed so greatly to the German defeat in Normandy.

Rommel in Normandy is a very important contribution to the literature of World War II. It will interest any military man, particularly one who aspires to high command and to perfection of leadership technique. Rommel was unquestionably one of the great captains of warfare. The tactics and strategy he perfected in North Africa provide a textbook of knowledge in the art of defensive-offensive warfare conducted with limited means and over wide areas. In Normandy, had Rommel been given command of all the German forces in the invasion area, and had he been given freedom of action in planning and conducting the defense, the outcome in June 1944 could well have been different.

Ruge has written a book about Rommel the soldier, and, of equal importance, he has given us an intimate portrait of Rommel the man.

Lt. Gen. E. B. Roberts
U.S. Army, Retired

Preface

*T*he success of the combined British-American invasion at Normandy
in June 1944 had the strongest influence on the Second World War and
the destiny of Europe for the subsequent decades. The landed armies
tied down and crushed the most powerful German divisions and for themselves directly and for Soviet-Russia indirectly opened the road to the
center of Europe. The large landing operation sealed the fate of National
Socialism and the German Wehrmacht. Because of its special significance, the Invasion has been treated in many books (a succession of
books), some seen from the viewpoints of the statesman (Churchill), the
political historian (Chester Wilmot), the generals (Eisenhower, Montgomery), participants on many levels, and of professional study groups
as well (Cross Channel Attack, U.S. Army).

Around the most outstanding figure on the German side, Field Marshal
Erwin Rommel, a whole literature has already sprung up. With the exception of Speidel's book *Invasion 1944*, most of them center on Rommel's leadership as commander of a division in the French campaign of
1940 and especially as commander in chief of the army in North Africa
from 1941 to 1943. Relatively little has so far been written about Rommel's plans for the defense against the Invasion in 1944 and about their
origin. The purpose of this book is primarily to give information on this
subject. It will show how Rommel handled his assignment when he received orders to examine the defenses of northwestern Europe, how he
employed his staff, the problems he faced, what he achieved, where

weaknesses and opposition existed and finally why it was not possible to parry the Invasion and if indeed such possibilities existed at all.

It is risky to write memoirs, intended to have historical value, a decade after the events from memory. This is especially true of events which in the meantime have been treated with bias in books, in the press and in so-called factual accounts.

The following pages treat Rommel's and his staff's work from the beginning of his assignment in November 1943 to Rommel's wounding on July 17, 1944, and several episodes from his personal life afterwards using not only the personal reminiscences of the author, who from November 1943 to August 1944 served as naval advisor to the staff of Army Group B (Field Marshal Rommel), but utilizing also the following documentation:

War Diary of Army Group B (cited as KTB).
"Daily Reports" Rommel, key words relating to his activities and thoughts, often only a few lines a day, written almost daily (cited as TBR).
The author's personal notes which starting on December 20, 1943, he recorded in shorthand almost daily (cited as PAV).

These three sources are a good combination. In addition I have used a number of letters, orders and reports. Together they make it possible to describe the events before and during the Invasion from the vantage point of Rommel's headquarters. If retrospective knowledge has been used, a special indication is made. The book does not claim to be a comprehensive description and critique of the Invasion, but instead is a contribution to the history of this time span and of the general on the German side who will always command a prominent place in our military history. The numerous details are intended as stones in the mosaic of the great battle which at some future time will be put together by a skillful hand.

The book was started in Tübingen in 1955. About three-quarters of it were finished when in 1956 the author went to Bonn. Here it remained unfinished for almost two years because of other obligations and was finally completed during vacation in the conviction that the conclusions to be drawn from it will be of value to the present situation.

Bonn, April 1959   F. Ruge

F. Ruge

The Assignment

The military situation in the summer of 1943 was tense. The previous four years of war had brought surprising and brilliant military successes in the war with Poland, in the Norway/Denmark operation, in the campaign against France, in North Africa, in the Balkans, and against Russia, as well as in cruiser and submarine warfare. The momentum gained by these successes, however, was insufficient to carry out the invasion of the British Isles, and was not exploited to drive Great Britain, Germany's main enemy, out of its position in the Mediterranean. In Russia, severe setbacks occurred during the winters of 1942 and 1943. North Africa could not be held and was completely lost by the spring of 1943, due to the large Anglo-American landings in November 1942, and because of superior Allied air and sea power. Simultaneously, enemy air power and radar paralyzed the U-boat war, blunting the only weapon that could endanger the enemy's sea power. The 1943 summer offensive against the Russian armies—supplied with American materiel—failed; concurrently, the Allies landed in Sicily and endangered the existence of an exhausted Italy. Mussolini fell, and the Badoglio government started secret negotiations with the Allies in order to find a way out of the hopeless situation.

In early September 1943 Italy changed sides and the Allies landed in Salerno. Field Marshal Rommel's quick action secured northern Italy and freed the rear of the Supreme Commander South, Field Marshal Kesselring. The enemy's failure to use his undisputed sea power for further amphibious operations enabled Kesselring to establish a defensive line

1

across the peninsula north of Naples. By August the Germans had withdrawn from Sicily with few casualties. In late September and early October they evacuated Sardinia and Corsica with similar smoothness. Transported to the mainland, these troops and their supplies slowed the enemy advance and ultimately forced a complete standstill at the Garigliano and the Sangro Rivers.

Meanwhile, in northern Italy Rommel had taken measures against an expected enemy landing. When the landing, which, especially during the first days, had excellent prospects for success, did not take place, Rommel was no longer needed there. Simultaneously, the indications of a major landing in northwest Europe increased: strong Anglo-American forces in southern Britain were in an advanced state of readiness.

Should they succeed in gaining a foothold on the European continent, they would force the already overburdened German Wehrmacht (armed forces) to fight on yet a third front. It could not be expected that their strength would be sufficient for this task. A complete defeat was certain. It was therefore of the utmost importance to prevent the Allies from establishing a beachhead. Until this time, appropriate defense measures had only been taken on a local level and without the aid of a comprehensive or general plan. No one had considered the overall problem of western Europe's defense. To analyze this situation, the OKW, *Oberkommando der Wehrmacht* (High Command of the Armed Forces), in early November 1943 assigned Rommel to check the defenses of the threatened coasts.

For this task, Rommel needed to supplement his staff with a high-ranking naval officer, and he requested me. His chief of staff, Major General Gause, an East Prussian with a dry sense of humor, had met me in the spring of 1943 at my headquarters, *Duropane* (hard bread), near Rome. We understood each other at once and soon discovered that we shared the same opinions about the confused and mismanaged situation. They did not coincide with those of the higher-ups. Due to my transfer in August 1943 to the officers' reserve (*Führerreserve*), I was ready for immediate service.

In the navy nothing was constant except change. During peacetime, a command seldom lasted longer than two or three years. This had its advantages, for these changeovers were often connected with a change of station and forced all officers to adapt themselves to new situations, both professional and human. An enlightened personnel policy guided the selection process and, in accordance with certain principles in command changes, an officer was advanced according to his abilities. This system was intended to prevent a person from becoming excessively one-sided or bureaucratic and was surely one of the reasons why pedantry seldom developed in the navy. It was more concerned with personal leadership than with personnel administration.

During the war, the navy increased in size to such an extent that, together with its many new tasks, these command changes became increasingly more numerous and unexpected. The flexibility one had previously attained in adapting to new situations was of great value. I realized this in early November 1943 when, quite unexpectedly, I was ordered to the staff of Army Group B (Field Marshal Rommel).

This was something completely new, because a naval officer had generally only cursory contact with the "Great Army" or the "Eighty-fivers" (a term employed by the navy because before the First World War, a battalion of the 85th Regiment was stationed in Kiel). As a rule, there were liaison officers to the coastal corps commands during peacetime but, due to personnel problems, the practice stopped almost completely after 1933. During the war, several naval officers served in the OKW, and liaison officers worked at the Army High Command, Luftwaffe High Command and army commands along the coast.

That did not indicate a total ignorance of army matters, since after the First World War many commissioned and noncommissioned naval officers had gained land war experience while serving in a free corps, a brigade, or in Kurland. After 1920, in addition to training on coastal batteries, the coastal defense units (later known as navy artillery units) trained in the field during a yearly exercise period at army facilities. In general, one can surmise that the transfer of thinking from sea to land is evidently somewhat easier than the reverse process.

Unofficial relations between the army and the navy were generally very good. In many cases a regular cartel system of cooperation existed between army and navy units; for instance, between the Ortelsburger Jäger and the First Mine Sweeper Flotilla, with which I entered Pillau in the fall of 1933.

The war gave me frequent opportunities for official and unofficial contact with army and air force staffs and units, especially during the operations in the Bay of Danzig during the war with Poland; during the preparations for "Operation Sealion" (the unexecuted invasion of Britain); in the garrisons of mine sweeper flotillas along the coasts of Holland, Belgium, and France; and finally, from February until August 1943 in Italy, during the final battle for Tunisia, the Allied landing on Sicily, and the subsequent evacuation of that island. I had never worked, however, inside an army staff. Aware of the differences in training and viewpoints, I approached the new assignment with reservations.

In the early morning of November 30, 1943, I arrived in Verona via the Brenner Pass, after traveling through the night huddled in the corner of a crowded railroad compartment. Rommel was on the road until evening. I stayed with his naval liaison officer in San Vigilio on Lake Garda. Towards evening I drove to the Field Marshal's quarters, the Villa Canossa, at the eastern end of the lake. He had not arrived yet, but he returned as I was removing my coat and a warm and manifestly unmilitary muffler. I reported in this irregular attire, but it seemed unimportant, since Rommel was apparently less interested in the uniform than the man inside it. Rommel appeared smaller than I had imagined him, rather serious, full of energy, and very natural.

Following a simple dinner with the immediate staff, Rommel and Gause informed me about our assignment. It derived from Führer Directive 51 and ordered:

1. The study of the defense readiness on the coast occupied by us, and the presentation of proposals concluded from this study.
2. Drafting of operational studies for the purpose of attacks against an enemy who had landed in western Europe. The operational studies were to consider the following questions, derived from a thorough study of the deployment, mobility, and combat conditions in the western sectors, with particular attention to these questions:
   a. Organization, structure, command, and assembly of all the armed forces for the attack, namely:
      1. The major reserves.
      2. The combat groups from unthreatened coastal sections.
      3. The combat groups from reserve divisions, schools, and military installations, and the Waffen SS located in the rear areas.
      4. The assembly of all combat-ready forces from all branches of the armed forces located in Germany.
   b. Planning and supply for all armed forces and Waffen SS units earmarked for action.
   c. Battle command in the operational area, with special attention to the possibilities for German and enemy panzer operations.

At first glance, this order seemed perfectly clear and unequivocal. It did not, however, answer the question as to how and when the transition from the theoretical plans for deployment and operational readiness to the state of combat command should occur—that is, the stage from inspector to commander in chief. For the moment Rommel had no command authority in the designated sectors. This point was not particularly emphasized during our conversation. For the time being we worked on the assignment's technical problems, which we had to resolve ourselves.

Written reports, always popular in official life for reference and support during moments of uncertainty, did not exist. The assignment was a new one for the German Wehrmacht, since, up to this point, they had not spent much thought on seaborne landings and defenses against such landings. During the First World War they had relied, and rightfully so, on the coastal defenses along the harbors and river estuaries and trusted in their powerful battle fleet to endanger any landing in its radius of action.

The Flanders coastline was short enough to permit its complete fortification and substantial garrisoning. Although the British had planned a landing at this location, together with a thrust of fast ships into the Baltic that could result in a landing, they only risked isolated attacks to block the ports of Ostende and Zeebrügge. The Germans undertook major landings only on Oesel in October 1917 and on the Aland islands and in Finland during the winter of 1917–18 against an already shaken enemy.

The Allies' major landings in the Dardanelles ultimately failed but gained them extensive knowledge, which they undoubtedly used to their best advantage. They could no longer be expected to fritter away their forces as they had done at that time; instead one had to reckon with the use of a concerted overpowering thrust combined with vastly improved means for a rapid landing. During the First World War, warships carried the assault troops who then were landed by boats under the protection of the ships' guns—a time-consuming and complicated procedure. It had originated during the time of the sailing ships, although the use of steam-powered boats and motorboats had modernized it a bit. The mass of the troops then followed on large transports and, with the help of larger boats, via makeshift landing stages, reached land. It took several days to land a single division on Oesel.

After the First World War the German army and navy, only 115,000 men strong, were too weak to effectively defend our extensive coastlines. Defensive measures against landings were limited to naval artillery on the North Sea and near Swinemünde and Pillau. Between the wars, neither the army nor the navy occupied themselves with the problems of amphibious landings on an enemy coast. The occasional small landing exercises were due to the initiative of local commanders.

The Second World War necessitated an early landing operation on a major scale in Norway. The number of troops constituting the first wave, however, was negligible—2,000 men in Narvik, 1,700 in Trondheim, 1,900 in Bergen, 1,100 in Christiansand, and 2,000 in Oslo—used together with air landing troops (as in Stavanger). Almost without fail, the troops reached land via undamaged harbors taken from the enemy in surprise actions. It was only during the preparations for "Sealion" that the military had to be concerned with the multitude of questions regarding a major landing on an open beach. They sought makeshift solutions since landing craft specifically designed for that purpose were not then available. Since the operation never materialized, we gained only limited experience.

The first to design craft and procedures specifically for a systematic, fast, and large-scale landing on an open beach were the Japanese. They surprised the experts in 1937 when, during their operations in China, they used newly developed landing craft designed for rapid unloading on the beaches. These craft displaced approximately fifteen tons and had flat bottoms, protected propellers, and bow ramps. They approached the beaches at right angles and dropped the ramp in such a way that the troops (up to 120 men per boat), light tanks, and trucks could reach land through the shallow water in the shortest time possible. Then they withdrew stern first for reloading from larger transports waiting in deeper waters.

This procedure was, of course, not suitable for every type of coast; cliffs and steep banks were difficult to negotiate. Nonetheless, even rocky coasts have surprisingly numerous spots with sandy beaches.

In the meantime, the Americans and the British had improved the Japanese craft and refined the Japanese methods, as demonstrated so clearly in their successful large-scale landings in North Africa, on Sicily and near Salerno. During the surprise attack on Dieppe in August 1942, the English left a complete collection of their various landing craft on the beaches, thereby giving us a good idea as to their qualities.

It was to my advantage that I had participated in the Oesel operation in October 1917 on a large torpedo boat which landed a company, and that shortly after the British attacks on Saint-Nazaire and Dieppe I had the opportunity to inspect the local conditions very thoroughly. Except for part of the coast of southern France, I was familiar with almost all the harbors and the coast to be inspected. During mine laying, mine sweeping, and convoy tasks I had frequently entered and left all the ports and sailed along the coast. This first-hand knowledge of the area was now very helpful.

We touched on all these points more or less extensively while examining the assignments according to Führer Directive 51. Rommel then summarized everything. He voiced his opinions and primary intentions very clearly, and, as I left for San Vigilio, I knew precisely what I had to do. On the whole, the Field Marshal was reserved, and not at all pretentious. I gained the impression that he possessed great objectivity and common sense, coupled with firmness, and I believed that we could work well together. With regard to Gause, I was certain of this.

Following our discussion, I was to fly to Berlin to receive the necessary instructions on the naval war staff's views, the status of the naval reserves, and the necessary naval maps, handbooks, tide tables, and admiralty staff handbooks. On the evening of December 2, I was to rejoin the staff at Silkeborg in northern Jutland. Until then, Rommel wanted to wind up his affairs in Italy. Undoubtedly, if an appropriate order from the OKW had arrived, our work in France, the prospective center of the expected attack, could have started five weeks earlier, in the middle of November. These five weeks would have advanced the work considerably, especially since during the winter time enemy aircraft disturbed the transport of fortification material far less than during the spring.

Early the next morning a car took me to an airport about one hour away. From there a plane transported me to Munich, where I had to find a way to continue my trip. The Luftwaffe (air force) personnel at Munich-Riem airport treated the single traveler with their usual kindness and consideration. After a few hours of waiting, I could continue the flight to Berlin on the plane of a Luftwaffe staff for air defense. It was an He 111, and, because the passengers included the commander and his complete staff, was considerably crowded. I found a seat far back in the windowless rear of the plane. It didn't disturb me, since a low cloud cover in the north prevented any sightseeing, and I was well supplied with English detective stories anyway. Just as the plane started to lift off, somebody shouted that they had forgotten the radio operator. He was collected, but as we discovered during the approach to Berlin, his presence did not make much difference, since his electronic equipment had ceased to function shortly after our departure from Munich. The news alarmed the whole staff; everybody started to navigate, and to fly by dead reckoning, followed by various attempts to drop below the clouds. Several times the plane ascended back into the clouds with a deep hum when, instead of the expected airport, inhospitable areas with houses and high chimneys appeared on the ground. Finally we landed. The airport we reached, however, was at the other end of the city.

During the following days I obtained the necessary books, maps, and other materials from the various offices of the Navy High Command. Simultaneously, I consulted the naval war staff experts regarding their opinions, especially with respect to time and location of possible landings, distribution of our forces, mine situation, current weapons development and whatever else seemed necessary. Unfortunately, I could not complete my activities. During the first heavy air attacks on Berlin (November 23 and 24) sections of the command buildings on Tirpitzufer burned out, forcing the Navy High Command to move to Ebverswalde. Because of the resulting limited work capacity, nobody had time to answer questions.

The fire also had destroyed my carefully collected data. I acquired substitutes from the mine sweepers in Cuxhaven. At the same time, I informed myself from the same source about the coastal artillery's condition. Since the beginning of the war, naval coastal artillery units had sent complete batteries to the occupied coasts as well as trained individual replacements. The home front at that earlier time had seemed completely secure. Now the situation was vastly different.

On the Helgoland Bight, to be sure, stood many antiaircraft guns, but only the bare minimum of the necessary heavy and medium batteries; specifically:

1 305mm and 1 170mm battery at Helgoland
1 280mm and 1 150mm battery at Borkum
1 150mm battery at Wangerooge
1 150mm battery at Sylt
1 150mm battery at Cuxhaven

In spite of these contributions which had bled the coast defense almost white, the navy had made it possible to release two 210mm batteries and two 150mm batteries for the defense of France. This contribution, however, exhausted the navy's heavy artillery.

Vice-Admiral Schuerlen, commanding admiral of the Helgoland Bight (killed in action as commander of a navy infantry division in 1945), briefed me on the situation in his command area and showed as a practical example the crew of a 150mm battery in Cuxhaven. Half of the crew consisted of reservists, mostly older gentlemen with civilian airs, and a very few young active specialists. Most of the rest was made up of men from "Volksliste 3," people of German descent from occupied territories who could only partially understand the German language, naval auxiliaries, older high school boys who were supposed to attend school while in service, Russians, and even antiaircraft women who operated the fire control equipment. All together this crew presented a motley and unusual picture and clearly indicated the scarcity of manpower. Surprisingly, everything worked reasonably well, but it was no surprise that, here or there, failure occurred.

First Experiences in Denmark

*R*ight on schedule, on the evening of December 2, I rejoined Rommel's staff at Silkeborg. The area was familiar to me. In August 1939, I had been with my command boat T196 for several days in Vejle, north of the Little Belt (area between the Jutland Peninsula and Funen). I had spent a quiet weekend at the summer house of the Danish commander of the mine sweepers, in a way a colleague of mine. However, the serenity of this wonderful forest and lake area with mild summer weather had already been overshadowed by the threat of war. Now it was winter and the situation appeared very bleak.

The assignment for Denmark was:

1. Inspection of the existing defense measures.
2. Study for the counterattack against an enemy landing with locally available forces.

December 3, 1943, was pretty much filled with lectures and meetings. General von Hannecken, the Wehrmacht commander in Denmark opened the day at 0800 with a general lecture. Lectures from the commanders of the navy (Admiral Wurmbach), Luftwaffe, the command of Army Coast Artillery Regiment 180, and the director of the Organization Todt (Civilian Building Corps) followed in short succession. After a quick lunch, Lieutenant General Wolff, commander of Air Force Administrative Area XI, gave a lecture in the afternoon.

The meetings lasted until evening. The overall impression gained was that Denmark's defense left much to be desired. On paper, six divisions were stationed on Jutland, with one training regiment and ten convalescent battalions on the larger islands. Of the six divisions, however, one was in the process of formation, three were grenadier training divisions, one was a panzer reserve division with only a few tanks of diverse types, and the last, a Luftwaffe field division, was undergoing retraining in bicycling. In reality Denmark had no combat-ready divisions. The Luftwaffe had a small number of fighters, bombers, and training planes; the navy had almost only defensive forces, such as mine sweepers, convoy and patrol boats—which did not, all together, constitute an imposing military force.

On the other hand, it was improbable that the main thrust of the attack would be directed at Denmark. The area was outside the range of the England-based fighter planes, and without strong fighter protection, a large-scale landing would be a precarious undertaking.

Uncertainty became manifest as to the direction of the enemy's attack. This complicated the defender's task considerably. We wanted to be strong at every possible location, yet it was only natural that every local commander considered his own area especially endangered.

At 2100, we drove to the staff train which had arrived in the meantime. I received a spacious sleeping room in a parlor car that had apparently belonged to a Balkan potentate. Gause's room and a large briefing room, probably the former dining room, filled the rest of the car. The Cyrillic script remained a mystery to us, so much so that we never unravelled the secret of the restroom's bell, which could be pulled in a sitting position.

During the night the train moved to Esbjerg, the only large port on Jutland's west coast. Before 1914, the British had made plans to land on that spot. Should they plan an operation against Denmark at all, Esbjerg would be a likely target.

An inspection of troops and positions had been scheduled for the morning of December 4, 1943, at 0800. The Field Marshal took breakfast with his staff in the dining car of the special train. I was already seated when he arrived at the table which I shared with him. He had a curious red spot on his face, and I asked him about its origin. "The spot always appears after I have used hot water," he replied. Rommel enjoyed the idea that we would now know when he had washed his face. Many a superior officer would not have seen the comical side of this situation.

At 0755 everybody was still in the dining car. At the stroke of 0800, however, I suddenly found myself alone. With a hasty jump I was able to catch a place in the last car of the long convoy. One got used to Rommel's tempo quickly; his absolute punctuality, his speed, and his efficient utilization of time were rather pleasant.

The first destination was the fortified zone around Esbjerg. Rommel had informed everyone that the work and duties should continue despite his visit; only local commanders reported to him. The majority of the defenses, mostly field entrenchments, were not especially impressive. Where a position was built according to fortification specifications, the many cubic feet of concrete stood in crass disproportion to the few light guns or even machine guns behind it. The best part of the defenses was a 200mm naval coastal battery.

During the afternoon we crossed to the island of Fanö, which dominated the entrance to the port of Esbjerg. Following a meal from the field kitchen, we watched a landing exercise in the northern part of the island. The completely flat, wide beach, excellently suited for amphibious and airborne landings, made the strongest impression. Here the concept of the obstacles against air landings and of the offshore obstacles first originated, for it became frighteningly clear that large numbers of men and materiel could be concentrated on such positions in a short time both from the sea and the air, and could quickly move inland.

Obviously something had to be done to prevent a sudden *coup de main* on the island, since whoever possessed it dominated the entrance to the port of Esbjerg. Since weapons and manpower were in short supply, the installation of obstacles on the wide beach seemed the best method to impede any landing of gliders. Wooden posts driven into the ground would have been ideal, but they were scarce in Denmark, a country known for its shortage of wood. One had to use the available local resources as much as possible. This led to the idea of installing the so-called Czech hedgehogs on the beach. They were tank obstacles consisting of three steel beams, each approximately one meter long and bolted together in the middle at right angles. They dated back to the beginnings of antitank defense, and modern tank forces condescendingly smiled at them. In the interior, the hedgehogs were useless, but imbedded between posts on the beaches, they could make a landing more difficult.

This spawned the thought to use them in water just deep enough to prevent their visual detection. This was not difficult, because the tidal change (the difference of the water level between ebb and flood tide) was less than one meter, in contrast to the mouth of the Elbe River where it was three meters, and at Normandy with a nine-meter difference. It was clear that the Czech hedgehogs would certainly not deal a deadly blow to the landing craft. But it could be expected that the sharp corners would rip holes in the bottom of small boats when they passed directly over these obstacles, and render them unusable for some time.

From this basic idea a sizeable number of other thoughts developed which subsequently led to extensive work in the west. By this time differences of opinion regarding the value of the offshore obstacles had developed, since various persons had serious doubts about their effectiveness. It should be pointed out, however, that these obstacles caused the enemy considerable headaches, forcing them to postpone the landing to the unfavorable time of low tide. In addition, the first landing wave had to make room in their already limited number of landing craft for special demolition squads (Chester Wilmot, *Struggle for Europe*, p. 194). The British traced most of their losses suffered during the actual landing to these obstacles (*Operation Neptune*, p. 151).

The days between December 5 and 12 were taken up with the inspection of the defensive installations along the entire west coast of Jutland, from Esbjerg via the heavy battery Hanstholm up to Skagen and along the eastern coast down to Frederikshavn. The daily schedule was almost always the same: In the morning the special train had moved to that day's point of departure. At 0800, which at this time of the year in Denmark coincided with the daybreak, the automobile convoy departed. The inspections continued until 1600 (dusk), interrupted only by lectures and a short lunch break.

The lunch was to be delivered from a field kitchen, but this was not always done, much to Rommel's annoyance. He was displeased by the complacent occupation life in this fertile land blessed with much nourishing food. At night we returned to the special train, which in the meantime had changed location. Immediately we analyzed the day's activities.

On the morning of December 9 it was the turn of the major Aalborg air base, the Luftwaffe field division, and the panzer reserve division, which was stationed in the interior of Jutland. That afternoon the Field Marshal and his immediate staff flew from Grove airport (middle Jutland) to Copenhagen for a tea with General von Hannecken and a dinner with Reichs Commissioner Dr. Best. These were by no means purely social visits, but included extensive discussions which rounded out the broad picture.

On the next morning we drove along the "Danish Riviera," the eastern shores of Seeland, to Kronborg Castle near Helsingör, which dominates the strait and is one of Europe's most beautiful places. The ghost of Hamlet had such a strong effect that he even captured a spot in Rommel's otherwise *very* short and sober daily reports. After watching a parade of the Copenhagen guard battalion, we flew back to Grove and reached the special train in Silkeborg shortly after 1600. This concluded the inspection tour. The report for the OKW on the state of Denmark's defenses, together with new proposals, was drafted at once.

The reports of the inspecting experts, who had sorted out a myriad of impressions during their tours, served as the basis for the draft. Through the daily discussions, in which the personality and experience of Rommel were always prominent, we already had formed clear ideas on how to tackle the problems of the defense. It was also evident that in view of the weakness of the occupation forces, which could receive hardly any support from the Luftwaffe and the navy, only partial solutions and stopgap measures could be applied under the best of circumstances.

The most logical measure, which every thinking soldier would have chosen, would have been to employ strong panzer units supported by powerful, tactical air power in a counterattack. However, this choice was not practicable here, because these units were simply not available on such short notice. The majority of the panzer divisions and Stuka squadrons were overcommitted in a gruelling battle on the excessively long eastern front. First-class, combat-experienced units had been senselessly expended in Tunisia and Stalingrad, and a smaller number deployed in Italy; France contained mostly units under training and regrouping. The only possible solution was to utilize even the most insignificant tactical and technical possibilities and from a considerable number of expediencies create something tolerably effective.

Out of this situation came Rommel's basic concept, articulated in the simple sentence: "The main battle line will be the beach." This meant that the defensive line should be as far forward as possible, to catch the enemy during his most vulnerable moment—during the actual landing and shortly thereafter. This theory was based on the knowledge that the dynamics of a military breakthrough on land differ from those of an amphibious sea landing, which actually constitutes a breakthrough as well—from the sea through the front of the coastal defenses. During a land battle, the enemy's offensive strength and impetus is strongest at the beginning of the operation. The momentum then decreases more or less rapidly, depending on the resistance encountered or the terrain difficulties. This leads frequently to a moment of weakness, which the defender's available reserves may use for a counterattack. Because of this, the concept of reserves positioned in the rear has always played a major part in a land war.

This is different during an amphibious landing, since the major moments of weakness occur during the actual landing and shortly thereafter. If the attacker successfully overcomes this moment, he usually forms a beachhead, that is, a defensive ring around his landing points. With enough troops and materiel supplied from the sea, he can achieve operational freedom with a "normal" breakthrough. Since the sea route is more efficient for mass transport than the land route, he who dominates the sea can consolidate his combat forces in a beachhead more quickly than his landbound adversary, provided that the unloading proceeds quickly.

Based upon his experiences in North Africa with the great defensive strength of English troops against panzer attacks, Rommel believed that it would not be possible to break up the enemy's beachheads again, especially since the German counterattacks would certainly lack the necessary air support. In addition, Allied air superiority would render rapid and timely panzer operations impossible. Rommel repeatedly indicated that in September 1942, his panzer force in North Africa, attempting to break through the El Alamein positions, was "nailed to the ground" by enemy air power for three days, although his own Luftwaffe was not much weaker. Since the power ratio in the air was now much less favorable, he considered it an impossibility—and future events would prove him correct—to move large units during the day without heavy losses. He expected that operational forces would be destroyed on the approach march.

Of all the German commanders, Rommel had gathered the most comprehensive knowledge of fighting against the British. From personal experience, he alone knew the progress they had made in tactics and weapons from 1940 to 1943. Friend and foe acknowledged his masterly knowledge of mobile warfare. Nothing would have been more probable than that Rommel now would have sought the solution in the same tactics.

However, he soberly judged the power ratio, expressed not so much in the number of men, that is, divisions (which OKW liked to use), but instead in their mobility, and in the number and quality of weapons, especially airplanes, armor and antitank weapons. In addition he made full use of his own experiences and came to the conclusion that, in view of these circumstances, a German counterattack against an Anglo-American beachhead would not be successful if, after the amphibious landing, the enemy had a few days' time to consolidate their position.

The result was for him the urgent necessity to give up the classical method of counterattack, and to oppose the enemy with all available means during the actual landing. He saw this possibility via a wide, flexible defensive belt directly on the coast, with the infantry in numerous strong points, protected by extensive mine fields. The lack of depth, which many critics objected to at once, was to be compensated for with an expansion toward the sea by means of the offshore obstacles and mines, and toward the land by putting all available panzer forces closely behind the defensive belt. Fundamentally this defensive plan originated as a result of the Danish inspection tour; details were later added in France.

During the inspection tours the following points had been noted in particular:

a. *A unified basic concept or idea for the defense did not yet exist.* The divisions had started to construct field defenses, sometimes near the coast, sometimes more distant, as the responsible commander judged the situation. Understanding of the impact of a major landing did not exist in all cases. Frequently one heard the uncertain hope of holding the enemy until reinforcements arrived and then shoving him back.

b. *The measures for defending the few large ports had been taken according to clear plans, although they had not been accomplished in every case.* These measures were based on the knowledge gained during the British raids in France. This meant that the batteries, which had been erected to protect the harbor, would be incorporated within the defensive zone. In Dieppe they had been located outside, a circumstance that enabled the enemy to eliminate them in a surprise attack.

c. *The commanding officers and the commanders of the Wehrmacht's different service branches apparently had good personal relations.* It was, however, clearly noticeable that the cooperation at the highest command level was inadequate. Consequently the three branches of the Wehrmacht followed different directives. This resulted, for instance, in a situation where several naval batteries or

Luftwaffe radars were placed in front of the infantry positions that were actually supposed to protect them. The authority of the Wehrmacht commander in Denmark was not sufficient to stop mistakes of this kind.

d. *No agreement had been reached regarding the basic principles of placing the artillery on the coast.* Probably nobody had made the attempt. Even later in France this was only partly resolved.

The navy was of the opinion that only by direct sighting methods would they be sufficiently successful against targets moving on the water. Therefore, the navy erected its batteries directly on the coast, accepting the risk that they would be taken under direct fire from the sea. The army, in contrast, was of the opinion that the batteries should be camouflaged and stationed in the rear areas with forward-positioned observers directing their fire, since forward-positioned artillery could easily be put out of action from the air as well as from the sea. Basically the task was to place the guns in such a way that they could fire at the enemy and hit them. An accurate battery, quickly put out of action, was of as little use as one which remained unharmed, but did not hit anything. Effective firing necessitated an efficient fire control system with the potential of following the target, which, at sea, could quickly move in any direction without delay. On the other hand, in order to stay alive, one had to avoid direct hits on the guns and the crew.

The navy had great experience with fire control against moving targets at sea. They knew the normal system used on board ship to be the most effective. It measured the distance from the target and intersected the target at one point. Calculators at once computed all the movements of the ship as well as those of the enemy, and theoretically concentrated the fall of shot of all guns on one point— actually in a narrow circle—with the target as the center.

The coast artillery usually lacked this complicated and expensive apparatus. Therefore, they endeavored to follow the enemy's movements by direct aiming. The batteries' technical equipment enabled them to achieve quick hits and to remain on the target.

The army artillery and also the army coast artillery were, in comparison, rather poorly equipped. The navy doubted—and later events would prove correct—the feasibility of quickly locating and holding a moving target during the delay caused by indirect shooting. The batteries stationed in the rear areas could only become effective the moment the enemy's landing craft reached the beach. This was a firm line on which they could zero in.

Either armor plate or camouflage could be used for protection against direct hits. Armored gun turrets, used by the navy on board ships and in the systematically built coastal defenses, offered small targets and gave dependable protection against splinters and even direct hits, except the heaviest calibers. Armored gun turrets, however, were no longer manufactured, because the precious material was in limited supply and was used primarily for the army's tanks. Placing guns under reinforced concrete, as was the case at many places in Denmark, protected against hits with almost equal effectiveness. The firing angle of the guns, however, decreased from 360° in the armored gun turret to 120° down to 80°, depending on the model. That was a considerable disadvantage, especially since the firing port was much larger than the small slit of the armored gun turret. Accordingly this put the operating crew in greater danger.

A well-camouflaged battery several kilometers behind the coast, however, had considerable chance of avoiding early discovery. Nonetheless one had to keep in mind that the enemy's powerful aerial superiority often prevented firing unless the batteries were willing to risk discovery and subsequent destruction.

In the final analysis, each method had its good and its bad points. The ideal would have been automatically directed and controlled batteries stationed in the rear area, with forward observers on the coast. But these were not as yet available and would not become so due to the limited resources and the time pressures. As a result there was no basic agreement between these opinions either then or later. As early as December 5, 1943, Rommel noted in his daily report: "Antipathy against the artillery's indirect firing methods seems to be universal in the navy."

e. *Sea mines in front of the coast can be an excellent means to stop and damage an advancing enemy.* They have the special advantage that, with proper preparation, they can create a serious obstacle in a very short time.

Off the Danish coast, only the entrance to the Skagerrak was mined. Parallel to the coast of Jutland, however, at a distance of 120–150 kilometers, an approximately 100-kilometer-wide system of mine barriers called the "Westwall" extended from the West

Frisian islands up to a point west of southern Norway. This belt was too remote to give direct protection, and for the most part had been laid down in 1939 and 1940. Since the life expectancy of the mooring cables was only a few years, it could be expected that the originally strong mine barriers had, by now, become extremely weak and thin. The British would have no difficulty in clearing wide passages. The closer the mines lay to the shore, the more difficult it would be for the enemy to sweep them, partly because of counteraction from land and partly because most mine sweeping equipment required a certain water depth in order to avoid touching the bottom and thereby suffering damage.

Without doubt, the best mine defenses were a string of moored mines farther out, a series of ground mines with magnetic or acoustic detonators closer to the coast in water between ten and thirty meters deep, and some special mines in shallow water. The necessity for the latter had up to that point not existed. The Mine Research Command were just in the process of testing coastal mine A.

Coastal mine A consisted of a concrete block filled with a fifty-kilo explosive charge, with an approximately two-meter-high Rommel-32 light steel frame on top. This carried in its point a lead-horn, the normal firing mechanism of a moored mine. Coastal mine A was cheap and easy to manufacture. The mine could, of course, only be activated if a ship hit it directly and bent the lead-horn. A so-called snag-line could enlarge the mine's range. This was a rope approximately twenty-five meters long, fastened to a lead-horn and held on the surface by pieces of cork. If a vessel touched the rope, the pull would bend the lead-horn and detonate the mine. In his final report on Denmark, Rommel requested that the manufacture of this mine be accelerated and that large quantities be stocked.

f. *A lack of striking power and flexibility was generally conspicuous among the troops stationed in Denmark.* It was of little consequence that, on paper, the units were almost complete, since they lacked experienced men and specialists. A typical example was the 166th Reserve Division, which was stationed in northern Jutland. Out of its 13,000 men, three-quarters were recruits; of the 273 required officers, only 170 were on hand; and of the latter only twenty percent were fit for active service (KTB—*Kriegstagebuch der Heeresgruppe B*, war diary of Army Group B). Such troops could perhaps defend themselves in prepared positions, but could hardly be used in an effective counterattack or in mobile operations. As a warning, the events of late fall 1914 were before our eyes. Then the flower of the German academic youth, the *Langemarck,* poorly trained, had tried in vain to break through the thin lines of the enemy, and had suffered heavy losses.

The situation was now aggravated by the motley assortment and shortage of arms. The slightest activity would result in ammunition resupply difficulties. The number of motor vehicles was equally insufficient, and horse-drawn vehicles were out of place in the age of the airplane and the tank. In Denmark, the classic country of the bicyclist, one looked to the bicycle for transportation. The 20th Luftwaffe Field Division reported with great satisfaction that their "mounted" units could ride 120 kilometers in twenty-four hours.

All these facts strengthened Rommel's decision to use the infantry in a primarily defensive capacity, and to use every possible means to make the defense more effective. The OKW's tendency to judge the effectiveness of divisions by their actual fighting capacity rather than by their combat readiness was already an impediment.

The lack of defense readiness in Denmark could be explained in part by the emphasis that had been placed on training and reorganization. Therefore, the troops in Jutland were stationed with practical training possibilities in mind rather than according to the necessities of coastal defense. As a result of his inspections, Rommel demanded a stronger concentration along the west coast and the location of the troops in defensible field positions.

If Denmark should be the target of a major attack, it could be expected that the enemy would try to bypass Skagen, move around Jutland, and secure landing positions on the east coast of the peninsula, since they would here be better protected from the weather than on the completely open western coast. Already during the first briefings the Commanding Admiral-Denmark called attention to this point.

The Skagerrak, approximately 100 kilometers wide, was covered by two 380mm naval batteries. They stood near Hanstholm on the northwest coast of Jutland and near Lindesnäs in southern Norway. It was doubtful that during hazy weather they could prevent the enemy from breaking through the center section. Additionally the Hanstholm battery, protected only by thin armored shields, was almost certain to be put out of action by massive bombing.

Quite a large number of mine barriers lay across the straits. They were not, however, strong enough to present a serious obstacle to well-trained mine sweeping units. Because of this, plans were worked out to strengthen them in such a way that an attempt to break through in one push was certain to fail. It was proposed to increase the number of mines considerably and to use especially low-lying mines equipped with magnetic detonators, which could not be easily caught by the mechanical mine sweeping equipment. The barriers were, in addition, to be protected by so-called explosive buoys. These had been developed based on experiences gathered in the First World War. They were anchored by simple devices a few meters under water. When the mine sweeping gear touched the mooring rope of the buoy, this "climbed" to the sweep cable and a small explosive charge broke the cable. This forced the mine sweeper either to fish the gear out of the water for repair, or to get new equipment ready. In any case, the run had to be repeated, much time was lost, and the mine sweepers were forced repeatedly to cross the real mine barriers behind the explosive buoys. This increased the danger of their striking a mine.

The barriers were strengthened during the next months, thereby eliminating at least one source of danger. A few days after leaving Denmark, I received a letter from Grand Admiral Raeder, in which, among other things, he wrote:

> I am greatly worried about the possibility of a major breakthrough into the Skagerrak, the capture of Jutland from the rear, and the occupation of southern Sweden. This could occur simultaneously with a major offensive in the area around Leningrad, where it is momentarily deceptively quiet since, at this time, the means are also not available as long as major attacks take place in the center and in the south. The protection of the Skagerrak and the Kattegat are of utmost importance, in my view, especially since the enemy probably has the means to render his own mines harmless. I bring these views to your personal attention. You know that I am by no means a pessimist.

Several weeks later the Leningrad offensive got under way. However, the attack on the Skagerrak did not materialize. The occupation of Jutland would have detached Norway, opened the way to the Baltic, and moved enemy air power close to the core of Germany. But the enemy apparently thought such an operation too risky.

The draft of the final report to OKW was ready by December 12, 1943. The operations officer of the army group read the report in the presence of the staffs of the Wehrmacht commanders and of Army Group B. Then, while the staff of Army Group B moved by train to France, Rommel flew to Herrlingen to spend several days with his family, and I went to the OKM (*Oberkommando der Kriegsmarine,* Navy High Command) in Eberswalde. There I reported on our experiences and discussed the reinforcement of the Skagerrak barriers, the construction of the coastal mines, the possible release of additional batteries, the organization of the reserves, and other things. The navy's means were limited, since everything was centered on the U-boat building program, which shortly was supposed to produce many boats of a new type with increased underwater speed.

Beginning in the West

As in Denmark, Rommel's task in France, Belgium, and Holland consisted of inspecting the defenses, drafting proposals for improvements, and studying the problem of an attack on a successfully landed enemy. Due to the size of the territory and the length of the coasts, the job was more extensive than in Denmark. Since the train's limited quarters were no longer adequate, we discontinued using it and found permanent quarters in Fontainebleau. The Field Marshal lived together with the chief of staff, the operations officer, and the aides in Madame Pompadour's little chateau. At first he was not too enthusiastic about drafting his plans and spending his leisure time in the house of this notorious lady, but he got used to it. The rest of the staff lived in several buildings nearby. For instance, our small navy team, which had in the meantime expanded to three officers and five noncommissioned officers and privates (driver, clerks, and navigation personnel), lived in a boarding house near the main chateau.

During the first few days, the immediate staff took their meals in the dining room of the Maison Pompadour, usually without the Field Marshal. He had arrived the evening of December 18, 1943, discussed the situation and the mission with the Supreme Commander West, Field Marshal von Rundstedt, the following day, and had already left early on December 20, 1943, for a lengthy visit to Schelde and Somme, since OKW considered this area the most threatened.

No agreement concerning the probable place of the main assault could be reached. It was to be expected that the enemy would not dispense with the effective support of their fighter planes. This meant that the attack could be expected anyplace along a 900-kilometer-long coastline stretching from Holland, approximately near IJmuiden, along the coast-lines of southern Holland, Belgium, and northern France to the Bay of Saint-Malo. The coast and beach conditions were not all equally favorable for a landing, but the areas which excluded landings were very few. All the Dutch and Belgium coasts had sandy beaches which continued to the area of Dieppe, except for a short section of steep banks on either side of Cape Gris Nez. West of Dieppe up to Le Havre, the beaches were mostly narrow and stony, with steep banks rising behind them—hardly suitable for landings. The Bay of the Seine consisted of sand, a few areas of rocky ground, and steep banks. Rocky banks predominated in the northern part of the Cotentin Peninsula on either side of Cherbourg, the major naval base.

On March 20, 1944, Hitler told the commanders in chief of the three Wehrmacht branches in France, the commanders of the armies and the fortress commanders, during an hour-long discourse (TBR—*Tagesbe-richte Rommels,* Daily Reports Rommel):

> It is obvious that the Anglo-Americans will and must land in the west. . . . At no point along our long front is a landing impossible, except perhaps where the coast is broken by cliffs. The most suitable and hence the most threatened areas are the two peninsulas in the west, Cherbourg and Brest, which are very tempting and offer the best possibilities for forming a beachhead, which would then be enlarged systematically by the use of air forces and heavy weapons of all kinds.
>
> Most important for the enemy is to gain a port for landings on the largest scale. . . . The enemy's total landing action can, under no circumstances, take longer than several hours or, at most, days, for which case the landing attempt at Dieppe is to be regarded as an ideal example.

Hitler's hypothesis did not change the opinion of the OKW that the enemy would try to cross over the narrowest part of the English Channel, landing in the vicinity of Calais. The belief still existed, dating from the time of "Sealion," that the operation was basically only an extended river crossing. Unfortunately, this idea was still very much alive and led to the result that when the Invasion occurred, this section was the best fortified and best manned along the coast. In the light of all historical experience, the massing of heaviest naval and army coastal batteries along the narrowest part of the Channel made it highly unlikely that the enemy would select this heavily defended area for their landing. A few nautical miles more or less made no difference during the approach of the participating craft. And weakly defended points were not difficult to find.

The Supreme Commander West, Field Marshal von Rundstedt, and his staff thought that a landing on both sides of the Somme Estuary was especially probable, since the broad beach and the wide, flat back country provided particular advantages for the landing of large numbers of troops in the shortest possible time. From the navy's point of view, however, this section did not seem particularly suitable, because it was too open to the prevailing westerly winds and the resulting heavy seas. Besides, there was no large port nearby, which would be an essential early target for such an operation.

The Schelde, on the other hand, seemed to offer certain prospects to the enemy, with the large port of Antwerp and the possibility of a thrust toward the Ruhr area. The other possibility was the Bay of the Seine, which was well sheltered by the Cotentin Peninsula against heavy western seas. It was later claimed that some naval staffs had called the Bay of the Seine unsuited for landings, allegedly because of rocky cliffs there. If any such doubts were voiced at all, they could only have referred to a few places. One look at the sea chart was sufficient to ascertain that the rocky parts constituted very limited areas, with large stretches of good landing beaches in between. And the particularly sheltered eastern side of the Cotentin Peninsula was only rocky in its northern section.

In Rommel's considerations these rocky cliffs played no significant role at all. At first, he was inclined to consider the area at the Somme Estuary as the most probable landing point, for the same reasons as Field Marshal von Rundstedt. The peninsula on which Brest was situated, which Hitler had mentioned in his briefing, was operationally too remote and offered, especially in the north, too few landing beaches. The longer Rommel worked on his assignment, the more he became convinced that the major thrust would occur in the Bay of the Seine. However, he considered it entirely possible that on almost any part of the coast supporting and diversionary operations might take place.

It should be mentioned in advance that the enemy air force hardly showed any interest in the back areas of the Schelde, but, in the course of spring, they increased their interest in the area behind the Bay of the Seine. As regards traffic, the enemy separated the western part of Normandy from the rest of France. In addition, the enemy continuously mined the areas off the Schelde and in the narrow part of the Channel, but not in the Bay of the Seine. All this pointed to the conclusion that the major landing would occur in the area between Le Havre and Cherbourg.

I remember a scene which took place several weeks before the Invasion. Rommel stood with several officers in front of the situation map, pointed to the eastern coast of the Cotentin Peninsula, approximately the area known as "Utah" where an American landing later occurred, and said to me, "You believe that the attack will take place at this point." I answered, "I think it very probable." To this he replied, "Well, yes, here they do have the best protection from the open sea against western winds and heavy seas."

Our work, however, started according to the directions from the Commander in Chief West, noted first in the following KTB entries:

December 18, 1943. Introductory conference of chief of staff and Ia HGr B (operations officer of Army Group B) with Ia ObWest (operations officer of the Commander in Chief West). Handing over working documents by the latter. 1115, conference Ia ObWest with Ia HGr B. Ia ObWest points out that, under all circumstances, even if it be only with small groups or at strong points, it is intended to hold onto the coast under any circumstances and thereby to force the enemy to disperse his forces. It is clear that this would be very difficult and occasion enormous air battles. Moreover, it is to be expected that the railroad network will be out of action. Despite this, the deployment of the operational reserves must proceed in orderly fashion (penciled on the margin: 'especially emphasized') and it is intended, even at the expense of other areas in the Western Command, to pull out as many forces as possible and to have them available for the decisive attack, which will be fought at the critical point with the combined power of all forces. This deployment would, in all events, according to careful calculations, require at least twelve to fourteen days. Available are, as far as is known at this time: six panzer divisions; six to seven infantry divisions. Available as commanding staff (*Führungsstabe*) are: First Army, General Blaskowitz; Panzer Group West, Lieutenant General Baron Geyr von Schweppenburg; as well as the artillery commander of the Commander in Chief West, and several other artillery commanders.

The main thrust of the enemy attack will most probably be in the sector from Normandy northwards. An attack on Artois, with the intention of breaking through to the heart of Germany, would certainly be combined with an attack on the Schelde. The enemy's capture of the Somme will be decisive for the overall operation.

An attack on Brittany must also be taken into consideration. The southern part of Brittany will be of less interest to the enemy, since at present the U-boat bases are not decisive.

An attack in the Mediterranean, in the area of the Nineteenth Army, must likewise be expected. This attack would be viewed as a holding effort. The enemy who has gained a foothold there will be attacked and destroyed only after the major battle at the main point has taken place.

Furthermore it was pointed out that: "The arrangement of the troop deployment for the counterattack would be the concern of Army Group B. The deployment had not been worked out in order not to encroach on Army Group B. Only the deployment areas had been determined."

So much for the war diary. Until the Invasion, the intentions and opinions of the Commander in Chief West, as recorded in the KTB, changed little, especially with regard to the area of landing. The first coastal mines A were, according to directions from the Commander in Chief West, prepared and laid in May 1944 near the mouth of the Somme, with the result that during the Invasion none of these very useful mines lay in the Bay of the Seine.

While the Field Marshal, together with some officers, visited the Fifteenth Army (General von Salmuth) at Tourcoing and the coast of the Schelde westward, I drove to Naval Group West (Admiral Krancke), to the commander of Security Forces West in Paris (Rear Admiral Breuning), and finally to the commanding admiral for the Channel coast in Rouen (Vice-Admiral Rieve) to inform them of Rommel's opinions and plans, and also to gain a picture of the situation and of the available forces. With respect to naval forces, little was available, at least insofar as combat units were concerned. There were five destroyers and three large torpedo boats on the Bay of Biscay, five old torpedo boats and some motor torpedo boat flotillas containing approximately thirty boats on the Channel, and a considerable number of U-boats in the major U-boat bases of Brest, Lorient, Saint-Nazaire, La Pallice, and Bordeaux. However, these boats, when submerged, were so slow that the improved enemy antisubmarine warfare defense presented a great threat to them. In view of the enemy's airborne radar surveillance, they could no longer move on the surface and attack as they had in the years of their greatest successes (1940–42).

In the spring of 1943, the submarine war practically collapsed because of the heavy losses. Boats with high underwater speed were still in the early construction stages and none were expected to arrive at the front in the summer of 1944. During an invasion, only the boats equipped with a snorkel could be used. This device allowed them to remain underwater continuously while still using the oxygen in the air for burning in their diesel engines. For the time being, this submarine arm had no prospects of deciding the war.

Only the security forces—that is, mine sweepers, submarine chasers, patrol boats, and gunboats—were plentiful in the west. They numbered altogether about 500 vessels, none of them over 1,000 tons and none equipped with more than one or two 105mm guns. The crews had combat experience and executed their manifold assignments successfully, even against a far superior enemy. But this fleet, consisting of small craft, could not endanger a seaborne landing.

Of the navy's four battleships, the *Bismarck* had been sunk in 1941; the *Gneisenau* lay in Gotenhafen, put out of service by a burned-out foreship. The *Tirpitz* and the *Scharnhorst* led dangerous existences in the northern part of Norway, where there was insufficient air protection. The weakness of the Luftwaffe made any commitment in the Channel totally futile. The same held true for the still operational four heavy and three light cruisers, primarily used for training. The *Scharnhorst* went down in the Battle of the North Cape on December 26, 1943.

Therefore, on the sea not much could be expected from the navy. Still in the experimental stages were small assault craft such as one-man torpedoes, crash boats (midget speedboats with an explosive charge in the bow, remote controlled by a second boat to ram the enemy), mini-submarines and frogmen. These were opportunistic weapons and even though they could surprise an unprepared enemy, the results might be good but hardly decisive. These weapons had been kept so secret that we, in Rommel's staff, became aware of their existence only weeks after the Invasion, when they appeared in the Bay of the Seine. By then the most favorable moment had clearly passed; moreover, the enemy quickly found preventive measures. During the first day of the landing their usefulness could have been considerable.

The naval coastal artillery, with a number of heavy and medium batteries near the large ports and the narrow part of the Channel, was in better condition. The batteries were modern and reasonably well manned. The navy's radar stations along the coast (during the Invasion proper, there were eleven in the invasion area) had fully caught up with the enemy's temporary advantage, and were quite good.

Early on December 23, 1943, I drove from Rouen to Boulogne, passing under some air fights. Near Abbeville a damaged English plane sped across the road right in front of us, headed for England. At noon I saw Rear Admiral Frisius, sea commander of the Pas de Calais (who defended Dunkirk fortress until the end of the war), and in the afternoon I visited the commander of the 2nd Security Division, partly to discuss the situation and the missions and partly to resume old relations. It was a great advantage that I knew almost all of the senior naval officers in France—several of them quite well—from earlier times.

In the evening I made contact with the Field Marshal and his company who were expected at the 191st Reserve Division in the small town of Montreuil, south of Boulogne. I arrived there shortly before them. The divisional commander, who had already assembled all his officers, commented, somewhat annoyed, on the costs of such high-level visits. For dinner the main course consisted of freshly hunted wild boar, which should not have considerably burdened his budget.

Before dinner Rommel discussed the results of his inspections, and during the meal he talked almost exclusively about the problems of coastal defense. With regard to our meals, Rommel was very much in favor of simple food, that is, food from the field kitchens. His wishes were not always observed. Occasionally some of his aides telephoned certain appropriate additions to the written inspection orders, thereby achieving the desired variation in the daily menu. To what extent Rommel noticed this is hard to say. He was a sharp observer who noticed a great deal, but did not always remark on what he had seen. It was not in his nature to waste time with trifles, and he was much too absorbed in his mission.

From now on I kept a diary. This was actually prohibited, and throughout the war up to this time I had not done it. But Rommel impressed me as such a remarkable personage that I thought it necessary to make notes.

On December 24 we first drove to the rear areas to inspect a second position under construction by two companies of the SS Hohenstaufen Division. The position used controlling hills cleverly and made a good impression. Then followed the inspection of a V-rocket firing ramp built in shafts tunnelled into a chalk cliff. For firing, the ramps were to be rolled out. It had apparently become known that the Field Marshal was on the road; we could deduce this from several *Türken* (mock exercises). Gun drills at noon on December 24 directly on a highway are rather uncommon. At one of the firing points, the staff of an engineer battalion was already organized for the Christmas holiday and allowed nothing to disturb them. Some female auxiliaries quickly seized the opportunity to ask Rommel for his autograph.

At 1400, after a conference at the staff of the 82nd Corps, which was in command of the coast from the Belgian-French border to the Somme, we started on the 300-kilometer-long journey back to our quarters via Amiens and Paris. At first we made good progress driving on empty roads. Then it turned foggy, and we lost our way in darkened Paris. Shortly after 1900 we finally reached Fontainebleau. After a simple dinner with the immediate staff, we followed the Field Marshal into a large hall where the staff and the guard platoon celebrated Christmas with harmless merriment.

December 25 was used to analyze the result of this first inspection tour. The overall picture resulting from the profusion we had seen and heard differed in many details from our impressions of the situation in Denmark, but fundamentally was very similar. Above all, here too there was no unified plan and design for a vigorous defense *on the coast*. Field Marshal von Rundstedt, Commander in Chief West, was of the opinion that it should certainly be made as difficult as possible for the enemy to land; he believed, however, that they could not be prevented from landing and forming a beachhead. But when the enemy advanced inland they would be stopped by panzer divisions kept in readiness in the area around Paris, and, in a swift operation, would be defeated and thrown back into the sea.

Already during his first discussion with Rundstedt on December 19, 1943, Rommel had expressed the strongest doubts about this view. He felt that, given the proximity of the enemy naval and air bases, this plan promised even less success than in Denmark. Rommel had outlined his own plan to defeat the enemy at the beaches, without evoking much enthusiasm. General von Salmuth, commander in chief of the Fifteenth Army, held a view similar to Rommel's. Salmuth, during the first meeting at his staff quarters at Tourcoing, pointed out that it would be necessary to "strengthen the coastline and keep the reserves close by. What was not there would come too late for the battle." Ideally, he wanted a panzer reserve division in the rear of every corps sector (KTB). The commanding general of the 82d Army Corps expressed a similar opinion. He also desired a strong force along the front line, although it meant sacrificing depth and availability of reserves. "The most difficult moment for the enemy occurs during the moment of landing itself; he has to be overpowered before he can reach the rim of the coast" (KTB).

The number of available forces was larger than in Denmark. Deployed along the 500-kilometer-long coast of the army area were nine divisions with three freshly organized divisions behind them. Farther back were the tolerably battle-ready 9th and 10th SS Panzer Divisions, and the 12th SS Panzer Division (Hitler Youth), also newly organized.

The divisions' strength and quality differed vastly. There were virtually no high-quality field divisions. Most of them were so called "stationary" divisions, some of which had been in France for years, training reserves for use on the eastern front. In some instances, these divisions consisted of nine battalions each; others were composed of only regiments of three battalions each and a seventh battalion. But the little flags on the maps did not reveal these differences.

The 156th Reserve Division, for instance, which occupied a fifty-two-kilometer coastal section, consisted of 14,000 men. The majority of the commanding officers, subordinate officers, and the cadre personnel had gained combat experience on the eastern front. According to its composition, this division could successfully defend itself, and some sections could even attack with limited goals. Given their equipment, however, they were not capable of undertaking a major assault in full strength. For this they lacked weapons, resupply capability, and other equipment (KTB).

In contrast the 18th Luftwaffe Field Division counted only 9,000 men, poorly trained, and a few noncommissioned officers. The army had contributed only two regimental and two battalion commanders. According to the division commander's opinion, the division could not become a fighting unit until young officers and noncommisioned officers were supplied.

The Luftwaffe field divisions, several of which were stationed along the Channel coast, were another story in themselves. During the winter of 1941–42, when the situation on the eastern front became critical, Göring had formed them from surplus Luftwaffe personnel and presented them to his Führer as a birthday present, so to speak. Most of the officers were older gentlemen who had seen action during the First World War. Junior commanders with land combat experience were missing here too. At the same time the divisions contained a large number of first-rate soldiers, since the Luftwaffe had plenty of manpower. However, these men could have been put to better use replenishing already existing infantry divisions. Their soldierly qualities would have combined well with the knowledge of the experienced soldiers and would have resulted in fine performances. As a result of their lack of experience, however, they suffered serious losses in battle without corresponding success.

Surprisingly, the Atlantic Wall, so highly praised by the propaganda, existed in harsh reality only in a few places. The newsreel pictures of the wall, repeatedly shown to the German public in all possible variations, originated almost exclusively from the Calais-Boulogne area, a remnant from the preparations for "Operation Sealion."

There the navy had placed the following heavy-caliber batteries:

Lindemann	3	406mm guns near Sangatte
Grosser Kurfürst	4	280mm guns near Gris Nez
Todt	4	380mm guns south of Gris Nez
Friedr. August	3	305mm guns north of Boulogne

In the same sector were also five heavy army railroad batteries with guns up to 280mm caliber. In 1940 the naval batteries had been permanently installed in armored turrets or under concrete as offensive weapons for the landing in Britain. They were later used to fire on targets in the Dover area and to relieve convoys which were under heavy fire from British guns while passing through the Channel.

The railroad batteries were placed farther back and relied on indirect firing methods. In the opinion of the local defenders, their disadvantage was that they could be removed at any time. The all-around defense of these batteries did not come up to Rommel's expectations. The coastline between the batteries was manned by insufficient infantry, as was evident in the fifty-two-kilometer-wide section of the 156th Reserve Division. In general, however, there was such a concentration of firepower on that point that an attack across the narrow part of the English Channel, as expected by the OKW for purely land tactical reasons, seemed highly unlikely as long as the batteries remained reasonably combat-ready. Subsequently no British plans were ever revealed that even considered attacking the German front at this, the strongest point.

The controversy between the army and navy about the most efficient use of the artillery became evident at once here too. The 82nd Army Corps complained strongly:

A special difficulty for the corps comes from the recent regulation of the command relationships, especially in our cooperation with the navy. The latter is responsible for command at sea; the army for command on land. The responsible coastal defense section commander is not in the position to decide which enemy force is the most dangerous and should be fought first. If the commander of the coastal area finds it necessary to use the army coastal batteries, the decision will be made by the naval coastal artillery section commander. The order from the Commander in Chief West abrogates the clear instructions of Führer Directive 40. The corps has nothing to say about the installation of the naval guns, which at present act parallel to the army guns for fighting targets at sea, but are unable to fire into the flank of an enemy breaking through on land. At the moment twenty-nine heavy-caliber batteries from the army coastal artillery and the naval artillery are on hand. (KTB)

Führer Directive 40 made the navy responsible for fighting the enemy on the water; the army would direct the struggle on land. At first glance, this gave the impression of a clear solution. But closer examination raised serious questions, such as: Who was to determine the moment of transition? What happened if the enemy landed at several points while his ships were still approaching the coast at other points? Who decided if it was more important for a coastal battery to fire on the companies already ashore or at landing craft that could considerably reinforce these companies with men and supplies? How could one overcome the natural inclination of each commander to consider his sector the most threatened point?

These were questions that the army and the navy had not taken into account before the war, and which could not, given the situation, be answered satisfactorily in such a short time. The majority of the army commanders had inadequate knowledge about war at sea and its peculiarities; the commanders of the navy had incomplete knowledge of land warfare in all its forms. No common concepts existed; nor was there even a shared language. Expressions used by the artillery differed from those used by the navy. The army, for instance, only made a distinction between light and heavy guns, with the dividing line at 120mm. The navy, in contrast, differentiated between light artillery (up to 105mm) and heavy artillery (200mm and up), while anything between 105mm and 200mm was called medium artillery.

During the first years of the occupation of France, the navy's responsibilities were limited to the construction of the heavy batteries along the narrow part of the English Channel and the artillery protection of the large ports. Each port was to be protected by two heavy, at least two medium, and several light batteries. This program had been executed to some extent. But the two main 380mm batteries for Cherbourg and Le Havre, *of all places*, were missing. The explanation for this omission was that at first the U-boat bases on the Bay of Biscay had seemed most threatened by surprise attacks and, therefore, had received priority before the ports on the coast.

The OKW gave the responsibility for the defense of the open coast between the ports to the army, which, in the summer of 1940, created the army coastal artillery for this express purpose. At that time, neither enough experienced personnel nor sufficient equipment were assigned to this new creation. The result was that the army coastal artillery unfortunately remained a stepchild in many respects. In the case of an enemy attack, it was under the orders of the division commanders of the various coastal sections, often officers who had never had anything to do with fighting targets on the water. As early as June 1, 1941, the army included the following coast artillery units:

- 4 artillery regimental staffs
- 39 artillery unit staffs (16 of them in Norway)
- 171 coast batteries (98 of them in Norway, with 62 almost completed)

To be sure, the navy was to guide the action against naval targets, through the local sea commandant. These were: on the Channel coast, the Naval Commandant Pas de Calais, whose area reached from the Belgian border to the Somme; the Naval Commandant Seine-Somme, in charge of the Orne area; and the Naval Commandant Normandy, in command from the Orne to somewhat west of Saint-Malo. The three commanders were subordinates of Commanding Admiral Channel Coast with headquarters in Rouen, who, in turn, was responsible to Naval Group West in Paris for the completion and instruction of the whole sector. To the west and south, reaching to the Spanish frontier, was the Commanding Admiral Atlantic Coast with headquarters in Angers, who controlled Naval Commander Brittany in Brest, Commander Loire in Saint-Nazaire, and Commander Gascogne in Rouen.

The geographical sectors of the commanding admirals did not correspond with those of the army. Nor did those of the naval commanders coincide with either the sectors of the army corps or with those of the divisions. Moreover, the communication channels between the army and the navy did not operate with the degree of efficiency which was absolutely necessary when firing at targets on the sea and in the fast-changing situations during a landing. A unified command, as envisioned in the Führer Directive, did not materialize. This would have been possible given an efficient central organization having clearly defined and effectively controlled responsibilities. However, the confusion in regard to command that existed in the west made a unified effort an impossibility. "Seams" or transition lines between zones are always difficult. The problems that arise can best be solved through close cooperation of all parties concerned and with good knowledge of each other's pecularities and needs.

Organization takes its name from the word "organ." In the coastal defense, two completely different systems had grown separately and now had to be joined. This unification was achieved only in part since the central top-level organization was not itself unified and no conceptual preparations had been made for effective coordination. Hence the result lacked coordination.

The purely tactical and technical problems could have been straightened out; the main obstacle was the unfamiliarity with the unaccustomed element—"water." The demand for total command made frequently by the army was no substitute.

In Africa Rommel had gained sufficient insight into the importance of the sea, and he would have been completely able to unify the divergent organizational threads and handle the situation here. For the time being, however, he was only an inspector and advisor and had no command power.

As in Denmark, it soon became apparent that the troops followed his ideas quickly and willingly, obviously with the instinctive feeling that Rommel, with his vast experience, could offer something practical and helpful in a difficult situation. It was not so simple with some of the higher commanders and their staffs, although Rommel was not the man to accept this fact easily. A large part of his work and his travels was devoted to convincing the reluctant ones, unfortunately not always with success.

Around noon of December 27, 1943, Rommel discussed the construction of the firing positions for V-weapons with the commanding general of the 65th Army Corps who, according to a special order, was responsible for them. In the afternoon, the Field Marshal, together with the chief of staff (Gause) and the operations officer (Colonel von Tempelhoff), drove to see the Commander in Chief West (von Rundstedt), to report the results of his inspections and to give his ideas on the conduct of the defense against a major enemy landing. The Commander in Chief West agreed only in part.

On December 28 the operations officers of the Commander in Chief West and the armies came to discuss the same subject with our operations officers. Rommel, together with Gause and the operations officer for the Luftwaffe (Lieutenant Colonel Queissner), drove to Air Fleet 3, Field Marshal Sperrle. The latter understood the situation clearly, especially the weakness of the Luftwaffe, and could give no hope that the situation would improve markedly. On the day of the Invasion, as it turned out, only ninety bomber and seventy fighter planes were ready for action in all of France. In contrast, the ration strength of the Luftwaffe units (including ground personnel, warning communication, service, etc.) amounted to more than 320,000 people.

The corresponding visit to Admiral Krancke, commander in chief of Naval Group West, at his staff building on the Bois de Boulogne followed on December 29, 1943. The discussion proceeded amicably, as did the subsequent lunch with the complete staff, although the discussion confirmed that the navy could contribute very little to the defense against a major amphibious landing. Heavy ships were totally unavailable, and light forces only in limited numbers. It seemed possible and necessary to strengthen the mine barriers in the English Channel.

In 1942–43, in order to counteract the many British strikes against our convoys, our torpedo boats, mine sweepers, and motor mine sweepers had, in numerous missions, mined the middle of the Channel with several barriers with anchored mines. Every expert knew that the strong current and the tidal changes would allow only limited effectiveness and that the swiftly moving waters would impair the anchor lines, allowing the mines a life expectancy of, at best, from one to two years. On our side of the Channel there were no German mines, but more than enough British mines. The enemy had, however, always bypassed the Bay of the Seine, an observation that strengthened our suspicion that they would land there. It was therefore reasonable to lay our own mines there, using all types—anchored mines with sweep cutters in between in the deeper water, ground mines closer to the land, magnetic, acoustic, and a mixture of both. There existed quite a collection of mine combinations—both difficult and easy to sweep. Directly off the beach, the mine barriers could be supplemented with coastal mines, of which we had seen the first in Denmark.

During the time when our convoys still passed through the Channel, it was reassuring to know that there were none of our mines there. It made the sweeping of British mines and keeping the passage clear much easier, but now no more convoys passed the narrow part of the Channel because the aim of the British coast artillery, firing with radar observation, was excellent and losses had become too great. But Navy Group West did not want to give up the free passage along our coast, to be able to move light naval forces. Therefore they planned to lay mines with timing mechanisms which would deactivate the mines after a certain time.

Now there existed only a timing mechanism for a maximum time of eighty days; it would have been necessary to lay new mines every three months. A 200-day timing device was under development and was expected to be ready before long. Since the invasion was evidently not imminent, the matter of mine fields remained temporarily undecided, although Rommel already categorically demanded the mining of the coastal approaches. This type of mining was vitally important for the necessary depth of his novel defense system.

The coast artillery was in better shape. Shortly before our arrival in France, the navy had relinquished two 210mm and two 150mm batteries, which were to be placed between the ports. It was up to the army to select the locations, while the navy was responsible for the installation and the operating crew. The OKW had supplied the Seventh Army and the Fifteenth Army equally in order to avoid envy. The Fifteenth Army put its heavy battery east of Calais, in an area that, in our opinion, was already well supplied with artillery. The 150mm battery was under construction near Houlgate, opposite Le Havre at the mouth of the Seine. The Seventh Army selected better positions. For the heavy battery they chose a position near Marcouf, southeast of Cherbourg, on the eastern coast of the Cotentin Peninsula; for their 150mm battery they selected a hill a few hundred meters behind the coast, north of Bayeux. During the Invasion both batteries saw action.

From December 29, 1943, to January 1, 1944, the results of all the inspections and discussions were combined in a "Report of the Defense Readiness of the Artois," in which Rommel, among other things, asked to be given full command over the troops along the coast, so that he could realize his plans better and faster. My contribution to the report was quickly finished. On the evening of the 30th, I was informed that a trip scheduled for the next day had been cancelled. Therefore I asked permission for a drive to Brittany to discuss matters of mutual concern with the naval commander (Captain Gumprich) and to do the same at the 3rd Security Division in Nostang near Lorient, where I also wanted to celebrate New Year's Eve. It seemed right and valuable to me to gather as many and varied impressions as possible from the entire area where the invasion might come, and not to forget the men over the material.

On December 31, we started early. Despite occasionally icy roads we made good progress. Because of air raid warnings in Rennes, we dispensed with lunch and arrived at Nostang at 1600. The weather was very mild. In the evening the staff's meteorologist and I walked for one and one-half hours in the singular countryside of Brittany amidst flowering Scotch Broom. Subsequently we discussed the necessary questions. After a simple and quiet dinner I joined the officers, whom I had known for years. Drinking a light punch, I listened to what had taken place. At 2400 I spoke a few appropriate words, and my friends became thoughtful. Then we went to the mess for a while.

On New Year's Day, the deputy division chief, Reserve Lieutenant Commander Notholt, and I drove to the small fishing port of Concarneau, known for its picturesque old fort, and took a look at the base where field gray and navy blue worked closely together. In the afternoon the naval commander of Brest briefed me about his area. There an order reached me to join the Field Marshal as soon as possible. Rommel was visiting southern Holland, about 1,000 kilometers away.

We started on January 2 at 0600. An earlier start would not have been expedient since driving in darkness was difficult due to the many antitank obstacles in the villages. We arrived in Antwerp at 2100.

Rommel was expected to arrive at Antwerp's 89th Army Corps during the afternoon of January 3. In order to use the time until his arrival, I drove to Cadzant at the mouth of the Schelde, where a heavy battery was under construction— albeit far from completion—and conferred with the naval commander of southern Holland, Captain Peters, and the commander of the battery. At the 89th Army Corps (General Baron von Gilsa), Rommel listened to the usual reports. The corps' district contained three naval artillery units with nineteen batteries, five army coastal artillery units with seventeen batteries, and six division artillery units with nineteen batteries. Our hotel was filled with the pleasures of the soft life behind the front which occasioned some disparaging remarks by Rommel.

The car put at our disposal took us on January 4, 1944, via the dikes and bridges, to the island of Walcheren. The island was of special importance, since it represented the key to the Schelde. The defensive construction lagged far behind, since for a long time only one battalion had been stationed on the island. The 19th Luftwaffe Field Division was now located here. Out of the approximately 600 planned concrete structures, only 230 were operational; the rest were to be ready by April 1 and required 40,000 cubic meters of concrete. The heaviest caliber was a 150mm naval battery near Westkapelle, where the shipping channel came especially close to the island. During the capture of this island by the Allies in November 1944, this battery fought well. Thirty thousand of the forty thousand inhabitants had already been evacuated from the island. No agreement had been reached with regard to creating swamps on the island. This was possible in many places for a large part of the island lay below sea level. The British later took advantage of this, when they broke the dikes with heavy bombs, submerging the island. With small craft they broke through the holes and attacked the batteries from the rear.

To save time, we crossed the Schelde near Vlissingen in a harbor patrol boat. In the port of Breskens on the southern bank, the boat ran aground on account of the low tide and shallow water. To the relief of all naval people present, it was soon free again. A meeting with Major General Neumann, the commander of the 712th Infantry Division in Ostbourg followed, then we inspected his sector, which extended to Blankenberge. In addition to the normal artillery, it contained three railroad batteries— one using the 203mm gun with a range of 36,400 meters, two using the 170mm gun with a minimum firing range of 13,000 meters and a maximum firing range of 26,500 meters. The guns looked impressive, but the KTB noted: "Fire control system: makeshift long-basis procedure; fire directed on moving point not possible because necessary instruments are lacking. Can now only be done on a makeshift basis. Successful only if enemy maintains a constant course." In plain language, these guns were hardly suited for firing at naval targets. They had, however, been erected for that very purpose.

We stayed overnight in Brügge. The following morning, the Field Marshal visited the cathedral and the city hall. This was the first occasion during our travels that he took time to relax a bit. He was especially impressed by Michelangelo's marble madonna and the exquisite craftsmanship on the sarcophagi of Charles the Bold and Mary of Burgundy. Our way back included a short stay at Tourcoing, because Rommel wanted to talk to General von Salmuth. We lunched as guests of the Fighter Squadron Schlageter in the area of Lille. The squadron commander, Lieutenant Colonel Priller, decorated with the oak leaf cluster of the Knight's Cross, made a particularly likeable and natural impression. His pleasant and natural demeanor was emulated by his officers. After a hectic trip via Saint-Quentin and Compiègne, we arrived safely at headquarters around 2000. Rommel drove a big Horch car. In my Mercury, a car that I had used previously during my service with the admiral commanding Security Forces West and which had been returned to me along with my chauffeur, Leading Seaman Hatzinger, I had trouble keeping up with Rommel on the straightaways, and only managed to catch up on the slopes. Fortunately most of the French countryside is softly rolling terrain.

The Work of the Staff

*F*rom January 6–15, 1944, Rommel did not undertake any major tours. This by no means implies that we were idle. The immense task of updating defenses in such a short time and with the available, often inadequate, means necessitated numerous and varied measures. The OKW solved the essential point of a clear command organization comparatively well. Effective January 15, it transferred to Army Group B power of command over the Seventh and Fifteenth Armies and the military commander–Netherlands "in all preparations for coastal defense and for coastal defense itself." Rommel himself remained under the command of the Commander in Chief West, much to our staff's regret since it would have been more useful for his task and more satisfactory for Rommel himself if he had been given full command in the west. Rommel did not comment on the decision. His sector of command was limited to an approximately twenty-kilometer-wide coastal strip reaching from the Zuider Zee to the mouth of the Loire. Behind it ruled the military commander of France, General von Stülpnagel, with whom Rommel had good relations. Both were subordinate to Field Marshal von Rundstedt, as were the First Army (General Blaskowitz) in southwestern France and the Nineteenth Army (General von Sodenstern) in southern France.

Rommel was assigned to examine the defense preparations of these two armies as well.

Rundstedt was not very independent either. In all major decisions— for instance, if he wanted to move a division—he had to consult OKW.

This necessitated an extensive exchange of teletype and telephone messages between the Fifteenth Army, Army Group B, Commander in Chief West and the OKW, as when the Fifteenth Army wanted to move the 344th Division to the coast north of the Somme in the former southern section of the 191st Reserve Division. The OKW finally authorized the shift.

The greatest disadvantage of the new command organization was apparent even before it was in force. It was impossible to reach unequivocal agreement on the conduct of the defense. By now all the higher staffs knew that Rommel wanted to seek the decision near the beaches. However, a strong opposition represented mainly by General Geyr von Schweppenburg, the general of the panzer troops in France, favored plans which kept the panzer divisions far back for a massive counterattack. During the French campaign, Geyr von Schweppenburg had successfully commanded an infantry corps and later in Russia a panzer corps. As an attaché in London, he got to know the British, their ways of thinking, and their army, very well. In the Second World War, however, he did not gain any combat experience against the British. On January 8, he came for the first time for a discussion with Rommel. Rommel informed him of his opinion that the enemy had to be beaten on the beaches, but failed to convince Geyr.

How unsatisfactorily the important question was clarified, how the operation should be conducted, and what friction resulted from it, is best shown by excerpts from the KTB:

a. January 10, 1944, 1800. Telephone discussion operations officer of Army Group B with operations officer of the Commander in Chief West: while discussing the necessity of an order for combat direction from the army group, the operations officer of the Commander in Chief West declares that the orders with regard to battle command have been issued exhaustively many times. There is no more any possibility of bringing other views.

b. The Commander in Chief West has declined the proposal made by the engineering general of Army Group B regarding the flooding of coastal areas in the required manner. It has been decided that only local flooding, which could be executed without interfering with telephone wires, cables, and other tactically and operationally necessary arrangements, should be considered.

2145. Telephone conversation chief of staff Army Group B with the deputy chief OKW Operations Staff, Lieutenant General Warlimont: Re inquiry by chief of staff of the army group whether Führer agrees with the Supreme Commander's idea regarding combat direction as outlined in the report about the defense readiness in the Artois. The deputy chief OKW

Operations Staff suggests that in view of subordination to the Commander in Chief West the OKW refrains from expressing an opinion, points out, however, that the Führer categorically believes that the enemy should be defeated on the beaches. The OKW has never advocated any other ideas. Moreover, with regard to the combat direction, the OKW is of the opinion that priority will have to be given to the evacuation of the coastal areas and flooding measures which can be executed at this point in time.

In conclusion, the deputy chief OKW Operations Staff suggests to clarify the basic questions about the combat direction with the chief of OKW Operations Staff (in plain language: General Jodl) during his presence at Western Command.

On January 12 Rommel had a conference with Rundstedt "with the express purpose of reaching an agreement—especially in the matter of combat strategy," since Rundstedt was leaving for a month's vacation on February 25, and Rommel had to substitute for him as Commander in Chief West.

The conference with Jodl took place the following day, and Rommel noted in his daily reports: "Met General Jodl, who shares my views of coastal defense for the most part."

Opposition to Rommel's plans was to be expected. It was a surprise, however, that in view of the special circumstances, and after the thorough joint discussion between Rommel, the Wehrmacht operations staff, and the Commander in Chief West, the OKW did not immediately and unmistakably decide the best method of coastal defense and create a clear foundation for all subsequent measures. Therefore, much depended on Rommel's powers to get his views accepted. In any case, precious time was lost by this procedure, and it did not always bring the necessary success. As members of his staff we soon made it our duty to brief all officers with whom we had close contact on Rommel's ideas. In the meantime, we had gained sufficient insight into the overall problem and the measures previously taken and were convinced that it was correct to fight on the coast.

An additional task for me was to further the mutual understanding between army and navy, and to alleviate either justified or unjustified local tensions. To get to the root of the evil—insufficient treatment of the problem in the past, and inadequate organization in the top levels at the present—was not possible, however.

It was not enough to create the psychological foundations for the coming battle; it was also necessary to bring in more resources—men as well as materiel. The extended front in Russia and the second front in Italy had strained the army to such a degree that it was almost impossible to make forces available for a potential third front in France. On the other hand sober, logical analysis showed that only total repulsion of a major landing would bring relief, and might even be used to effect a reasonably acceptable end of the war, despite all the demands for "unconditional surrender" by the statesmen on the other side. With regard to manpower, this meant that all reasonably trained available personnel would have to be used. The navy could only be of indirect help, since navy personnel were generally insufficiently trained for modern land war. And it would have been a mistake to repeat the sad experiences of the Luftwaffe field divisions. It seemed possible, however, to replace army training units stationed in Germany and in the occupied territories with naval training units. The first proposals of this sort went to the Navy High Command in early January.

The materiel situation was likewise not rosy, since the battle fronts required an immense amount of supplies, and much equipment remained behind during the retreats in Russia. The forces in the west had to put up with armaments more variegated than those ever accepted by any other army. The weapons came from every imaginable arsenal in Europe. Some divisions had up to 100 different types, and rarely the same as its neighbors. For many types of arms, ammunition was no longer manufactured. When the one or two basic supplies which were still at hand were fired, one could practically throw the gun or the machine gun away. Of course, this made training with live ammunition very difficult. It would have been much better had the weapons been scrapped after the victorious campaigns. Now it was too late.

Rommel's past experience had taught him to put the greatest value on extensive mining in order to slow down and break up attacks—especially by armored units—on his insufficiently equipped infantry. The ultimate goal of his plan was the mining of the western shoreline with 50 to 100 million mines. When we arrived in France 1.7 million mines had been laid, with a monthly supply of only 40,000. The home production increased constantly, but because more had not been demanded earlier, it took weeks and months until larger amounts could be detached for the west.

To bridge this gap, an assiduous search began for stopgaps, for which we planned to use old ammunition, captured explosives and shells. When first approached, all responsible officials answered that captured ammunition had, according to order, been scrapped. Not quite unfamiliar with

the habits of bureaucracy, we were not satisfied with this answer and continued our search outside official channels. Success was prompt. By January 9, General Meise was able to report that captured French explosives for approximately eleven million mines was readily available. Only the cases and the fuses needed to be manufactured. We also discovered quickly that several hundred thousand shells for ships' guns (up to the heaviest caliber) were still stored, partly in ammunition dumps of the French naval bases and partly in the bunkers of the Maginot Line. Makeshift fuses were not difficult to manufacture, and shells buried around the resistance points provided better protection than none.

Another problem that occupied the Field Marshal was the transfer of staff quarters closer to the probable invasion front, necessary in order to shorten the approach route in case the situation became serious. Rommel believed that Fontainebleau, sixty-five kilometers south of Paris, was situated too far in the rear. It is remarkable that his first request was a forest camp near Laon, which meant direction northeast towards the Artois. On January 7 the office of Hitler's adjutant informed Rommel that Hitler had rejected the request. From then on, occasionally, Rommel and, more frequently, Generals Meise and Gehrcke (our recently arrived communications officer) would scout the area northwest and west of Paris in the direction of the Bay of the Seine. They searched for solid caves, many of which existed in chalk and gypsum cliffs, so we could find protection during bombing attacks. Rommel kept his eye on a naval subterranean torpedo arsenal. He inspected it while I was away, but did not get it.

I used the time of relative quiet to travel to Holland for two days, since I had not yet spoken with the commanding admiral, Vice-Admiral Kleikamp, and the chief of the 1st Security Division, Rear Admiral Winter. Their staff quarters were located near Utrecht. When we arrived in the evening, a pilot awaited us at the city's perimeter according to schedule. He got lost at once. Moreover, his car had neither stop nor signal lights.

I spoke with Kleikamp about Rommel's basic ideas for approximately one and one-half hours. Winter came for dinner and we continued the discussion until 2300. Above all, we deliberated over how we could requisition personnel and mines from the navy.

The following morning I condensed the information into a report, with proposals based on facts, and sent it to the OKW. Then I drove to Admiral Winter, who gave me the opportunity to inform his staff of Rommel's ideas. On my journey back, Winter accompanied me as far as Antwerp. Greatly concerned, he told me about the slackening of the duty concepts and forms in some of his flotillas, although during action the men performed excellently. These were matters that necessitated the steady and energetic influence of all superior officers.

Surprisingly, Fontainebleau had its own naval garrison, for a motor transport detachment with approximately 500 vehicles was stationed there. Its task was to provide rapid transportation for naval authorities in France. Originally the detachment had had a load capacity of 740 tons, but this had just been reduced to 560 tons in order to save personnel. The commander, an engineer officer and former officer on a destroyer who was no longer fit for ship duty, now used his automotive expertise to the best advantage. He demonstrated to us the departure of his unit under battle conditions, which worked superbly. The whole unit was trained to evaluate its quarters as fast as possible in case of impending air attack. So that they and all their vehicles could reach the protection of the surrounding woods in a few minutes, the commander had cut several passageways through the walls surrounding the barracks, an act that had aroused the anger of the local military administration.

The days at headquarters were well filled with telephone calls, teletypes, conferences, and visits at different agencies in the area around Paris. The weather was beautiful—a clear sky and a light frost—and we used the opportunity almost daily for walks in the woods surrounding Fontainebleau. With its many large and small rocks, ravines, springs, and observation points, the countryside offered much variety. It was here that the Field Marshal began his "armed promenades." When he was in command of the Goslar Jägers he had acquired a taste for game hunting. Now, using his occasional free hours for walking in the woods, he would carry a hunting rifle in the hope of shooting something.

There was no closed season for wild boars and the town commander, himself a hunter, gave his gamekeepers instructions to scout the woods for sows. I received a hunting license—certain things were surprisingly orderly during the fifth year of war—and a machine pistol, which, adjusted for single shot, could perhaps just make the grade. By no means did I intend to devastate the game population. But the watching and observing gave my walks through the woods a new stimulus.

One day a big boar passed in front of me across a clearing, much faster than one would have thought possible. In any case, he was under full cover again when I had finished my deliberations with the result that perhaps it might be worthwhile to shoot him. But the boars were too clever for the other hunters too, and remained entirely undamaged. One day, when we gathered in a clearing after unsuccessfully scouting through a small wood, a majestic stag came out of the wood so close that we almost could touch him. As if he well knew that it was closed season on deer, the stag proudly and calmly stared at us for a few minutes. We could easily count his twelve tines before he disappeared noiselessly into the brush.

Our table company in the Pompadour consisted usually of the Field Marshal, Major General Gause (chief of staff), Major General Meise (of the engineers), Major General Gehrcke (signals), Colonel von Tempelhoff (operations officer), Colonel Lattmann (artillery), and Colonel Krähe. Included later were Lieutenant Colonel Staubwasser (intelligence), Colonel Freiberg (personnel officer), Lieutenant Colonel Queissner (operations officer Luftwaffe), Lieutenant Colonel Olshausen (deputy transport officer), the two staff officers (First Lieutenant Hammermann, later also Captain Lang and the Prince of Koburg), and myself. Queissner and I were usually called the *Hilfsvölker* (auxiliary tribes), but we knew how to defend ourselves.

Our ages, experiences, and interests differed greatly, but precisely this difference created the mutual interest and diversity of our table conversations. Rommel usually talked about military matters and his experiences with people of all kinds. He was, however, not bent on dominating the conversation and understood how to listen to others. He had a good sense of humor, even when he was the butt of the joke. He was no prude, but so-called humor of a certain kind was not tolerated in his presence. I cannot remember ever having heard in his staff a dirty story of the kind which seems unavoidable in some groups of males. Once, during an inspection tour, a commander whom we visited made an attempt in that direction, but stopped cold when he saw the expression on Rommel's face.

Rommel drank little and did not smoke. He usually retired in the evening between 2200 and 2300, a habit which he compensated for with an early rising. He insisted on simple food, a demand that slightly troubled the officer in charge, who, before the war, had managed a world-famous hotel. Only once was the chef allowed to show all his talents. That was when an important person came to visit us from Germany through whose influence Rommel hoped to gain an improvement in the supply of certain scarce weapons. We could hardly eat our way through the many courses, while the guest tucked the food away without any difficulty. The unusual culinary display, however, did not result in a substantial increase of arms.

Generally no fuss was made about guests. Nonetheless, they enjoyed their stay. Rommel usually invited only one guest; occasionally two, but seldom more. On these occasions I moved one chair down from my usual place on the right of the Field Marshal and got to know our headquarter's important visitors from the left-hand side, so to speak.

Our first visitor, who arrived at noon on January 9, was Colonel Hesse, well known for his writings, especially his book *Feldherr Psychologos* (Military Psychology). He was now the field commander at Saint-Germain. Our lively discussion centered first around the influence of First World War literature on the attitudes of the soldiers of the Second World War, especially the youth, upon whom Jünger, Beumelburg, Rommel (*Infantrie greift an*), and others had exerted a strong influence.

Personally, I understood trench warfare in France in all of its horrors only after reading Jünger's *Stahlgewitter* (Storm of Steel). We then talked about sculptors, starting with Rodin. Hesse viewed him as Breker's precursor. I found Rodin much superior to Breker. During the debate about the "Burghers of Calais" we could not determine the location of the original. Our discussion then moved to the collections at the Louvre. Some of them were then at Chambord Castle, where I myself had seen the crates. Gause remarked that they might have been moved to Germany, to which he received the reply, "It had not been known that the Reich Marshal (Göring) had visited France in the meantime."

In our circle we spoke quite frankly and openly, since we trusted each other implicitly. The trust was never misused. We had no NSFO (National Socialist Political Officer), and we would not have one for the foreseeable future. In this group of people with their many different backgrounds and dispositions I always felt a harmony that springs from an inner kinship. It seemed that the harmony was spontaneous, but when in July 1944 Rommel lay seriously wounded in the hospital, we became strongly aware that the harmony had been greatly due to the influence of his personality. Almost imperceptibly he had molded us into this unit, an indication of a true leader. Titles and beautiful speeches cannot compensate for the lack of this talent. When this is missing, ambition soon will flourish at the cost of comradeship. There will be no united group; it will disintegrate under pressure to the detriment of the whole.

The table conversation those days was dominated by North Africa. Rommel spoke about the unsuccessful attack on Tobruk in 1941, the major offensive in 1942, and the successful surprise attack on Tobruk. With his dry humor, Gause, who had been Rommel's chief of staff in

Africa, added the human highlights to Rommel's tactical and operational descriptions. This included the story about the regimental commander who had come directly from Germany and, en route to El Mechili, had made hotel reservations for his staff and himself. Gause assigned him to the third hotel on the right side of the main street. All of El Mechili, however, consisted of only two huts. The OKW, too, became the target of our ridicule, because they had inquired sternly if it was true that the troops of the Africa corps had looted the shops in Bir Temrad. All of Bir Temrad consisted of a hole in the ground filled with some water and a gasoline barrel turned upside down holding a sign post.

Hammermann was somewhat unhappy; he insisted that he had now listened to the capture of Tobruk for the fifteenth time. This did him no harm, and to the staff's newcomers the descriptions were useful, because they provided lively examples of Rommel's leadership. They revealed that even his most daring and apparently spontaneous operations had been carefully considered in advance, and their chances for success had been soberly weighed. Time and time again, Rommel's main consideration emerged: confronting the enemy with new situations and surprising him in order to save bloodshed. Once Rommel had made his decision, he carried it out with lightning speed.

As much as Rommel liked to talk about his campaigns, there was no trace of boastfulness in it. He liked to discuss his mistakes, since one could learn from them. The man behind the stories was not a mere expert or trooper or a *miles gloriosus,* but a highly talented soldier who attempted to solve his military tasks responsibly, keeping human casualties to a minimum; a man who, despite his fame, had remained a modest human being with an engaging personality.

Under the guidance of this personality's unobtrusive influence our group quite naturally gravitated towards each other despite our differences. We got to know and understand one another, and the awareness of our common task under the leadership of such a commander did the rest.

Offshore anti-landing obstacles (drag curves and tetrahedrons) shown at low tide.

Concrete tetrahedrons on the beach, with wooden drag curves visible in the background.

Mine attached to obstacle. Mine detonated when struck by ship or landing craft.

Stakes with mines on top shown at half tide.

Stake with mine and crossbeam. Obstacle was submerged at high tide; mine exploded when a ship touched the cross beam.

Raft with mines attached to damage landing craft and ships. A Czech hedgehog is visible behind it.

Offshore obstacles to hamper landing craft.

Concrete anti-tank obstacles. Note the use of barbed wire as antipersonnel defense.

Heavy coastal gun in camouflaged concrete emplacement.

Guard with machine gun in mined sand dunes.

After Assuming Command

*E*ffective January 15, 1944, the chain of command regulations changed Rommel's status from that of inspector back to commander in chief. This gave him more work and responsibility, but also the right to give orders in questions of coastal defense instead of only making proposals and suggestions, as up until now.

It was characteristic that the first order he issued decreed the erection of offshore obstacles, which several staffs had strongly opposed. Rommel also sent the order to OKW, as an addition to his report on the defense readiness of the Artois region.

On the same day General Blumentritt, chief of staff of the Commander in Chief West, reported that State Party Leader Sauckel had visited him with orders for the requisition of one million Frenchmen for work in Germany. Rommel opposed this measure at once and repeatedly later on, with some success, because it seemed to him disastrous for the situation in France and the situation in general.

Indefatigably, Rommel continued the inspection tours in order to gain a personal picture of the defense readiness. During two inspection tours, he had familiarized himself with the situation in the sector then considered particularly threatened, between IJmuiden and the mouth of the Somme. Now he turned his attention to the left flank of the Fifteenth Army, from the center of the Bay of the Seine, where the Orne River formed the demarcation line of the Seventh Army, to the mouth of the Somme. On January 16, we drove to the 711th Division whose com-

mander, Major General Reichert, had his command post in a small castle
northwest of Pont l'Evêque. During the conference the Field Marshal
clearly outlined his opinions and intentions. The division had already
given much thought to the defenses and had signed a contract with a
civilian firm for planting stakes as offshore obstacles. There was some
difference of opinion regarding the employment of the artillery and it was
decided that "the artillery would be employed in fighting the enemy on
the water as well as after reaching the shore" (KTB).

An apple soufflé, made for the Field Marshal from Normandy's boun-
tiful apple treasures, highlighted the simple lunch. In misty weather we
drove west through the lovely undulating French countryside to Cabourg, a few kilometers from the Orne. The coastline was dotted with
resorts, some with well-known names, such as Deauville and Trouville-
sur-Mer. In the interior there were only a few villages, but many farms
of prosperous appearance, similar in design: a giant barn with a shallow
U-shaped ground plan dominated the farm, enclosing the main house
located parallel to the road.

Cabourg lies on the west bank of the mouth of the Dives. At this river,
William the Conqueror gathered the fleet with which he sailed for England in 1066. Had his invasion been unsuccessful, it would probably not
have been necessary for us in 1944 to protect ourselves from his descen-
dants' unpleasant intentions. The defense status of Cabourg was not very
impressive; clearly the necessary dedication was lacking. Further east the
situation improved, with a good deal of concrete construction; however,
the possibilities for outflanking the enemy on the steep grades of the
"Labyrinth," a group of picturesque cliffs and ravines, had not been exploited to the best advantage. The view from the domineering height of
Mont Canisy, 112 meters above sea level, was impaired by the hazy
weather. On top stood a main battery with four 155mm guns of French
origin built into concrete on wheeled gun carriages. In winter 1940–41,
when I was there for the first time, on a walk from Trouville-sur-Mer,
the hill had been populated by only a few sheep.

Now Deauville looked less attractive than it had then, and in Trouville-
sur-Mer where I had been quartered, the landing jetty had disappeared.
In picturesque Honfleur there was time for a brief look at the harbor.
The resistance nests along the whole route made a generally good impression, but throughout, the mining was still much too weak. Our tour ended
after dark west of Rouen at the staff quarters of the 81st Corps where
Major General Gümbel substituted for the absent General Kuntzen. The

corps sector contained approximately 250,000 mines and one man would place about ten mines a day. Rommel immediately demanded that this amount be doubled.

On January 17, conferences followed at the 17th Luftwaffe Field Division station in Bolbec. We inspected this important port on the major road to Le Havre later that day. At the division many noncoms stood in rank and file, because there were more corporals than privates; they even had a Luftwaffe field artillery regiment. Here a French firm worked under contract on the second line. The Field Marshal corrected many misconceptions and again outlined his points of view clearly and impressively.

We had conferences at the command post of the commander for the defense section Le Havre and then in the command post of the naval commander Seine–Somme. Rear Admiral von Tresckow was not present, and we met instead with the commanding admiral, Vice-Admiral Rieve. The main support of the defense towards the sea was the 170mm naval battery at Saint-Adresse, but due to the emplacement the battery could not fire toward land. North of the city a 380mm battery was under construction, which was to be ready in the spring. While inspecting Naval Artillery Unit 266, which manned the naval batteries, I met my former clerk, a capable man who was now a lieutenant commander and battery commander.

The army's coast batteries were not too well equipped. In particular, starshells for night firing were lacking. Up to now the navy had helped out. As in other bases we had visited, the port entrance was here, too, protected by rope barriers, nets, depth charge throwers, and makeshift mine barriers which were detonated from land.

Our next destination was Fécamp, where large strongpoints were under construction east and west of the town. The local regimental commander reported to us, and denounced all the navy in Fécamp as bureaucrats. Now, the harbor captain, with whom he most likely did most of his business, was an elderly and mild-mannered gentleman. Also stationed here was the 15th Patrol Boat Flotilla, the strongest unit at the place, which since 1940 over and again had proved itself under the severest conditions in the convoy service. Intervention in a conciliatory form led to a general hilarity and détente.

After a quick lunch at the soldiers' mess, we continued for Saint-Valéry-en-Caux, where in 1940 Rommel with his 7th Panzer Division had pushed a British division towards the sea and forced them to surrender before they could leave the mainland for England, as they had done at Dunkirk. The British commander had been especially indignant that he had had to surrender to an officer junior to him.

We climbed the hills to the left and the right of the small, considerably destroyed spot to reach a battery position and a Luftwaffe radar. Rommel severely admonished the reporting first lieutenant because the operating crew had failed to report an air attack to the base commander (army). However, he caught the wrong person, because the lieutenant had just returned from leave and was therefore completely innocent. But in principle Rommel was correct, because the omission was a sign of deficient team thinking and of insufficient cooperation.

The indecision about the best method of defense was demonstrated in Fécamp where bunkers on the beach had been walled up and in Dieppe where they were unoccupied. South of the mouth of the Somme, we even found some bunkers that had been blown up because the commander had moved the main defense line to a ridge several kilometers from the beach.

In Dieppe, every participant in a conference held in the officers' mess received a cup of genuine coffee as a special treat. As was often the case, Rommel, in the fervor of discussion, forgot to drink his coffee. Meise longingly watched the slowly cooling cup. Behind a large situation map, I poured part of its contents into his cup. When the Field Marshal finally reached for his cup, he was visibly surprised to find it half empty.

After a thorough inspection of Dieppe's relatively strong fortifications—here one had learned the lessons of the 1942 British raid—we drove after dark to Abbeville. At dinner, Rommel described in absorbing fashion his thrust with the 7th Panzer Division into the lateral extensions of the Maginot Line where he used the order: "Broadside right, broadside left, as in the navy." The breakthrough, executed during a moonlit night, was successful and led deep into the rear areas; occasional resistance was broken by a few broadsides. Rommel captured Avesnes and the bridge over the Sambre near Landrecies and opened the way to Arras and Lille.

A few weeks later, for the attack across the Somme, he used a partially destroyed railroad bridge near Abbeville where the defenders sat in the hills at some distance from river and bridge. On the other bank, Rommel went some distance up the river and then attacked where the defenses were weakest. In this manner he penetrated sixteen kilometers into Weygand's position system on the first day.

Already as a young officer, Rommel had trained himself to surprise the enemy and to attack him where he did not expect it. He related how once during maneuvers, he had received an assignment to capture a bridge and hold it against his friend Schneckenburger (killed in October 1944). Both were lieutenants at the time and both led full companies. Schneckenburger was known as a good tactician, and the bets stood against Rommel. He quickly occupied the bridge and blocked the road in the direction of the enemy, using only a sergeant and twenty-five men. He himself advanced along the edge of a forest at some distance from the road. When, according to operating rules, the enemy closed in on the bridgehead and deployed, Rommel attacked him from the flank and "destroyed" him.

We were lodged in civilian quarters. Not everybody reconciled himself to his bed, made in the French fashion with the blanket tucked under the mattress on both sides, creating something like a sleeping bag into which one had to crawl from the pillow.

One of the day's results was further search for heavy shells urgently needed for conversion, with the help of full fuses, into mines to roll down the steep slopes of this coastal section. On January 18 the inspection started at Treport, where the division commander was not too well informed. The relatively strong army coast artillery did not have enough communications equipment; only one battery had radios. Therefore, the fire of the batteries could not be centrally directed and one had to rely on the individual battery commander's estimate of the situation.

A major landing seemed unlikely here because at the foot of the steep slopes the stony beaches were narrow and the high terrain could only be reached via deep and narrow ravines. Minor operations and surprise raids, however, could occur. The ravines had been well mined and covered with barbed wire. Flanking possibilities, however, had not always been exploited fully. In Cayeux-sur-Mer, south of the mouth of the Somme, we found an abandoned battery position with perfectly good concrete bunkers, which had been partly blown up. This made Rommel very angry.

In the afternoon Rommel conferred with Salmuth at Montreuil-sur-Mer. Subsequently we drove to Hardelot-Plage, where SS engineers had installed good mine fields. Again we stayed overnight at the "Soldiers' Home" in Le Touquet-Paris-Plage. Some good English books were in the reading room.

At 0800 on January 19 we started for Berck-sur-Mer to inspect more mine fields and positions. Much had been accomplished already, but compared to the enemy's expected attacking power, it was not nearly enough. After a speedy drive we reached Fontainebleau early in the afternoon.

Three days of hard work at headquarters followed. In addition to questions about materiel (especially mines, offshore obstacles, artillery, and ammunition), the main points discussed were:

1. The formation of combat zones in which the generals responsible for the coastal sections had unrestricted command.
2. Transfer of command for both sides of the mouth of the Somme to the 67th Corps to reduce responsibility to a single command agency.
3. The formation and reorganization of the panzer divisions.

Except for the usual exchange of telephone calls, the first two points did not create any particular difficulty. The following fortified coastal defense sectors were declared "fortresses" effective immediately:

The Netherlands: IJmuiden, Hook of Holland.

Fifteenth Army: Dunkirk, Boulogne, Le Havre.

Seventh Army: Cherbourg, Saint-Malo, Brest, Lorient, Saint-Nazaire. Army Group B applied for the additional installation of fortress garrison headquarters at Vlissingen, Ostende, Calais. This meant strengthening all these places in such a way that they could also hold out against attacks from land. So far they had only been fortified toward the sea. It went without saying that the order did not result in instant fortresses, since in most cases the construction was still far from completion.

Point 3—formation and reorganization of the panzer divisions—created difficulties at once. During a telephone conversation with Jodl on January 20, 1944, Rommel discussed the participation of the 21st Panzer Division "without delay," which was subsequently more clearly defined by him as "during the first hours of the enemy landing." Jodl agreed with Rommel. But later he telephoned to the chief of staff of the Commander in Chief West that in his telephone conversation with Rommel, he, Jodl, understood the "participation without delay" as applying to the infantry only. The operations officer of the Commander in Chief West informed the operations officer of Army Group B of Jodl's interpretation. The operations officer of Army Group B at once pointed to Rommel's conviction that under all circumstances the mobile units should be moved up closer in order to be able to participate in the first hours of the fight. The operations officer of the Commander in Chief West emphasized that the Commander in Chief West would reject this idea in any event, because the fast panzer units also had to be available for other operations, especially since surprises from the enemy were to be expected.

Later, a slight shift of the 9th and 10th SS Panzer Divisions and the 21st Panzer Division towards the coast was granted, "but these divisions had to retain the rearward Seine bridges under all circumstances" (KTB).

During the morning of January 21, Gause, Meise, Tempelhoff, and myself, together with other staff members, participated in the final discussion of a resupply exercise organized by Western Command. It was well directed and General Wagner, the army's supply general quartermaster, discussed it very clearly. Particularly instructive was how much bringing up supplies depended on the railroad. Subsequently I drove at once to Vice-Admiral Schirlitz, the commanding admiral of western France, who later defended La Rochelle. His headquarters were still at Nantes. Using secondary roads for the most part, we drove in mild spring-like weather via Chartres—with a short rest for a visit to the cathedral, regrettably devoid of the beautiful glass windows—Le Mans, La Fleche, and finally along the southern bank of the Loire to Nantes, where we arrived at 1800. Without further ado we discussed the situation. Schirlitz talked for about one hour and then wanted to adjourn the meeting, since he had to drive to Posen the next day for an instruction course. However, he did not succeed in getting away, which gave me the opportunity to give my unshortened talk.

Next day I arrived shortly before the Field Marshal at Seventh Army, General Dollmann, at Le Mans. Brigadier General Pemsel was the chief of staff. Both men were very personable, but until now they had had little to do with naval matters. Their navy liaison officer was away. In the most cordial manner they told me immediately that there was too little naval artillery in their sector. I fought back and pointed out that, except for the ports, the defense of the coast was exclusively the task of the army and that the navy had already furnished heavy artillery to the army for the protection of the ports.

After Rommel's arrival, Pemsel gave an excellent report with very clear maps. He considered every landing possibility, which were then examined in detail. The discussion revealed unequivocally that the section from the Orne westward approximately to the Bay of Saint-Brieuc (about fifty kilometers west of Saint-Malo) gave the enemy excellent landing possibilities. A large scale landing further west on the northern coast of Brittany was very unlikely. Seventh Army considered cutting off Brest by a double landing only expedient if this coincided with a similar operation against southern France, in order to join the landed forces on both sides of the Loire and in this manner sever a large section from France. Special difficulties for a major landing in the Bay of the Seine were not mentioned.

The troops in the army sector were equipped with ninety-two different weapons, to which belonged 252 types of ammunition, of which forty-seven were no longer manufactured. Of heavy antitank guns the thirteen divisions of the army had only 170 of 75mm and sixty-eight of 88mm and above on hand.

In the afternoon we drove in rain and hard squalls at constantly increasing speed, via Rennes to Guingamp, for a visit with the 74th Corps, General Straube. Again we billetted in civilian quarters. The introductory conferences were similar in content to those at the other corps commands. At 0730 in the morning of Sunday, January 23, 1944, we started the round trip through the western section of Sibiril (west of Roscoff) via Saint-Pol-de-Léon to the old sailing port of Paimpol. The section contained no large ports. The northern coast of Brittany is ragged and rocky and almost everywhere open to winds from the northwest; the roadnet is much thinner than in Normandy. A major landing here was very unlikely. But a number of sandy bays offered good opportunities for small landing operations, and it was understandable that the responsibility for a 510-kilometer coastline greatly troubled the commanding general.

The resistance nests of the corps were spread out along the coast, with distances up to seven kilometers between them, and of the 217 shore batteries, 157 were not yet under concrete. The corps had laid 106,000 mines in its district, but supplies were at a standstill. The Field Marshal immediately allotted 20,000 mines from the supplies which Army Group B had made available.

In the evening we heard the news about the landing of Anglo-American divisions in Nettuno, fifty kilometers southwest of Rome, behind the lines of Monte Cassino. It need not be mentioned specially that our staff followed this operation with the greatest interest, especially the failure of the counterattack carried out with relatively strong panzer forces, twenty-five days after the landing.

On January 24, after staying overnight in Guingamp, we inspected the eastern section of the 71st Corps, extending from Saint-Brieuc to east of

Saint-Malo. The weather was rainy and stormy. The 721st Infantry Division for special employment under the command of Brigadier General Count Stolberg-Stolberg occupied here a sector 250 kilometers long with some eastern battalions. The men made a surprisingly favorable impression, but it seemed odd when they reported in Russian. The quality of these troops obviously depended very much on the officers' ability to deal with them, and, naturally, on the development of the situation. There were no illusions concerning their behavior in case of reverses.

In Saint-Lunaire, west of Dinard, we had a lengthy discussion regarding placing an army coast battery with Russian 122mm guns on turntables. Two positions had been selected, one in the rear and one on a dominating hill near the coast. The commanding general wanted the guns located in the rear, while the commanding admiral desired them to be emplaced on the coast. The sea commandant proposed a compromise—three guns on the coast and three in the rear. The most expedient solution seemed to be to find two more guns and thereby get two batteries of good firing power. Since the casemates had not yet been built, it was understandable that the general in command wanted to put them in covered positions in the rear.

Our main interest in Saint-Malo was in the fortress La Cité, an exceptionally sturdy construction in Vauban's style. With the removal of 15,000 cubic meters of granite, tunnels extending 1,500 meters had been created. They connected all battle stations while shafts at right angles to the main shafts provided space for reserves, ammunition, and storage. Much concrete, probably 30,000 cubic meters, had been built into the battle stations. So far, this was all very nice, for La Cité was situated inside the port entrance and completely dominated this and the port. But it was only armed with two (PAV—*persönliche Aufzeichnungen des Verfassers*, personal notes of the author) or four 75mm and 70mm guns and several smaller automatic weapons (KTB). In contrast, the naval battery on the island of Cézembre, exactly off the port entrance, was completely unprotected. With its four 190mm guns it possessed an incomparably higher firing power and could protect the port and its entrance just as well as La Cité.

In pouring rain we inspected positions near the fishing village of Cancale on the western shore of the Bay of Mont-Saint-Michel and an army coast battery near Dinard. During the evening I talked with the naval officers who organized and protected the convoys to the Channel Islands. They complained about the lack of cooperation in several respects.

On the morning of January 25 I intentionally arrived fifteen minutes before the Field Marshal at our meeting place outside of Dol-de-Bretagne in order to discuss with the commander of the 179th Reserve Panzer Division, Major General von Boltenstern, the possibility of luring the Field Marshal to Mont-Saint-Michel, so that after all the inspections of resistance points, mine fields, and battery positions, Rommel would be able to see something quite special. Boltenstern was very helpful and added the inspection of a guard there, consisting of one corporal and a handful of men, to our program. But Rommel did not take the bait. When Boltenstern read him the day's scheduled stops, and, without revealing the strength of the position, mentioned Mont-Saint-Michel, Rommel, with a faint smile in my direction, had it scratched off the list. Well, then it could not be helped.

The division was incomplete and could only deploy one panzer company. They had more tanks, but transport was not available, especially for ammunition. One foot battalion was completely combat-ready; so was a coastal defense battalion, a situation which somewhat contradicted the definition of a fast mobile unit. The rest of the men, including some recruits, formed two regiments. Lacking were antitank weapons, communications equipment, and transportation for part of the artillery. On the situation maps at supreme headquarters, however, the division appeared as a proper panzer division.

Near Tinteniac, Reserve Panzer Reconnaissance Unit 1 demonstrated its combat-readiness and made a favorable impression. The unit trained replacements for four panzer divisions, but in the previous three months it had received only forty-six recruits divided into small groups. It lacked hand grenades, ammunition for the French rifles, and a change of clothing, which, in rainy and damp Brittany, was of particular necessity. The training for motorcycle units was hampered by the poor condition of the motorcycles, but the instruction of drivers went well because gasoline was allotted amply. Should the situation have become serious, provisions were made to create from the 179th Reserve Panzer Division and the 155th Reserve Panzer Division, situated further inland, and several other detachments, a combat group, *Polster* (padding), consisting of two panzer companies, which were to be combat-ready within twelve to fifteen hours.

At noon we were in the staff quarters of the 179th Reserve Panzer Division at Rennes. Our way back home was interrupted by a short discussion of the results with Brigadier General Pemsel in Le Mans at Seventh Army. General Dollmann had gone to Posen. Among other things, Rommel promised the army 400,000 mines by the end of February. The situation in Saint-Malo was clarified to the extent that the port commander and his personnel would only be used in the defense, after the unserviceability of the port had been assured.

Upon our return the operations officer, who had remained at Fontainebleau, reported that for reasons of the general situation OKW had not approved the transfer of the panzer divisions closer to the coast (TBR).

On January 26 Lieutenant General H. Geyer—now retired—visited us as a civilian. Before the war he had been Gause's superior as the 5th Corps' commanding general. Geyer was a Swabian like Rommel, who valued him greatly and had invited him to visit the headquarters. As commanding general, he had stopped his corps before Moscow without orders, initiated an orderly retreat, and in doing so, probably saved the majority of his troops. As a consequence he had been sent home as "too old." Geyer, who during the First World War had been a valued coworker of Ludendorff in the supreme army command, and according to general opinion was one of the army's best minds, had very clear opinions on operational command questions. During the conversation he put the question: "Why do the soldiers in the highest command collaborate with this type of leadership?" It was answered with the reply that all of them but one lacked combat experience. Geyer was not satisfied with the answer, and remarked, without doubt correctly, that this was a question of character.

While talking about the defense against invasion, Geyer, without knowing Rommel's views, said that considering the limited resources the reserves had to be far forward. He had done the same with his corps in Russia because of the extension of the front. Reserves were a function of numbers and space. Very few people could correctly evaluate figures, however, and most had a subconscious fear of them. The fact that one square kilometer contained one million square meters would seem odd to such people. Rommel, who up to that point had not said much, looked to the engineer and asked: "Meise, how many mines do you think that would take? I figured on 65,000."

The next subject was safety and concerned peacetime maneuvers. During an exercise with live ammunition, Geyer and two other generals had received light wounds. The commander of the maneuver promised, during the ensuing discussion, to be much more careful in the future to prevent a repetition of the incident. Geyer's standpoint was that, on the contrary, they should risk still more; besides, nothing like this would probably happen again. He also condemned the exaggerated safety measures during the throwing of hand grenades, since they made the soldiers insecure. In this connection one could add that accidents occurring during the navy's mine sweeping exercises that had been executed under combat conditions had produced valuable experiences which in the war saved much blood and materiel.

The cooperation between Luftwaffe and panzer units made for another conversation topic. Geyer wanted an independent Luftwaffe for strategic purposes only. Then we talked about conducting peacetime maneuvers, and about the rose-tinted glasses through which the present situation now was often viewed. More topics were the landing at Nettuno and the question whether in modern mobile warfare the commander should be with his troops in the front lines. The question was answered in the affirmative. Other subjects were the effectiveness of carpet bombing and how to combat panic, and finally the unsuccessful attempt to lower the generals' average age after the first Russian winter. Many generals were then dismissed, but due to the promotion of old colonels, the average age rose allegedly from fifty-five years to fifty-eight years.

On January 17 I drove to Navy Group West and discussed with the chief of staff, the operations officer, and the department heads a number of questions, especially regarding the craft for laying mine fields and getting more artillery for the Seventh Army. In the afternoon I went to the command quarters of Security Area West, when I suggested improved armor plating for the vessels as protection against air attacks. If necessary, makeshift shields could be made from ship-building steel, as we had done in 1941–42. At least they protected against splinters and gave the operating crew a sense of security.

During the morning Rommel had a discussion with General Geyr von Schweppenburg about the employment of the panzers. In the afternoon he drove to the Commander in Chief West's staff quarters, where he had another discussion "which proceeded in mutual agreement, but unfortunately did not change the obstructions that originated from there during the actual execution of the plan" (TBR).

The Netherlands sector was asked by telephone to accelerate the laying of its mine fields for, during the last ten days, their numbers had increased only by 1,700, despite reserve stocks of 33,000. The problem of the "combat zone," in which the troop commander had unlimited power of command, was not yet clarified. The Fifteenth Army reported bitterly: "The army does not intend to pillage this area or to conduct confiscations, but instead wants only to act in the interest of the troops, without being forced to get prior permission from the military commander" (KTB). Gas masks were required for the eastern battalions. The Commander in Chief West's intention to remove batteries in order to form some kind of artillery division started an extended discussion. Rommel even had to waste his time about the acquisition of butter for the troops stationed along the coast.

Not even an attack of lumbago could keep Rommel from his inspection tours. On January 29 he visited the 84th Corps, the Seventh Army's right wing, which in its sector included the coast of the Bay of the Seine from the Orne westward, all of the Cotentin Peninsula with the major naval port of Cherbourg, and the English Channel Islands. Unknown to us, we entered for the first time the section that would be hit by the concentrated force of the Invasion. It is certain that if others, especially the OKW had had a different attitude as to the probable place of the invasion, and if our work had started in France instead of in Denmark, we could have come to this area several weeks earlier and started our work accordingly earlier.

General Marcks, coming from the general staff, was widely acknowledged as a strategist. His address was clear, distinct, and surprisingly optimistic. He was severely impeded physically, for he had lost a leg in Russia, and had to use an artificial limb.

Including the Islands, his corps occupied a sector of 400 kilometers. For this he had five divisions. One of them, the 319th Infantry Division, normally at full strength, was stationed on the Channel Islands. Those given to jest already called it the Canada division, since, in view of enemy superiority in the air and on the water, there was not much chance to take the division back to the mainland after an enemy landing.

The 716th Division, between Orne and Vire, occupied a front line of ninety kilometers with two regiments forward. Adjoining to the west, the 709th Infantry Division occupied 220 kilometers of front line, with all three regiments forward. Both divisions continuously gave up trained men; their ages ranged up to forty-five years. Officers and NCOs were of good quality; most of them had gained combat experience in the east. In reserve behind them were the 243rd and the 352d Infantry Divisions. The 243rd, a stationary division, consisted of three regiments each with two battalions—one horse-drawn, one with bicycles, and one completely motorized but still being organized. So far the 352d Infantry Division had only four battalions and four batteries ready for combat. The 1021st Grenadier Regiment, strengthened by two batteries, the future core of the 77th Infantry Division, was also billeted in the corps area.

With regard to the coastal conditions and the landing possibilities, General Marcks reported (KTB):

> In the Bay of the Seine the coast is flat and well suited for landings. The east coast of the Cotentin Peninsula, excluding some steep areas, lends itself well to enemy landings. Along the west coast several major bays make enemy landings possible.
>
> *The Channel Islands create special problems: unsuitable for enemy landings; outlaying reefs; well-built defenses. The artillery located there only partly blocks the passage to the mainland. Particularly endangered is Alderney Island which can easily be neutralized. Also strongly alternating currents between Alderney and mainland. Possibilities for airborne landings: in view of the Cotentin's hedgerows and terrain, limited to rear area of east coast, area of 243rd Infantry Division, and the flatlands around Caen.*

Rommel was of the opinion that the enemy had enough small ships and did not depend on large ports. With regard to combat leadership, Rommel said that the cheapest battle would be fought on the coast, which led to the conclusion that all means should be used to prevent the enemy's disembarkation. He urged increased mining, also by the infantry, and stressed the necessity of moving the artillery of the reserve divisions far enough forward that it could fire on the beaches.

On our way back we received unclear reports about the sighting of many vessels west of the mouth of the Gironde. Several hours later it turned out that they were fishing boats. After lunch we inspected the construction site of a battery east of the mouth of the Orne. While our group stood openly in the middle of that place, two British fighter planes approached us directly at low level. First I watched them; then, when the operations officer next to me dove into full cover, I did likewise. The Field Marshal remained standing; the fighters did not fire.

We then drove in a westerly direction along the coast. We saw much that was good, for instance, some well-placed flanking guns, and noticed much that was quite poor. In the 716th Infantry Division's right sector, the strongpoints on the coast were 600 to 1,000 meters apart: in the left sector, there were gaps of even three to three and one-half kilometers. Even if some of this coast was very steep, this was obviously much too far apart. Lacking generally were a clear understanding of the dangerous situation and the determined will to prevent the enemy from reaching land.

Rommel's orders had not yet penetrated to the troops. On January 3, the Seventh Army reported that they had not forwarded the order for major mine laying and inshore obstacles to the corps' staffs, because the movement of additional workers and necessary materiel had first to be clarified by the commander of the army engineers. This problem was now solved very quickly.

The inspections had to be discontinued when darkness fell. We drove to Saint-Lô, the 84th Corps staff quarters, where General Marcks gave a dinner for a small group. His chief of staff, a middle-aged Austrian, was very well versed in military and naval history. The discussion was animated but always returned to the problem of coastal defense. In his daily report, Rommel summarized his impressions as follows: "Generally, the troops do not do enough work to complete the positions. The urgency is underrated. The inclination to form reserves everywhere results in a weakening of the coastal front."

At 0800 the next morning, we started for our inspection tour of the area from the mouth of the Vire to Cherbourg. The roads were especially bad. The commander of the 709th Infantry Division reported, and then Rommel explained his intentions.

When we reached Quineville shortly after low tide, Rommel noticed stakes and antitank obstacles far outside on the foreshore. When asked, a lieutenant replied that those things had been around for quite a while. Rommel at once marched towards them. It turned out to be an experimental installation of 1941. Of four stakes imbedded in concrete, which were much too long, three had remained effective. Some curved antitank obstacles, simple stakes, and stake triangles had also survived. Apparently somebody back in 1941 had had thoughts similar to ours; a pity that we had not known about them. The Field Marshal beamed, since this evidence clearly answered the much debated question as to whether the offshore obstacles would last long enough.

Except for some flooding, not much had been done north of the mouth of the Vire. Farther north, the situation was better. The army coast battery near Morsalines (four French 155mm guns) made a favorable impression. The large naval battery at Marcouf (four 210mm guns) was only in the early stages of construction. Here Rear Admiral Hennecke, the sea commandant of Normandy, joined us, having been detained by fog. We found him well informed about his sector. I drove with him in his car to use the travel time for exchanging ideas. The archaic fortress of Saint-Vaast was also in the process of being turned into a strongpoint. We noticed repeatedly the excellent locations of the Vauban solidly built fortresses, which made them suitable for our purposes.

Temporarily left behind, we missed the so-called "East Corner" with the "Hamburg" battery (four 240mm guns in casemates) and rejoined the others at Fort de la Roule, high above Cherbourg, where we had a beautiful view of the city and the port.

The waterfront of the so-called fortress was thirty kilometers long with forty resistance nests; the land front fifty kilometers with eighty resistance pockets, mostly uncompleted. The sea front was strong enough to beat off an attack from the sea. But, how to find the troops needed to occupy the land front remained unanswered.

In a rather large group we ate lunch at the soldiers' mess ruled by old Sister Barbara, who had created the establishment. Here the port commander gave afternoon coffees for officers of all branches of the Wehrmacht, a useful venture, worthy of imitation.

How inadequate cooperation could be was revealed to us immediately after lunch. At the harbor we found the ruins of a hotel and a large navy concrete air raid shelter, which had recently been blown up in order to clear the field of fire. I protested vehemently that the navy had given its permission for such an inexpedient procedure, especially since the bunker had existed before the combat positions had been determined. Now rubble was strewn about without particular improvement to the field of fire. Rommel very clearly stated his strong opinion that this action was impractical and not to his liking, a subject he brought up several times later.

After the inspection of the port facilities and the sea commandant's report concerning his defense measures, we left Cherbourg and drove to the Luftwaffe's special installations near Vauville, close to the west coast of the Cotentin Peninsula. It was very hazy and, to our regret, we could see very little. The west coast was well suited for landings; however, because of the gradually rising banks, it provided for better defenses than parts of the east coast.

Our destination for the evening was again Saint-Lô. After I learned that the Field Marshal had canceled an inspection of Mont-Saint-Michel scheduled for the next day (I had some part in this plan), in order to confer with the commanding general of the 2d Panzer Corps, Lieutenant General (SS) Hausser in Alcenon, I parted company and drove to Hennecke's staff quarters at Tourlaville, southeast of Cherbourg, since we still had a lot to talk about. Hennecke expressed a fear that he might get too many weapons. That would have been the first time! Actually, when he did finally receive the arms he was able to utilize everything.

Captain Wetzel of the Mining Office–Cherbourg explained a very simple and yet effective offshore mine with a lead cap fuse, which he had built from available parts. Several of the mines had been submerged for a few months off the northern coast east of Cherbourg and had withstood heavy storms quite well. They were simple and useful weapons. Mass production was immediately requested, but the mines of this type were not completed in time for the Invasion.

We discussed very thoroughly the question of making the larger ports unserviceable, which was particularly important for Cherbourg, an unloading port for the largest ships. Together with his staff, Hennecke had developed many ideas. But some measures could be made more effective, with the aim of preventing the unloading for as long as possible, while not destroying other port installations. We also agreed to obstruct the very small ports on the west coast—with mines, for instance—but not to destroy them. Our reasoning was that a large port like Cherbourg would quickly be repaired by a conqueror under the stress of necessity, whereas nobody would be interested in rebuilding the small ports. If a major landing should succeed, the few supplies that could enter through these lesser ports would be negligible. The same policy could later be put into effect for the Brittany ports. For the moment it was not clear who would take the responsibility for making the ports unserviceable. At the top, nobody apparently wanted to take on the job.

The next morning, January 31, there was fog, particularly thick, in the flooded area around Carentan on the mouth of the Vire. I was Hatzinger's only passenger and, to get out of the fog, we drove further inland. Behind Saint-Lô, the weather cleared, and we found real spring conditions with wonderful sunshine, steaming earth, flowering pussy willows, and green meadows. A country blessed! Typical Norman hedges abounded everywhere, similar to the Holsatian hedges, especially suited for partisans. However, partisans were notable only by their complete absence.

During dinner in the headquarters, the Field Marshal once more commented disapprovingly about demolishing well-preserved bunkers to clear fields of fire. From this starting point, the conversation shifted quite effortlessly to naval customs, and specifically to the frequently used call, "Ahoy." To the assertion that in France "Ahoy" was pronounced "Ahoa," one of the colonels, obviously deeply impressed, uttered "Oh, how interesting," to everybody's amusement. From there to the question of tracer ammunition and flare guns, it was only a short step. Then it was time for the movie: "A Man with Principles."

The following two days were spent working through the findings of the inspection tours. Concerning the navy, a regulation was drafted on rendering ports unserviceable and another on the defense of the Bay of Saint-Malo. Patrol boats were to close the gaps between radar installations. Rommel sent a letter of thanks to Admiral Wurmbach, who, in his function as Admiral–Denmark, had reacted efficiently to many of Rommel's suggestions.

During the morning Rommel met in Paris with Blumentritt, the chief of staff of the Commander in Chief West. When he returned he was a bit distressed that we had waited for him. Table talk: mines. The 191st Infantry Division had submitted maps showing planned and executed measures, which made it clear that much progress had already been made. In the afternoon the Field Marshal had a conference with general staff Colonel Höffner and a representative of the railroad on transport problems. February 2 was again filled with conferences, telephone calls, and teletypes. After lunch, in beautiful weather, we again undertook an "armed promenade" without any hunting results, but it was good to stretch one's legs and to sort out one's ideas.

On February 3, Rommel drove with Meise and me via Beauvais to Hardelot-Plage to inspect an experimental field of offshore obstacles. The practical troops there, averse to unnecessary physical exertion, had determined that they could install the stakes with a fire engine hose and thereby save much time and labor. Without much physical labor, it took only three minutes to install one stake, as compared with forty-five minutes when using a pile driver. The installation of the stakes was excellent. On some there were already flat land mines, which in theory should have been waterproof. In order to make certain, they received an extra-thick cover of tar. In contrast the Czech hedgehogs quickly sank and could only be used with a plank for support or higher up on the beach. On the average a work detail managed 100 stakes a day, which meant that a fifty-kilometer-long obstacle strip (the average length of a division sector) would take 850 men a month to install. A difficulty was that the hoses were several years old and burst frequently under pressure.

Together with General Sinnhuber, the commander of the 67th Corps, we inspected a number of installations along the coast between Boulogne-sur-Mer and Calais. Near Wissant and Sangatte, Belgian "gates" (antitank obstacles) were just brought to the beach. For small boats they would certainly represent a most uncomfortable obstacle. Further east, in the flatlands, flooding had just begun. With its own resources, the corps produced 300–400 mines daily; other supplies arrived only sporadically. The maximum number of mines placed in one divisional sector, with the help of the Waffen SS, was 4,900 mines a day.

On several occasions Rommel again explained his principles for the defense. Late in the afternoon he discussed the results in the hall of the officers' mess in Calais, where we stayed overnight. Rommel invited the sea commandant, Rear Admiral Frisius, and Major General Ellfeldt, who was to take over a division, for dinner. Quite obviously both men were experts in their fields, and Rommel liked them. Only temporarily did he become a bit sharp when the general not only rejected the idea of all paperwork in general but also refused in particular to supply the army group in time with the necessary maps and plans for the defense.

On February 4 we started our work at 0800, with a brief lecture by the port commander of Calais; inspection of the port defenses followed. Rommel then surprised a company, which was excavating dugouts on an unused airfield far behind the coast. It considered itself as the regimental reserve. This did not suit him at all, for the distance to the beach was five kilometers, and much more useful work was to be done up front. We then visited again and unannounced the command post of the 47th Division in Aires. The division commander was out inspecting his troops. His operations officer not only looked good; he also was well informed. The division was thoroughly occupied with mining, but had not yet received an order for the installation of offshore obstacles. Rommel quickly outlined his ideas and instructed the division to keep in close contact with the port commander in Calais, who was under their tactical command.

In Tourcoing, Rommel confered with von Salmuth for quite a while, partly in council, which gave me time to talk with the naval liaison officer. In the afternoon we drove back to Fontainebleau with Meise as navigator. The Field Marshal talked first about mines and shore defenses, and then about many other things. He related how, as a lieutenant colonel and liaison officer to the Youth Movement leaders, he had, in the interest of the youth and the schools, attempted to bring about cooperation between Minister of Education Rust and Youth Movement Leader Baldur von Schirach. As the son of a school principal, Rommel wanted to preserve respect for teachers and to prevent the schools from becoming an object in the power struggle between two top party officials. Rommel succeeded in bringing the two together at one table, but nothing came from the meeting.

Two days' work at headquarters followed. On February 5 Rommel drove to Blumentritt, and in the afternoon I went to the command quarters of Security Area West to discuss mining possibilities and other things. From 1800 to 2100 I attended the opera, enjoying Mozart's "The Magic Flute," and then, somewhat elated, drove to Navy Group West, where Admiral Wever had taken over from the vacationing Krancke. I discussed many details with Wever and the chief of staff, Rear Admiral Hoffmann. Shortly after midnight I was back at Fontainebleau.

During breakfast on Sunday, February 6, Rommel telephoned about the laying of mines at threatened points on the coast. I got Lieutenant Reischauer of the navy group, whom I knew well, and he arrived around noon. In the meantime Rommel went hunting for a short time and then talked with General Warlimont (Jodl's deputy from the Armed Forces Supreme Staff) about coastal defense and the chain of command in the west. Then it was Reischauer's and my turn. We discussed all possibilities of mine laying, but we could not, of course, give any orders. After the Luftwaffe representative, Lieutenant Colonel Queissner, had stated his problems, we went to lunch. Warlimont sat between Rommel and me. He remembered me from Italy, where in the spring of 1943 at my staff quarters, *Duropane*, Gause and I had informed him about the situation without mincing words. In the afternoon I drove to Paris to meet Rear Admiral Voss, the permanent naval deputy at Führer Headquarters. He arrived late from Toulon, due to an air attack there. I gave him a clear picture of the situation, informed him of Rommel's plans, and outlined the resistance against him.

The first three weeks after Rommel had assumed command had shown how disparate and weak the defenses against a landing still were, especially in western Normandy. The only exceptions were the large ports. At the same time it was confirmed that the measures found in Denmark lent themselves equally well to France—measures such as offshore obstacles, mining, emplacement, and the placing of all troops in resistance nests. The immense amount of work still to be done in order to execute these measures had grown more apparent with time. The Field Marshal had not made any progress in the question of bringing the panzer divisions forward.

To the Mediterranean and to the Bay of Biscay

*R*ommel's assignment to examine the defenses of western and southern France was still valid. Therefore the next trip was to include these areas. After a more nourishing breakfast than was the custom at the Maison Pompadour, we left at 0600 on February 7. The Field Marshal, together with the intelligence officer and the Luftwaffe operations officer, took the Horch, with Meise and me in the Mercury. A number of men from the combat squadron—armed to the teeth—followed in two open cars. One of them soon got lost, but rejoined us late that evening. At high speed we drove first to Dijon, at times along the Burgundian canal, which was, like all French canals, too narrow for modern shipping. At dawn we passed by the flat hill on which stood Alesia, whose conquest by Caesar also decided the fate of Vercingetorix and Gaul. Driving through the hilly countryside of the Beaune to Chalon-sur-Saône, the missing corners of several houses showed that room had been made for the transport of naval landing craft, motor torpedo boats, and small mine sweepers. Since the Burgundian canal was too narrow, the boats had to be carried overland from the Seine to the Saône in special vehicles. Various villages were constructed so that the passage of such large vehicles was prevented. Thus, some houses had to be removed, either totally or partially. The damage was reimbursed in cash on the spot, with the result that in some places additional houses were offered for dismantling.

After we had passed the picturesquely situated Lyon, we took a short rest on the right bank of the Rhone River and ate the sandwiches we had brought along. A cool mistral blew, and we had to warm ourselves with the names of the wine types listed on large signs which lined the road: Pomard, Chambertin, Beaujolais, Clos Vougeout, etc. The well-known Parisian restaurant Reine Pedauque had a private vineyard in this area. Changing to the other side of the river near Tournus, we passed quickly through Valence; Montelimar, the town famous for nougat (without time out for nougat); and Orange, with its Roman triumphal arch; arriving in Avignon around 1630—earlier than expected. The commander of the Nineteenth Army, General von Sodenstern, whose headquarters was located high above the town west of the river, delivered a clear and excellent report. It was gratifying how he had completely grasped, adopted and disseminated Rommel's ideas. After the report, Rommel outlined his own ideas very impressively. I listened to the reports from the rear of the room, close to a window overlooking the Pont d'Avignon and the Palace of the Popes.

We were Sodenstern's guests for dinner at the Hotel Europe in the center of town. Next to me sat a colonel who had been in China a long time and who knew Colin Ross very well. This gave material for conversation, which in Sodenstern's presence was never wanting anyway.

Since that evening nobody showed any interest in a stroll through the moonlit town, I at least took a look at the outside of the popes' palace by dawn on February 8. At 0800 we started; first to the Alpilles hills, then via the Port-de-Bouc to the hills west of Marseilles, and then through the Camargue, the completely flat area at the mouth of the Rhone River, to Port Saint-Louis where we watched a demonstration of flamethrowers against landing craft. The Camargue had changed its look compared to earlier days. The masses of stones which had previously covered the wide flatland had been gathered into thousands of rock cairns as a defense against airborne landings. For lunch we stopped briefly at the headquarters of the 4th Luftwaffe Field Corps, Lieutenant General Petersen in Montpellier, and then continued westward.

A new problem was the absence of tides in the Mediterranean. This complicated the installation of offshore stake obstacles considerably, which could not be installed with a pressure hose but had to be driven into the ground from rafts. On the other hand the constancy of the water level allowed for a relatively narrow belt of obstacles. This could most quickly be installed by using concrete and steel tetrahedrons, assembled on land and thrown into the water from rafts.

Otherwise the tasks and concerns were the same as on the Channel, except that the defense was thinner still. Except for the towns and the widely spaced resistance nests, not much had been done. Altogether, the Nineteenth Army had six divisions for the defense of a coast approximately 500 kilometers long. The 277th Infantry Division, the westernmost division, had to defend a 200-kilometer-long section.

The port town of Sète, whose main defensive support was a 150mm battery of the naval artillery, was well fortified. Our visit to the port of Agde, farther west, was too short to allow more than a superficial impression of the newly formed army coastal artillery school. After dusk we arrived at Narbonne and retired after dinner and reports.

On February 9 we started at 0600 with low clouds and rain. Without any rest to speak of and unfortunately without a view of the mountains, we rapidly drove west via Perpignan, Feux, Tarbes and Pau north of the Pyrenees. At times we drove in the foothills of the Pyrenees, and in deep ravines on winding roads, we climbed to a height of 600 meters without getting more than a glimpse of the scenery through falling snow and ragged clouds. During a so-called lunch break (eating sandwiches while standing), it became apparent that only Rommel's and my car had enough gasoline to reach the Atlantic coast. We received the last fuel reserves and drove on to Bayonne where we arrived at 1400.

The commanding general of the 86th Corps gave his report immediately, followed by Rommel outlining his principles. Without a rest, we drove to the Spanish border, along the way inspecting several army and navy positions having motley equipment. Near Hendaye we walked up to the border and, after a look into Spanish territory, turned back immediately. Without rest, we drove on the straight, modern road through the flat, wooded and swampy terrain of the Landes to First Army's headquarters at Bordeaux, which we reached around 1900. While driving into town our Mercury forced aside a car without plates, which had tried to approach Rommel's car from behind in a suspicious manner. Later it turned out that it was the city's guide, who had awaited us at the wrong location and who had tried to cut in front of Rommel's car. We found First Army headquarters without his help; in any event, Rommel's safety was more important.

We lost no time at First Army headquarters. We had barely put our luggage into our rooms when the discussion with General Blaskowitz began. That only an experimental strip of coastal defense obstacles was under construction, although the army had received Rommel's constant proposals and suggestions, indicated how uncertain the success of mere advice was without the authority to give orders. At 2100 we had an evening snack quite casually. At 2200 the supply officer of First Army reported on the supply situation. Then came the army staff signal communication officer discussing his work, and finally the commander of Fortress Engineers IV reported on the continuous construction in First Army area. During this less than stimulating topic sleep overcame several of the listeners. That finished the day.

Departure at 0800 on February 10 was a comparatively leisurely time. On our way to the mouth of the Gironde we saw several positions on the wide sandy beach of the Atlantic coast, among them one manned by Indians. The Fortress Gironde–South was well equipped with artillery—two 280mm railroad guns with a firing range of 29,500 meters and one army coast battery consisting of six 152mm guns. On the land front the resistance posts were, however, up to three and one-half kilometers apart and were manned partly by Cossacks. The harbor station of Le Verdon with a pier for large steamers had been prepared for demolition. After a meal from the field kitchen we crossed over to Royan on the northern shore. The crossing took a good hour and, in a lively westerly breeze and some swell, some of the passengers came very near the edge of seasickness.

The sea commandant and later defender of Royan, Admiral Michahelles, joined our party at Gironde–South and the chief of the 4th Security Division, Captain R. Lautenschlager, at Gironde–North. The construction here had progressed well; ultimately, the fortress held out until the last days of the war.

After the conferences and lectures, which followed the usual course, I drove with Lautenschlager to La Rochelle, to discuss his problems with his staff.

The next morning (February 11) I returned to Rommel's group, who were inspecting positions in and around La Rochelle. Here too the construction had made good progress, and this fortress also held out until the war ended.

Subsequently Rommel drove to Le Mans for a conference with General Dollmann, "in whose command mining and the construction of coastal offshore barriers has now started with maximum effort" (TBR). Independently I drove to the commander of U-boats West, Captain Rösing, and visited him at his staff quarters near Angers, to discuss with him the part his men and boats would play in the defense. It was confirmed that the prospects for U-boats taking an effective part in the defense were dim, because the first boats capable of high underwater speed were still on the stocks, and the old, slow submarines would not stand a chance against enemy antisubmarine weapons. Only boats equipped with snorkels could even expect to survive, but there were not many of them. Using the ground personnel of the submarine arm in the defense constituted a very poor alternative.

Later in our trip I inspected a subterranean food supply depot near Tours on the northern shores of the Loire. Before the war, the French government had run a motor factory here in a subterranean stone quarry (a soft stone that hardened when exposed to the air). The German Luftwaffe removed the machines and placed them somewhere above ground, thereby gaining 50,000 square meters of bomb-proof storage space. Actually that was much too valuable for a food supply depot.

In the evening, Rommel had a lengthy phone conversation with Jodl, during which he discussed the following points (KTB):

1. At the First and Nineteenth Armies generally everything in order; however, the western part of Nineteenth Army and the center of First Army is too thinly defended. Proposal: move troops from the interior to the coast.
2. Before his leave, Field Marshal von Rundstedt ordered the formation of an artillery division by pulling out batteries. Since these units are insufficiently motorized, timely combat commitment on the coast seems doubtful; therefore further weakening of the already not too strong coastal defense is untenable.
3. Chain of command unclear since orders are given by: Field Marshal Sperrle as deputy of Rundstedt in his position as Commander in Chief West; Rommel as deputy of Rundstedt in his position as Commander Army Group B; the chief of staff of the Commander in Chief West; and (especially thorough but lacking combat experience) the operations officer of the Commander in Chief West.
4. Mine supply improved.
5. Detailed report about the impending visit at Führer Headquarters.

The Fifteenth Army proposed testing the offshore obstacles with small boats to determine their effectiveness. This was not quite as simple as it sounded. Genuine obstacles with mines could not be used for such tests, and the gentlemen from the army often had no real conception of even a small boat's momentum. If such a boat would flatten the stake obstacles without incurring much damage, which in a simple case was completely possible, this could result in disappointment with unfavorable effects on our future work. Above all, many lacked the perception of the effect the mass of obstacles would have on the great number of landing vehicles. Several tests were later run at various places, but the results were not conclusive.

Further points were: the naval units on land would have to mine their positions themselves. The artillery division would not be formed; instead, units would be pulled out for maneuvers. Outlines would be issued showing the appropriate use of a stationary infantry division in a coastal defense section.

At lunchtime (February 12), General Guderian, in his position as inspector general of panzer troops, visited Rommel for a discussion on the employment of panzer units in the support of coastal defense. "The inspector general shares the commander of the army group's point of view, that the intervention of the panzer units during the first hours of an enemy landing will have to be guaranteed" (KTB). Rommel remarked in his notes: "Guderian agrees with me on the mining and the forward deployment of the panzer reserves."

At lunch Guderian proved to be a bright and entertaining guest. I talked with him about his *Tigerfibel* (Tiger primer), the first official German service regulations in rhyme. Guderian was visibly pleased, and this started an animated conversation on a great variety of subjects.

On the morning of February 13 Rommel was in Paris in order to discuss with the staff of the Commander in Chief West how the alarm readiness on the coast could be increased without hampering training. Seventh Army reported that they had no wood for the offshore obstacles. Their woodcutters were already working in the Vosges. Moreover, Seventh Army wanted the mining of several bays on the west coast of Brittany. This was understandable, but was, because of the especially heavy surf there, not easily done. Moreover they complained that the combat orders for the light naval forces (vessels in the vicinity of the landing area were supposed to attack the landing fleet at once), had been sent to them by chance. The army command had a considerable talent for not utilizing its naval liaison officers.

On February 14 and 15, Rommel drove to the 9th SS Panzer Division and then inspected the sector from the Somme to west of Dieppe. In many places construction had progressed well. The 348th Infantry Division had so far laid 160,000 mines in a stretch of thirty kilometers. The 21st Panzer Division, stationed in the rear area, had fifty-four German and twenty-eight French tanks and thirty-five assault guns at its disposal.

On his way back Rommel stopped at Auberville to have a look at the quarters he occupied in 1940. He then visited the castle of La Roche-Guyon on the Seine, fifty kilometers south of Paris, which had been selected for his new staff quarters.

The next two days brought telephone calls about antiaircraft detachments, the transfer of various battalions, the moving of the 9th SS Panzer Division and the 271st Infantry Division behind the coast in the Nineteenth Army area and participation by Rommel and Guderian in a war game of Panzer Group West. The navy released seven 88mm and 150mm batteries for this use. As a result of the last trip, the Mediterranean coast and southern France had moved into the spotlight. Deliberations were made on the possibility that the enemy might first land in southern France. A conference with all the senior commanders in chief west, which was to take place at Führer Headquarters on February 21, was postponed indefinitely.

We went hunting without success, except for the sighting of a few wild boar. In the evening of February 14, we celebrated Gause's birthday in harmonious company. Rommel gave a very affectionate speech in honor of the birthday child.

On February 18 Rommel, Meise and I drove to the west coast of Brittany. We left headquarters at 0700 and drove first to Paris to pick up General Blumentritt. The inspections began at Saint-Nazaire, where the town had been destroyed virtually beyond recognition. But the harbor was still fully intact as a base for submarines and security forces. The commanding general of the 25th Army Corps, General Farnbacher, reported first. The sector of his southernmost division, the 275th Infantry Division, was definitely the most variegated we had so far encountered. The division, still in the process of formation, consisted of little more than one divisional and one regimental staff, one artillery unit, and two battalions of old men. Therefore, the sector was provided another regimental staff and one battalion from the 343rd Infantry Division, and had retained two battalions of the previously removed 243rd Infantry Division. In addition, it contained twenty-seven companies of fortress cadre troops, seven eastern battalions, one Russian bicycle detachment, and one Russian company of engineers. One Russian cavalry regiment was on loan to the Normandy sector for installing mines.

Each of the major fortresses and ports of Saint-Nazaire, Lorient, and Brest had one battalion of infantry. This scarcely sufficed to guard the extensive land front and its valuable installations with infantry patrols.

Available as reserves were smoke-laying troops, barrage balloon crews, dock police, and dock workers. The latter, however, could be removed at any time. The best was the coastal artillery, with one army coast artillery detachment each in every fortress; one to two heavy-caliber, two to three medium-caliber naval batteries and, for all three, sixteen naval antiaircraft batteries.

After inspecting several strongpoints, to which I added unofficially the prehistoric monoliths of Carnac, we spent the night at Quiberon, at the outermost point of the narrow peninsula that closes Quiberon Bay to the west. On November 20, 1759, an English fleet of twenty-three ships of the line, commanded by Hawke, had pursued a French unit of almost equal strength into this bay and had defeated them at dusk in a hard battle fought between the cliffs and reefs during a raging northwest storm. This exemplary naval accomplishment secured English naval superiority for the second half of the Seven Years War.

Back home, Gause, in a telephone conversation with Warlimont, tried unsuccessfully to achieve some progress in the question of command of fast mobile units. "OKW does not desire their movement from the present areas" (KTB).

February 19 started with a conference in the soldiers' mess at Quiberon. We discussed the defense of Saint-Nazaire, followed by ways of confusing the enemy during his approach to the coast and during the actual disembarkation, such as using false navigation markers and artificial smoke. Finally the discussion shifted to the utilization of submarine personnel for land fighting, and the paralysis of ports, with special emphasis on preventing the unloading of larger ships.

Blumentritt joined me in my car during the next part of our drive. He told in a witty and entertaining manner of his job as chief of staff for Rundstedt, who, more or less, was the connecting link to Marshal Petain. First we visited a base on the mouth of the Etel, southeast of Lorient, and then Port Louis, the old harbor town, situated on what can well be called the Fjord of Lorient, founded during the time of mercantilism when navigation to the Orient started in a grand manner. Now the

French war port served as a German submarine base from which Dönitz had for years directed the submarine war in the Atlantic. The town was well defended by artillery, and the installation of fortifications facing inland had, thanks to technical aid from the large shipyards and workshops, made excellent progress. Rommel was very pleased that the Organisation Todt had manufactured large numbers of concrete hedgehogs for use in offshore obstacles. The submarine bunker formed more or less the core of the defense, similar to Saint-Nazaire. Artillery could not make any impression on the seven-meter concrete ceiling; this could, at best, be done with special bombs of the heaviest size. Both fortresses held out to the end of the war.

Via the smaller port towns of Concarneau and Audierne, which I did not yet know, we reached the broad bay of Douarnenez with its wide sandy beach, so far only sparingly equipped with beach obstacles and defended by one Russian battalion only. From the Pointe des Espagnols, south of the entrance to Brest, the view onto the large roadstead and the main war port of Brittany was beautiful and instructive. Near Camaret we inspected a 220mm army coast artillery battery, which guarded the outer approaches to Brest. After dark we reached the soldiers' home— Morgat, on the Bay of Douarnenez. Following the conferences and evening meal, Meise and I sat together for a while and discussed the impressions of the inspection trip and our tasks. Both of us had met many acquaintances, and both of us, as always, had disseminated Rommel's ideas. Meise remarked that we were sent out like the Apostles and had to act accordingly.

On Sunday, February 20, it was still dark when we started for Brest, and, as was often the case, we arrived there ahead of schedule. As in the other major ports, the defensive installations facing the sea were excellent; towards land they were well constructed but thinly manned. In hazy weather and pouring rain we drove to the Fjords Aber-Benoit and Aber-wrach on the northwestern coast of Brittany. They were quite well defended, although entirely unsuitable for major landings. They could only be the target of small diversionary actions or raids. Farther east, the Bay of Goulven, several kilometers wide, was well secured by flanking guns placed in the rocks and by a dense barrier of obstacles.

Accustomed to the rain, the Bretons strolled in large numbers, the farmers in their Sunday best, with black, round, wide-brimmed hats with long ribbons. The shape of the women's white headdress changed with the area.

Toward noon we drove inland to the Monts d'Arrée, a chain of hills rising to 370 meters, about thirty-five kilometers east of Brest and twenty kilometers south of the port of Morlaix. The 353rd Infantry Division, still in the process of formation, occupied the hills, and the deputy commander reported to us on the situation and his assignments. The main task was the securing of an intersection formed by secondary roads. It was not quite clear to us what the enemy would be looking for in the center of Brittany, far from the main roads. One had the impression that, in some plans, the Monts d'Arrée served a purpose similar to, although less important than that of the Plateau de Langres during the Allied campaign against Napoleon in 1814. In a very cold tent we ate a slightly warmer stew. Rommel, for once, showed manifest dislike for one of our higher-ranking hosts. It was told afterwards that he had torn Rommel's book, *Infanterie greift an*, to shreds in a review, certainly an unfair critique of this vividly written book.

During our drive back, Rommel stopped once more at the Seventh Army. Because of bad gasoline in his car we arrived late. During the conference, in which Blumentritt also participated, it became apparent that "Dollmann was now absolutely for Rommel's ideas" (PAV). Not so much the Netherlands commander. When, during the next morning, Gause announced Rommel's visit for the beginning of March especially for the inspection of the offshore barriers, the chief of the general staff informed him that "the installation of offshore barriers was still in the experimental stages, the results of which would show beach conditions to be conducive only for stake obstacles." In plain language, two months had been wasted. At the same time it turned out that the order for making ports unserviceable had still not gone through.

Warlimont replied to the question as to where and how the panzer divisions should await the enemy that "the draft of the order lay before the chief of OKW that, by means of oral discussion, should clarify deployment structure and location of the mobile units between Commander in Chief West and Army Group B. A more active participation of the commander in chief of Army Group B (Rommel) is recommended. The bulk of questions should be clarified between the two chiefs of staff of the army groups (Blumentritt and Gause)" (KTB).

With this we were back exactly to the point where we had started. The OKW even rejected the transfer of an instruction staff from the Channel Islands to the mainland, and the Seventh Army had to make do with an instruction staff of eastern troops.

Simultaneously, Rommel, in a personal letter to the subordinate armies and to the Wehrmacht Commander–Netherlands, commended them on their accomplishments and emphasized the necessity of continuing *by all means available* the large-scale mining and coastal offshore barriers according to a clearly outlined plan.

Working Out Details

*T*wo months after Rommel's arrival in France, the work was proceeding generally according to his suggestions and in the intended direction. With all his energy and great tenacity, he had devoted himself to his task and developed a novel defense system. In order to impress his ideas personally upon troops and staffs and to familiarize himself with local conditions and situations, he had become an indefatigable traveller. His plans had been well received by the troops; some of the most important staffs were, however, not yet convinced. The OKW had acknowledged Rommel's logic, but had been unable to arrive at a clear direction—not for the first time. Much detailed work was still to be done to bring troops and materiel to the important positions, to convince the reluctant, and to strengthen the defense decisively.

Now Rommel went home for ten days, to rest and to reexamine his thoughts far from the routine staff tedium. I used the time to visit a number of naval staffs, partly about matters of defense and rendering the ports unserviceable, partly to clarify questions of alert units of the navy and to try to free more forces for the west.

I started my tour on February 23 in Le Havre with a visit to Admiral von Tresckow. There I met my former flag lieutenant, Lieutenant Commander (Reserve) Kloess, a native of Siebenbürgen, who had served in the Austrian navy. As a qualified shipbuilder he now directed the shipyards of Le Havre together with twenty-three German foremen and master workmen. He handled the 12,000 French workers so intelligently that they produced excellent work without the slightest sabotage up to the day when the approaching Allies took the town under artillery fire.

In Rouen I spoke first with the port captain, who knew the orders and had already taken the appropriate measures, and then with the commanding admiral and his staff.

On February 24 in Boulogne I witnessed an attempt to test a stake barrier with a 120-ton British landing craft. Nothing happened, because the water level was already too high and the craft passed over the stakes.

I had discussions first with the port commander, then with the commander of the 2d Security Division at his staff quarters, and then drove on to Utrecht to visit Kleikamp, the commanding admiral in the Netherlands. We lost time in Utrecht because we did not know that the staff building was located at the town's entrance. The first person we asked for directions was a German sailor, who, with a loving bride on his arm, seemed to be a resident. However, he replied that he was here only on a trip. Two Dutchmen did not know the address of the staff, a third one knew it so well that we became suspicious and did not believe him. Finally we found the office of the town commander and, with the aid of a city map, determined that we only needed to drive a short distance to reach our destination.

Conferences with Naval Commander–North Holland (Captain Stöphasius) at the naval base of Den Helder followed on February 25. The subjects discussed were mines and rendering port facilities unserviceable. Then we drove over the dike that closes the Zuider Zee and via Groningen and Nieune-Schans to Leer. There we took one of my men, who up until now had officially protected us from partisans, to the station in time to catch a train for home. In the dusk we reached the Sengwarden command post, north of Wilhelmshaven, now the headquarters of Navy Command North. Admiral Förste, the commander, had just returned from Hamburg. There followed a long conference in the briefing room, with Rommel's sketches, about mines, barriers, obstacles, and the deployment of the forces. This was very useful because it revealed that none of this information had reached Sengwarden via official channels. With regard to alert units, it also revealed that Navy Command North had no power of command; OKW had put the second admirals (responsible for personnel) under its own orders and supervised them directly. At the moment, thirteen navy rifle battalions formed the front line on the Helgoland Bight. Officially they assembled only in case of an alert, but in reality some battalions already existed.

There were three types of navy alert units: "A" was to be ready for immediate action, "B" needed some time for preparation, and "C" was used only in an extreme emergency. In Germany and the rear areas the three groups totalled approximately 100,000 men. In the North Sea area, group "A" was 3,800 men strong. These alert units were inadequately equipped with arms and ammunition. Navy Command North lacked 30,000 rifles, and it was expected that this number would increase to 45,000 since every man ordered to the western area took his rifle along, and none returned. Ammunition available for each machine gun had decreased from 4,500 to 1,500 rounds.

The orders for the alert units' commitment appeared impractical. At collective places in Germany the men were to be outfitted in field gray uniforms, equipped with arms, and then moved to collection stations in France. There the combat units would be formed. This procedure failed to take into account the human values in a unit where the men know each other and therefore will perform better.

A better procedure would have been to store arms and uniforms at the unit locations and assemble and train the units there. In the case of an alert, the men could then be quickly outfitted and armed and, under their own officers, sent to the west. Even platoons and other small groups assembled in this manner and later formed into larger units represented a gain because of their inner cohesion.

The navy had transferred much coastal artillery to the occupied areas. As already mentioned, the German Bight had only two heavy and five medium batteries left. Although a major landing was hardly to be expected in this area—difficult for navigation and landings—the defender had to consider what could happen and what steps should be taken if the enemy for once acted in a completely unexpected way.

Between the conferences we had potato pancakes and bread, and lively conversation. Here, the style of life was refreshingly simple and the morale good, although nobody closed his eyes to the dangers of the situation. This was due to the admiral's flexibility and versatile nature.

On February 26 I visited the second admiral–North Sea, Rear Admiral Engel, in Buxtehude. With his voluminous personnel bureau, he occupied an immense barracks, populated almost exclusively by friendly girls giving the Nazi salute.

Again, alert units were the subject for discussion. Because he only provided personnel and had nothing to do with arms and transport, Admiral Engel could not add anything of substance. While we were still in discussion, one of his experts returned starry-eyed from Hamburg, from a conference on alert units. According to him things looked a bit different again, somewhat like I had heard in Sengwarden, with collection camps in Germany and in the western area, with final formation only in the west.

While staying with the coastal commander–German Bight, I wrote a report about the defense of the Helgoland Bight and the alert units with proposals for better organization and sent it via teletype to Navy High Command. I was anxious to achieve the transfer of as many naval land units as possible to the rear area in France in order to free parts of the army for the coast.

On my way back to headquarters I stopped in Belgium at Camp Beverloo on March 1 to speak with the commander of a naval training regiment stationed there. His orders for action in case of alert were again different. It was to be hoped that the concerted effort of all participants would result in gradually creating some degree of order.

On March 2 I discussed with an official of the military administration in Brussels ways and means to improve street markings for night driving. It was certain that, in the event of invasion, most of the automobile transport would be forced to drive at night with dimmed lights. The street markings were not adjusted for night driving, which became quite apparent during every night drive on empty streets in a passenger car. At almost every intersection and road crossing, one had to stop and search for the correct direction. Much precious time would be lost in an emergency if nothing was done to change this. In the cool of the sunny afternoon I drove via Mons, Laon, and Meaux (where I passed a very unpleasant and vulgar anti-German monument) back to Fontainebleau. While I was away, Captain Peters had arrived from Fontainebleau. I knew him from Cuxhaven where, as sea commandant, he had gained much experience in coastal defense. He was full of enthusiasm for his new assignment as my closest co-worker. We complemented and understood each other well. He soon took over liaison to the naval staffs in Paris and the task of influencing their advisors.

Gause, in the meantime, had made several trips to the coast, and had conducted many conferences and made numerous phone calls. The 67th Corps, at the mouth of the Somme, complained that no agreement could be reached with the navy about the direction of the fighting on the coast, so I should quickly visit them. General Peltz, the commanding general of the 9th Air Corps, had reported during a conference that his corps should be committed only at night since heavy reaction during daylight hours prevented his planes from getting through. He estimated that in daytime action his forces would not last longer than two days.

The Seventh Army had tested a captured 120-ton British boat on an offshore obstacle barrier of wooden stakes and Czech hedgehogs. In the process several wooden stakes broke, and others were knocked over before the boat came to a halt. From this experiment, the army concluded that it would be necessary to attach mines to the obstacles. We did not object to that decision.

The 16th Luftwaffe Field Division in the Netherlands had begun to buy automobiles to get motorized, but had to stop these efforts because of protests of the Reich Commissioners of the Netherlands.

On March 2 Western Command and Navy High Command occupied themselves with naval alert units. To the subordinated commandos, Western Command pointed out that "these units will first conclude their special tasks and can only then be used as combat units in local emergencies." This applied especially to the ports. There it was important that the few men of the port office, and communication and signal units, etc., first saw to it that work continued for as long as possible, and then installations that could aid the enemy were to be made unusable.

The naval training units in the occupied areas were available for flexible use, but only after "obtaining agreement from the appropriate naval authority." I was under the impression that during my travels I had convinced these agencies of the urgency of quick deployment and therefore took the agreement almost for granted. Thus, an order from Navy High Command which created a new and rather unpleasant situation regarding these units was all the more surprising. It said that, effective immediately:

> Tactical units, instructor units, training units, and schools situated in Germany and in the occupied areas can no longer be used for the formation of alert units. They can only be used for local defense if their immediate garrison is directly threatened by the enemy. The training units of the 2d, 3rd and 6th Naval Training Regiments are, therefore, no longer available as flexible alert units to the military commanders and the Wehrmacht Command–Netherlands.

The naval training units were mainly trained men for submarines under construction, which from the summer of 1944 were to come in large numbers, and men for the mine sweepers which were needed to guide the submarines safely out to and back in from deep waters.

Western Command answered: "In case of threatening danger, even the last armed man will have to be used for the tasks which Western Command considers necessary. Western Command cannot supply replacements for missing naval forces."

The navy was still under orders which made submarine war its main task, and it was understandable that they greatly desired to commission these new boats as soon as possible. It remained to be seen, however, whether they could be built as fast as planned. On the other hand, all reports very plainly indicated that an enormous army with numerous landing craft was gathering in England, obviously for a large-scale operation in northwestern Europe.

It was also understandable that the navy suspected that naval units might be utilized locally and thereby be withdrawn from their actual duties much too early. But against such misuse one could get protection by other means. On the whole, the main problem was to muster as much strength as possible against the gathering storm. In this situation it was neither from a military nor a psychological viewpoint correct to deny oneself in favor of such a distant goal, especially since Führer Directive 51 unequivocally ordered concentration on defense in the west.

Immediately, I drafted a proposal for "small conciliations." In it I suggested that the naval training units should be available at a predetermined radius of approximately 100 kilometers around their garrisons, for security measures during an alert. My proposal was sent directly to Navy High Command, while Navy Group West was informed of it.

On March 3 Gause had an extended talk about matters of deployment and transportation with the experts at Western Command. In the afternoon, Rommel, Meise and Tempelhoff returned by plane from Württemberg. Landing at an airport near Paris, the plane blew a tire, luckily without serious damage. At Fontainebleau, Major General Schmundt, from Führer Headquarters, awaited the Field Marshal. During dinner Rommel was very cheerful, despite his remark that once more certain people were making things difficult.

In the afternoon of March 4, a beautiful day, we were hunting for wild boar. Two Frenchmen with their dogs tried to move the game into our direction. They succeeded three times, but the boar continuously broke through at spots where somewhat inferior hunters awaited them.

Admiral Krancke had invited Rommel and me for dinner with Grand Admiral Dönitz in the house of Navy Group West in Evry, between Paris and Fontainebleau. Dönitz and Rommel had a good conversation. They touched on the most essential points without pursuing any problems too deeply. Quite obviously the two very different "big lions" were assessing each other. Moreover, the circle of participants was too great to allow for profound questions. Unfortunately the matter of the alert units was only touched upon, not seriously discussed.

On Sunday, March 5, General Reinhard Wühlisch and Vice-Admiral Kleikamp arrived at Fontainebleau from the Netherlands to discuss combat direction in their area, the deployment and employment of reserves, minings, offshore obstacles, and flooding. Afterwards Rommel wrote in his notes: "In the defense area of the Netherlands not much has been done to comply with the army group's proposals and intentions." This did not, however, cloud the lunch to which he invited his visitors, and Rommel was a charming host.

Following Schmundt's visit, Gause had an extended phone conversation with Warlimont, once more about moving panzer divisions to the coast. Warlimont stated (KTB):

> The chief of the general staff of the Commander in Chief West (Blumentritt) had been informed of the army group commander's wishes. OKW could not come to a direct decision, and therefore recommended making the commander's wishes the subject of discussion between the two commanders; or, the two chiefs of staff of the army group, thereby arriving—with regard to the chain of command—at an acceptable solution, satisfactory to both parties. In view of the overall situation and the pressure on the other fronts, OKW cannot place the available mobile divisions in the area of Western Command under the command of Army Group B, especially since these units represent the only motorized reserves available to the OKW. It is not impossible that the development of the situation will force the withdrawal of one or the other of the mobile units in the near future. In the opinion expressed to Army Group D (Rundstedt), OKW expressly emphasized that Panzer Group West has to perform that which the commander of Army Group B deems necessary in regard to training.

Gause pointed out "that experience had shown that in the case of a landing, quick action was absolutely necessary." He emphasized the difficulties "now inherent in the order to request the release of mobile units in such a case. Moreover, the army group does not intend to tie the mobile units down in any way and they are at the moment only deployed in a way that guarantees their flexibility."

Warlimont promised to send Gause a copy of the OKW's letter to Blumentritt. Gause asked that Rocket Launcher Regiment 101 be equipped with mortars of a larger caliber, and also passed on Rommel's wish to report the results of his inspection tours to Hitler personally.

In the morning of March 6, we started on a four-day trip to the coasts of Normandy and Brittany. Gause, Meise and I accompanied the Field Marshal first to the 711th Infantry Division, whose energetic commander, Major General Reichert, apparently had his troops well in hand. His sector, between the Seine and the Orne, had a coastal length of twenty-four kilometers. Of the available 40,000 mines, 25,000 had been installed, and four kilometers of the offshore area were already well sown with obstacles. The only annoying thing was the revelation that somewhere someone had tested simple stake obstacles with a 300-ton ship. The vehicle had pushed some of the stakes to the side or crushed them without noticeable difficulty. No other result could be expected, since the stakes did not contain any mines. On the other hand, a ten-ton boat actually became stranded on top of the stakes, to everyone's satisfaction. Rommel prohibited any further tests, and declared himself satisfied with the result. He knew perfectly well that topping the stakes with mines was the best method to make them really effective. Unfortunately the supply of flat land mines—the only mines suited for this purpose—was limited. An additional handicap was that the mines were officially watertight, but nobody was certain that they would remain so under the changing water pressure caused by the tides.

Some of the gun emplacements for the coastal artillery were finished; others were still under construction. There was a painful shortage of radio equipment for communication between observation posts and the resistance nests. We did not expect telephone connections to survive a heavy shelling. The 716th Infantry Division (Major General Richter), whose sector joined on the left, made preparations to transfer the left half of its much too wide sector to the 352d Infantry Division, effective March 15. This meant the doubling of combat strength on the coast. But a thirty–forty kilometer stretch for each of the two divisions was still too thin. It is remarkable that this reinforcement, which caused the Americans great difficulties during their landing, remained completely unnoticed by their intelligence service. Even an enemy who had superiority in the air and who, moreover, with the help of the inhabitants, had the best sources for his intelligence service, did not know everything.

In February the division had laid 62,000 mines and hoped to reach 100,000 for the whole sector by March. Eight kilometers of the offshore obstacles were complete. The stakes had to be driven in at some spots, since the soil was too hard for installation with a water hose. Belgian gates were a good substitute for the stakes in these areas. The concrete work was not progressing satisfactorily, apparently because Organisation Todt allegedly had not received the blueprints for constructing the casemates.

We concluded our inspection at 1800 with a conference at the officers' quarters of the division in Caen, in which General Marcks also partici- pated. Afterwards we were together with the divisional staff and then spent the night at a hotel in Caen.

March 7. At 0730 we drove to Riva Bella (*Ouistreham*) on the mouth of the Orne and then along the coast westward, accompanied by General Marcks and the commanders of the 716th and 709th Infantry Divisions. Rommel inspected the offshore obstacles, some positions and strong- points, and the few floodings which the terrain allowed in the sector of the two divisions. Rommel's verdict was (TBR): "Layout of mine fields and development of offshore obstacles for the most part unsatisfactory." In the sector directly west of the mouth of the Orne there were no ob- stacles at all. As a consequence he gave strict orders that each battalion sector, independent of its neighboring sectors, had to start the construc- tion of obstacles. He also demanded deeper mine fields, for the present up to 1,000 meters, and ordered the fields to be rounded out with dum- my mines.

For lunch we once more made a brief stop at the soldiers' mess at Ourville near Cherbourg. An inspection of the west coast of the Cotentin Peninsula down to the small port of Carteret followed. There were enough sandy beaches for major landings almost everywhere. Behind them the mostly rocky banks rose rather steeply. Even taking into ac- count that a decisive landing on the west coast was improbable because it was entirely open to all western gales, so limited an operation in con- nection with a major landing on the eastern shore was entirely possible. Now this part of the coast was especially weakly manned: one battalion's sector was only twenty kilometers wide. Rommel ordered that even the last reserve company be moved forward. The solution here was well- armed and mined resistance nests which could overlook the ten-kilo- meter-wide, crescent-shaped bays sufficiently and could cover them with artillery. In between, the high banks needed heavy mining and the beaches needed to be filled with obstacles.

When we reached the small Norman town of Coutances, the boundary of General Marcks' command sector, the general bade us farewell. We continued to the small port of Granville on the eastern bank of the Bay of Mont-Saint-Michel, where we took a brief look at the port. Unfortunately the road along the coast was closed because of mines. We therefore had to use the main road further inland and arrived after dark at Dinard, a seaside resort on the west bank of the Rance opposite Saint-Malo, after traveling via the city of Dinan. General Straube (71st Corps) welcomed us at the Villa Mond, owned by the British economist and politician by the same name. It was a splendidly furnished place, complete with, among other things, fine china in glass cases. In an endeavor to entertain the Field Marshal, Gause showed him several beautiful pieces of antique Sèvres china and talked enthusiastically about this famous company's newest products. Rommel listened patiently, and said, chuckling: "Maybe they could manufacture mines for us." Sacrilegious perhaps, but the porcelain was waterproof and antimagnetic, and therefore well suited for small, enclosed containers. As usual, Rommel retired around 2200. The rest of us gathered around the fireplace for a while, and I later withdrew to the library. Most informative was the motto of a book plate: "Make yourself necessary."

On March 8 we left at 0730. In Belle-Ile-en-Terre (in contrast to Belle-Ile-en-Mer opposite Quiberon), we had a conference with the commanders of the 266th Infantry Division (Morlaix area) and the 3rd Parachute Division, stationed in the rear area. The division had been replenished and the soldiers had finished one-third of their training. However, they lacked heavy weapons. Five eastern battalions of little combat value were employed in the 266th Infantry Division area. Again Rommel discussed his conviction that the battle had to be fought *on the coast*, which necessitated the forward deployment of all available forces even during this time of preparation.

In the small Bay of Saint-Michel near Lannilis, north of Brest, we subsequently inspected a giant offshore obstacle of iron stakes, wooden stakes, Belgian gates, drag curves, mined floats, anchored mined posts, iron rails in concrete, Czech hedgehogs, buffers, mined wooden stakes, and rollers that looked like porcupines. Here the corps commander, divisional staff, and the troops had effectively cooperated to put into effect the suggestions Rommel had given them on his first visit. The Field Marshal was happy; I had certain reservations. The anchored floats and beams covered with mines theoretically adjusted excellently to the tides, but the moorings were too weak to withstand a powerful sea in a real storm for very long. Once they broke loose, the builder was in for a big disappointment.

Flat land mines, moreover, were very hard to get. Therefore, the navy had developed coastal mine A and surface mine A to accomplish the same purpose. These exposed a far smaller area to the sea. From an overall point of view, it would have been more expedient to concentrate on these mines. Unfortunately, in spite of all efforts not much progress had been made in this respect. For stationary stake obstacles there were no flat land mines. I proposed saws and a kind of can opener made of strong steel as substitutes, which could also be used on the drag curves, designed to stop small craft. I had no illusions about the adequacy of these substitutes. The logic behind them was that while a boat damaged by these obstacles might not sink, the crew would not want to move about in a damaged boat and would therefore keep back accordingly. It was one of those makeshift measures which did not bring much by themselves, but had a certain value when coordinated with the stopgap measures.

Because the soil was very soft, the Belgian gates had sunk deeply. After we had splashed in the water long enough, we drove to the mine fields in the rear area. Here Rommel was less satisfied. The mines were laid in too regular a pattern and, above all, were too close together so that one mine explosion would set off the others, and shelling could easily result in opening a gap. On the coast northwest of Saint-Brieuc, Rommel criticized one of the commanders severely, because he felt himself too weak to hold his position. This was a characteristic example of inadequate grasp of the situation. Certainly, with his few men, he could not stop a major landing. But on the rocky coast this was a technical impossibility, and, in view of the poor interior road net, highly improbable. Against a small operation, however, his forces were sufficient.

We stopped for a short lunch at the attractive soldiers' mess of Le Val André, the villa of a French politician with a beautiful view of the sea and the cliffs in warm sunshine. In the afternoon we ferried to Saint-Malo, inspected the defensive nest "Osteck" and from a hill viewed Cancale with the wide Bay of Mont-Saint-Michel. Not much had been done here, mainly because of the lack of personnel. Rommel suggested the use of two companies from the SS geological battalion, whose existence surprised most of us, and to employ the inhabitants for good pay. In addition, the attempt should be made to obtain one more battery from the navy. During dinner at the Villa Mond, Colonel Aulock, the commander of Fortress Saint-Malo, was very amusing and frank. One had the impression that his personnel file carried the remark: "Not a simple subordinate," which in such a personality was no disadvantage. With easily guided subordinates one can perhaps administer in the long run, but never lead.

For March 9, it was planned to drive a short way along the bay east of Cancale and then inland to visit the staff of the 155th Reserve Panzer Division at Fougères and Seventh Army at Le Mans. I had ceased to suggest visits to Mont-Saint-Michel. But while inspecting a position several miles away, Rommel, with a glance in my direction, exclaimed: "Today we'll have a look at Mont-Saint-Michel." With visible joy he absorbed the beauty of the abbey's classic Gothic granite, uniting fortress, monastery, and place of pilgrimage under one roof. In a rare moment of relaxation he enjoyed the abundance of beauty offered by the medieval architecture and also the view over the wide bay from the various observation points. All this did not, however, prevent him from turning to me, as we were leaving the granite rooms and halls, and, while stepping through a portal, remarking with a twinkle in his eyes, "Good bunker."

Although it was not even 1100, we disregarded our usual habits and took an early lunch at the famous Poulard restaurant. We ate the customary crêpes, prepared over the wood fire of an open fireplace in a long-handled pan right before our eyes. The innkeeper herself supervised the proceedings, since she apparently noticed that she had a special visitor. But only when we left did she discover who her guest had been.

Near a massive castle and an old fortification with a tower we entered the medieval town of Fougères shortly past noon. The combat group *Polster* (padding) had in the meantime changed its name to *Falke* (falcon), and almost reached the strength of a small panzer division. The antitank battalion of the 155th Reserve Panzer Division alone had approximately sixty tanks, types III and IV. The continuous loss of trained personnel unfortunately diminished the combat-readiness of the unit severely. The engineer battalion was working somewhere near Bordeaux.

At Seventh Army, Rommel expressed his satisfaction with the progress made so far, but stressed the necessity of continuing work in all sectors, or even to begin it. For the commitment of the 352d Infantry Division to the west of the 716th Infantry Division, Rommel proposed only a partial forward movement of the division on the beaches, so that the division could easily be redeployed. Rommel's proposal, which partly contradicted his own orders, was possibly influenced by the desire to mitigate the difficulties which the OKW imposed repeatedly. For the west coast of the Cotentin Peninsula, a kind of defensive sector with heavy minings and offshore barriers was discussed. The army's stockpile of mines amounted to 100,000; another 170,000 were on their way. Five engineer battalions, working on bunkers for preparing and launching guided missiles, were lost to the coastal work force. The army planned to use the complete 275th Infantry Division on the west coast of Brittany, and moreover to regroup their troops in order to free forces for Cherbourg and Brest. The army reported that the fortresses would, within a few days, be completely stocked with food but not with arms and ammunition.

Other problems needing attention were the prevention of the undesired Sauckel action (transporting Frenchmen to Germany for work), at least in the entire coastal area, and the transformation of the resort Bagnoles-sur-Orne in southern Normandy into a hospital town. "Troops" there consisted only of a female signal detachment of the Luftwaffe.

Rommel remarked in his notes: "As a result of these inspections I have gained the impression that much has already been done on coastal defenses, but if the army group's plans and intentions had been studied more carefully, much more could have been achieved, so that with continuous mining and installation of offshore barriers a disembarking enemy would be stopped right on the beaches."

It took Seventh Army longer than Fifteenth Army to adjust to Rommel's thoughts and plans and turn them into reality. As Rommel once pointed out, Fifteenth Army was six weeks ahead of Seventh Army in coastal defense, a lead which it retained until the Invasion. Since the Invasion attack struck almost exclusively on the front of Seventh Army, the loss of six weeks had crucial effects.

At the New Headquarters

Soon after arriving in France, Rommel had decided that Fontainebleau was much too distant from the coast, and had looked for quarters located more conveniently to the probable invasion front. Initially the search went in the direction of the English Channel. Rommel asked OKW to assign to him an already existing headquarters near Soissons, northeast of Paris. Prepared for Operation "Sealion," it was centrally located behind the coastal arch reaching from the Schelde to the mouth of the Seine and nearest to the mouth of the Somme (150 kilometers air distance).

By the time his application had been denied Rommel had already changed his mind about the best location. He now selected La Roche-Guyon, a small town with a castle about fifty kilometers from Paris, on the north bank of the Seine on a river bend, near the small town of Mantes, away from the main traffic but close to several major roads. It was slightly farther from the English Channel than Soissons, but was a good 100 kilometers closer to the Bay of the Seine and to western Normandy.

On March 9 at 1900 we arrived at our new quarters. The castle, built between the twelfth and the seventeenth centuries, stood at the foot of the riverbank's slope; the oldest part, a tower built around the year 1000, capped the hill above. Over the years, the inhabitants had tunnelled several passages and caves into the soft limestone, which our engineers now had transformed into communication centers, briefing rooms, and alert quarters.

The castle itself, while historically and artistically valuable, was neither especially large nor grandiose. Only part of the staff found shelter in the castle; the rest were lodged in the village. In keeping with the old customs of chivalry in war, the inhabitants were not forced to leave their property.

By chance I had already met the owner of La Roche-Guyon and his family in 1941–42. It was nice to return to the familiar house, although the changed circumstances and the inherent dangers to the inhabitants gave food for thought. At the moment this could not be altered, but several things were made easier, and it can be reported that the castle and the inhabitants later survived the storm.

March 10 officially served for getting accustomed to the new surroundings. In the morning Rommel received General Jakob, general of engineers and fortresses at Army High Command, and another high-ranking engineer officer. In the afternoon General Wimmer, the commanding general at the Luftwaffe field command Belgium–Northern France, arrived for a conference. We naval people installed our work and briefing rooms in an adjacent building, in which the men also lived. The two officers were quartered in a comfortable house at the village, a few minutes from the castle. My room in the castle had a large window facing the Seine. Presently it was quite cool since the whole wing had apparently not been heated in years, and the walls, several meters thick, exuded a remarkable cold. And the operation of the medieval fireplace required some learning. Wood, however, was not scarce, and after a few days sufficient warmth had seeped into the walls.

Already, on March 11, Rommel, accompanied only by the intelligence officer, went for two days to the sector from the mouth of the Somme to Calais, which OKW and Western Command still considered as the most likely invasion place. North of the Somme the 344th Infantry Division had both their regiments well forward, with the reserves directly behind. Mine barriers at a depth of one kilometer were to be finished in fourteen days. Of the thirty-four kilometers of offshore obstacles for high water, twenty-one kilometers had been completed. Then the construction had been stopped because of an apparently misunderstood order from Fifteenth Army. This aroused the suspicion that it could be the result of the experiment with landing craft against offshore obstacles. Rommel corrected these "misunderstandings" with great vigor, and emphasized the necessity of extending the obstacles far into the water down to low tide.

Already the 344th Infantry Division and the 49th Infantry Division, adjoining on the north, had developed a kind of land front of large mine fields, for the time being partly dummy installations interspersed with resistance nests, occupied by reserve, transport, and supply units. Behind this there still existed a second line of divisions. The 49th Infantry Division had eight mines for each meter so far. The second mine barrier (Riegel), located five kilometers behind the coast, was completely planned and most of the area had been fenced in. The required mines had already arrived. Rommel wanted the belt to be eight kilometers deep, with 100 mines for each meter. Our overall impression was that the tasks had been generally well recognized and that the work had proceeded accordingly.

The results of the second day were similar. The day started at Boulogne, where the fortress was manned with 4,500 soldiers armed with 488 machine guns, fifty-one mortars, forty-one antitank guns ranging from 25mm to 88mm, ten guns up to 100mm, twenty guns of 194mm, ten antilanding guns of 75mm, seven permanently installed 50mm guns in turrets, twenty antiaircraft guns of 88mm, nine antiaircraft guns of 37mm, and twenty-four antiaircraft guns of 20mm. In addition, the port entrances were protected with nets, observation mines, and depth charge throwers. In January 26,000 mines and in February 54,000 mines had been installed in the fortress area. The sea front was very strong; the land front almost completely constructed and sufficiently manned with infantry. Of course, the 439th Infantry Division behind him made the life of the commander easier.

According to the KTB, cooperation with the Luftwaffe was good, and also with the lower naval staffs. There is no comment about the upper levels. In the journal entry, Rommel developed his ideas concerning a modern fortress and expressed his conviction that an enemy assaulting Boulogne should be beaten on the water, owing to Boulogne's good fortifications and strong defenses.

The neighboring 47th Infantry Division had installed obstacles only on twelve of fifty-five kilometers. Part of the area had a steep coast, not suited for landing. The plan was to finish in three months. Other defense possibilities were good: sixty-two batteries covered the section of the division, and part of the 349th Infantry Division stood behind it.

Inspected at the port were experimental fields of obstacles, constructed by the local navy, some with automatic alarm systems. The considerable effect of the Czech hedgehogs on the bottom of a 120-ton landing craft was demonstrated. The navy people denied the deadly effect of a flat land mine on such a craft, partitioned into forty sections. Rommel pointed out that even though the craft might not sink from running onto a mined stake, the crew's shock and alarm would be considerable. After a conference in Boulogne's officers' quarters, he also inspected the 326th Infantry Division's command post. He expressed "his satisfaction about the status of the defense efforts. They were of the greatest importance because, in case of a landing, the defense battle had to be won under any circumstances, since this would decide the fate of Germany and of Europe for the next 100 years" (KTB).

At headquarters a request of Seventh Army regarding the utilization of the 352d Infantry Division in the Bay of the Seine had, in the meantime, been regulated in such a way as to allow them to fire on the beach not only with the artillery, as Rommel had originally suggested, but with all weapons. The 352d Infantry Division received orders to take charge of the complete western sector of the 716th Infantry Division. But even this change still left the coast in this sector much weaker than the sector north of the Somme, quite apart from the missing divisions in the second line.

On March 13 Rommel had a conference with the military commander of northwestern France regarding his assignments and the utilization of his forces. In the beautiful spring afternoon we undertook an armed promenade through the rolling countryside. From the castle we walked over meadows and through the woods, without any hunting success, except for a bunch of wild primroses. The walk reminded me vividly of another a year previous, also in the shadow of a threatening invasion; together with several Italian admirals, through Campagna north of Rome, where we had found the wild cyclamen in bloom.

On March 14 Rommel went on the road again, accompanied by Meise, Major Behr and me. Behr drove with me. He had come from Russia, had been decorated with the Knight's Cross in Africa, and was an excellent type of the younger officer of the general staff. While we were driving to the 81st Corps' command post (General Kuntzen), Gause ordered via telephone from Seventh Army that the Netherlands and the corps commands in between provide detailed maps of their final plans for May 1.

General Kuntzen reported the situation of his corps very clearly and subsequently touched upon a number of details. Rommel found the troops still too dispersed. Once more he outlined his thoughts very thoroughly: "The commander in chief desires a land defense that within this divisional defensive position includes the artillery positions as well. . . . In the defense of the land front the division can only depend on itself, since reserve divisions can be withdrawn. The area of the division will form a fortress. Then there will be no objections to withdrawing all the reserves in the fall for use in Russia" (KTB).

Subsequently we visited the sectors of the 245th Infantry Division and the 17th Luftwaffe Field Division east of Le Havre. The coast here was steep, with deep ravines from the beach to the undulating country behind. The beach was narrow and largely covered with small rocks. An attack here was not overly promising and, therefore, was unlikely. On the other hand, the difference between the tides was slight, therefore secondary operations utilizing the protection of the cliffs were not impossible. Intelligence had moreover reported British exercises in overcoming this type of terrain. Therefore, plans were discussed to barricade the ravines, to install roll mines, and to blast whole sections of the steep cliffs. Several times we lost our way, which showed that not every division commander knew his sector in sufficient detail.

The small ports of Yport and Etretat seemed adequately defended. Towards evening we approached Le Havre from the north, and inspected the construction site of the casemates for a 380mm naval battery. One gun was in position, but was shortly thereafter severely damaged in an air attack. None of the battery's guns were ready for the Invasion. They could have fired on the English landings immediately west of the Orne.

We inspected the beach, with very good obstacles. Beside the entrance to the port, barges had been scuttled, a sensible measure, which, however, forced our craft to navigate accurately when entering the port.

The fortress commander's report showed that here too weapons were sufficient and the seaward defense was quite strong. On the land side, work had begun, made easier by the fact that Le Havre was situated on a headland, but not enough workers were available. Rommel acknowledged the good work, but demanded that the 17th Luftwaffe Field Division, adjoining to the east, accelerate the construction of offshore obstacles and increase mining operations.

Fortress commander General Leutze and sea commandant Rear Admiral von Tresckow joined us for dinner at the soldiers' mess. Leutze was about to take over a new command, a change regretted on both sides.

Rommel was in an especially good mood—although he was never actually in a bad mood—and told delightful stories about his first impressions of the navy. That was in 1919, when he was stationed in Friedrichshafen as company commander. A company of so-called red sailors was transferred there from Stuttgart, where they had been too troublesome. Although only a handful had actually sailed the seas, they all wore the blue navy uniform. Rommel had received the thankless and vaguely defined order of somehow coping with them. The sailors at once rejected Rommel's *Pour la Mérite* in their Swabian dialect as *Blechle*, a small piece of tin. But they were a sharp group, and, if treated correctly, in many respects unexpectedly level-headed. Although they demanded that one of their friends, a sergeant from Rommel's company, be released from detention, Rommel was able to talk them out of it. Applying a mixture of firmness, kindness, alertness, and occasionally extreme roughness, Rommel controlled and transformed them into a useful troop. Under his command they proved their ability fighting communists in the Ruhr. Later on several transferred to the police. They formed a delegation, went to Rommel and asked him to transfer with them to the police, so they could continue to serve under his command.

During an early breakfast on March 15, the discussion turned to landing possibilities on coastal cliffs. Rommel was somewhat shocked by the lack of readiness and comprehension in some divisions. In light fog we drove to Bolbec and the 346th Infantry Division, stationed here in the second line. The staff resided in a nicely situated mansion. Major General Diestel reported that his infantry stood in a broad front behind the 17th Luftwaffe Field Division: one regiment was completely mobile; the two others had one horse-drawn battalion each. The two other battalions and the supply trains were provisionally motorized, the men rode bicycles, and the artillery regiment was horse-drawn. One battalion worked on a second position. Rommel considered the construction of this position a mistake, because it was usually not manned and could, in case of an airborne enemy landing, easily be used by the enemy for his own protection. The division did not have clear combat orders. It was deployed in such a way as to destroy an airborne enemy landing from resistance nests on dominating points. The division was also prepared to send its regiments to the coast along selected routes. One battery was ready to fight airborne landings immediately. Rommel demanded this of all batteries, and requested the division to move forward so that its front line stood at the upper entrance of the ravines to the beaches. Furthermore he suggested the preparation of earthslides by blasting.

Until now the troops had lived in quarters near the villages, with the majority living right in the villages. Rommel was for removing the troops from them completely because the villages offered the enemy excellent targets (the same applied to the subsequently visited 84th Infantry Division). The average age in the division was thirty-three years. The boot supply had improved; the food was good, but a bit meager for the younger men and the *Ostkämpfer* (men who had fought in Russia).

The 84th Infantry Division, still in the organizational process, was only partly combat-ready. The commander was an old Africa fighter, which led to reminiscences about Tobruk. Despite the lack of weapons and equipment, training had progressed well, as became apparent during well-executed battle exercises with live explosives and hand grenades. The Field Marshal gave a short talk to the battalion which had done the exercise, expressed his satisfaction over its demonstrated dash, and his confidence in the men, whom he knew would do their best to help win the battle in the west in case of a landing.

Early in the afternoon we returned to staff quarters. Gause in the meantime had coordinated with Western Command and Seventh Army the employment of the 352d Infantry Division on the western part of the Bay of the Seine, and the transfer of the SS geological battalion to the Bay of Mont-Saint-Michel. According to an agreement entered into by Western Command and the SS Führer Headquarters, the battalion could only be employed undivided. Gause had negotiated the allotment of drag curves for stopping smaller landing craft and the delivery of antipersonnel mines and antiaircraft protection for railroad shunting yards. The next day we received an allotment for 10,000 drag curves. There were no fuses for antipersonnel mines and two million of these mines without fuses were stored in Germany. Gause, however, arranged that the other mines allotted to the west were sent by "Lightning-Arrow Transport." At the moment, this was the highest priority in transport matters. In transport, as in production, it was a high art to obtain such a high degree of priority.

At noon Rommel had a conference with General Geyr von Schweppenburg about the condition and the operational possibilities of the mobile units of Panzer Group West. Once more their points of view did not coincide. With similar results, I had, simultaneously, a one and one-half hour conference with the commander of Navy Group West. We first discussed the coastal mine A, the start of production and distribution—much too slow for my taste—and the principles of its use. The main bone of contention was, however, the division of responsibilities. Up until now Navy Group West had been lord and master in naval matters in the west for all practical purposes, with the exception of the submarine war, which was under direct orders from Berlin. Somehow I did not fit into this arrangement, and the commander in chief wished for me to be put under him. He denied my right to make proposals directly to the chief of the navy, as I had done in the case of the alert units.

But I was not his subordinate, nor was the matter of the alert units only of interest to Navy Group West. The higher staffs in Germany, at least in the North Sea area and the Navy High Command personnel office, were concerned as well. Unfortunately, at the moment my position was somewhat weakened because some time ago my deputy had committed a tactical error in the war of competition by giving an order to the commanding admiral–Channel Coast concerning the allocation and disposition of permanently mounted light naval guns. We were not at all entitled to do so, and I had personally clarified the matter long ago with Admiral Rieve, with whom I was on good terms. The deputy was no longer with me; instead, an experienced man from the coastal artillery now took care of these affairs. Nonetheless I was again reproached about the matter.

I strongly fought back, for it was an advantageous position, which I did not at all want to give up, that I could report directly to OKM when I thought it necessary. I had always, of course, informed Navy Group West of my exchanges with Navy High Command. As expected, we could reach no agreement, but all proceeded in conciliatory fashion.

Lunch at the command quarters of Security Area West in the circle of my old staff was a welcome compensation. Then, accepting the invitation of some friends, I drove to the large engineer depot in the north of Paris near the Seine. There I could watch a new manufacturing process for reinforced concrete. Its manufacture was run by a Mr. Hoyer from the Sudetenland (lost in the air raid on Dresden in February 1945). Even during the First World War, reinforced concrete had been used in shipbuilding to save steel. The success was moderate, because the concrete with the steel rods (as now used in the construction of modern buildings) was heavy and inflexible. Ships built of this material suffered damage easily. Hoyer, with a technically very elegant solution, had improved the process considerably. Instead of the steel rods, which still were as thick as a finger, he used piano wire, thereby decreasing the weight considerably. The actual trick was to put the wires under stress before they were pouring the concrete. Hoyer did this with a special device. Once the concrete had set, the wires were released and would have shrunk.

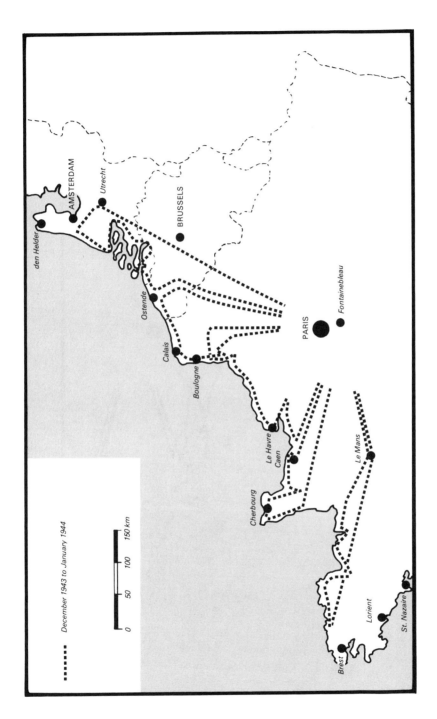

Field Marshal Rommel's inspection tours

Field Marshal Rommel's inspection tours

February to March 1944

0   50   100   150 km

den Helder
AMSTERDAM
Utrecht
BRUSSELS
Ostende
Calais
Boulogne
Le Havre
Caen
Cherbourg
Le Mans
PARIS
Fontainebleau
Brest
Lorient
St. Nazaire

The concrete, however, prevented this and, while locking the wires in place, was itself under stress. Therefore, construction parts of Hoyer concrete could bend without breaking until the prestress was equalized. This gave such construction considerable elasticity. One limitation was that the wires had to lay completely straight in the concrete, since otherwise they could not be stressed. The designers had to take this into consideration and design the concrete sections in such a way that they consisted of flat planes or parts curved in only one direction. The best method was flat planes since the wires could be put under stress crosswise.

For building barracks, one merely joined flat hollow parts. The single parts were poured in such a way that one man could handle them. The air in the hollows acted as excellent insulation against heat and cold.

Riverboats of about 1,000-ton-capacity were the maximum accomplishment. Several were already in use, and one was under construction. The ship's draft was only a few centimeters more than that of a steel ship of the same size, while the saving on steel was over ninety percent. Now Hoyer was starting the mass production of tetrahedrons for offshore obstacles. Each side was separately poured and then assembled at the beach, simplifying both manufacture and transport.

In the nearby engineer depot, Brigadier General Habicht of the naval fortress engineers showed me a revolving turret built of standard reinforced concrete by his engineers. He had chosen this method because he could not obtain panzer steel and the firing angle of guns in concrete emplacements was not sufficient and the firing slit was too large. After the capture of Toulon he had ordered the removal of the roller bearings from the turret of a battleship sunk in shallow waters. He used them in the demonstrated experimental turret.

The lower surface of the roller bearing (several meters in diameter) was mounted on a circular concrete base, approximately two meters high and mostly buried in the ground. On it was a movable platform for a gun up to 150mm size, standing under a strong concrete cupola. The gun fired through a slit only wide enough to allow a few degrees of traverse to each side, much narrower than normal slits of 90–120°. The rough direction of the turret was achieved with the aid of a simple turning device, operated from the base by a few men with a crank-handle. Precise aiming was done by the gun captain with the gun's laying mechanism.

This was much more primitive than the intricate swivel mechanisms used on board, which, independent of the movement of the ship in a seaway, had to revolve the turrets absolutely evenly. But it was entirely sufficient for the coast, and it was unfortunate that the construction of these turrets had not made any progress in spite of several applications Habicht had sent to fortress construction officials. The roller bearings presented a problem, since extra large lathes were needed for their manufacture and only a few of those existed. Without adversely affecting other production, four could be built in France each month. That would have meant a dozen batteries a year had production started early enough. The production of a few months could have changed the situation on the threatened coasts considerably. The first battery was under construction, but was not completed when the Invasion began.

Driving back I stopped at the navy hospital Eaubonne, north of Paris, and visited its chief physician, Fleet Surgeon Dr. Heim. He was not only an excellent surgeon, but also saw the problems of his patients from their human and psychological sides. From 1940 to 1942 he had directed a hospital in the vicinity of Boulogne, where I had frequently visited various of my men. Then and now our discussion centered on the "inner cohesion" (innere Gefüge), a phrase which did not then exist in words, but certainly was perceived as a problem. Dr. Heim and I agreed that under the continuous stress it had already deteriorated tremendously, a process which we knew would continue.

Heim was of the opinion that young officers and older men had the best morale. Many of them were ill and worn out but almost always willing and grateful. The morale of the female members of the Wehrmacht was seriously deteriorating, despite all attempts at supervision. Among the men, including the officers, alcoholism was on the increase. The fast buildup of the Wehrmacht and the following immense expansion, especially in the army, had catapulted many people into positions of authority with responsibilities they could not handle. But, on the whole, it was astonishing how well the apparatus still functioned.

Rommel had been ordered to Führer Headquarters at Berchtesgaden for March 19 and 20. Colonel von Tempelhoff, the operations officer, accompanied him. Because they were forbidden to fly, they drove to Paris on the evening of March 17 and spent the night in the special train which would take them to Führer Headquarters the following day. Rommel used the preceding days to draft the results of his activity and his opinions on the direction of fighting both for the troops and for the discussion with Hitler.

In this memorandum it was noteworthy that Rommel, at this point, still was not certain where the invasion would strike, and wanted to accelerate the work on the less threatened coasts. This was also reflected in telephone calls, conducted by Gause, with the aim of transferring the 12th SS Panzer Division to the northern bank of the Seine in order to have one combat-ready unit on either bank (the other was the 10th SS Panzer Division). In addition, Rommel wanted to transfer the 21st Panzer Division, whose withdrawal from the Western Command area had been cancelled, to Brittany, where defense was especially weak. Probably the wide dispersal of the fast units was connected with the fact that intelligence reports so far did not at all give a clear picture of where the blow would fall.

The most important problem for Rommel was and remained the command of the most mobile units. He discussed it with Hitler personally after the general conference. Rommel believed that he had succeeded, and when he returned to La Roche-Guyon on March 21 he noted in his daily report: "Satisfied with result. The Führer has completely accepted the commander's (Rommel's) opinion regarding the defense of the coast and agreed to a change in the command organization." Later events showed that Rommel had been too optimistic; the promise was never kept.

Rommel's absence gave me an opportunity to drive to the naval front. Since decisions without him could hardly be made and special surprises were not expected, I took along Captain Peters to introduce him. On March 18 we started at 0600 and, in fog and darkness, we drove southwest to Angers, our first destination. The driving was at first difficult; Hatzinger frequently had to stick his head out of the window to find his way. After Vernon we found ourselves on two badly bombed airfields which had been built across the road.

At the engineer school in Angers we inspected, under the commander's expert guidance, all types of land mines and mine detectors and witnessed the laying of mines and mine detecting in the so-called "mine garden," partly because mines were a most important topic, and partly to be able to answer questions of the shore-based naval units, which had to lay the mines themselves. Once more the similarity between the mine war on land and at sea became apparent.

Subsequently we drove to the commanding admiral—West Coast, Vice-Admiral Schirlitz, who had moved to the hamlet of Erigné several kilometers south of Angers. He had assembled his complete staff and several other men. For seventy-five minutes we discussed neutralizing port facilities, mining on land and in the ports, emplacement of guns under concrete, and a number of smaller points. I used this opportunity to repeat Rommel's principal ideas, which were understood and acknowledged completely.

In the afternoon we drove in beautiful, warm spring weather via Nantes to Saint-Nazaire to sea commandant Rear Admiral Mirow. After wandering about for a while, we found his quarters near the water. The conference was similar in content to the one held earlier.

Continuing our drive the next morning (March 19), we first saw the offshore obstacles on the wide sandy beach of La Baule, a resort on the northern bank of the mouth of the Loire. Half of the wide bay was already filled with obstacles. Unfortunately it was the wrong half, with cliffs which made a landing improbable although not impossible. However, work proceeded quickly so it could be expected that the other half without cliffs would also soon be protected.

From La Baule we drove on minor roads via the small fortified town of Guérande to the main road, which we reached at La Roche-Bernard, to Lorient. There we took a quick look at the plaque in a rock above the Villaine River in memory of the *Couronne,* built here in 1634 on orders of Cardinal Richelieu, the first triple-decked dreadnought of the era of the sailing ships.

At noon we arrived at the 3rd Security Division in Nostang, twelve kilometers from Lorient. With the chief of the division, Captain Bergelt, I discussed the laying of the coastal mine A, which would possibly have to be done with his boats. Other topics were making his machine guns and 20mm guns mobile for land warfare, and his men's close-combat training and equipping them for fighting on land. Actually, there were no orders to do so, and it was debatable if this concerned me at all, for in the case of an invasion the task for the security units would be at sea. But it was to be expected that boats would be confined in ports or be put out of action. Then their crews would find themselves ashore, and the better they were trained and equipped, the more useful they could be, especially since their combat morale was high. After the installation of bases in France I had, in the winter of 1940–41, started close-combat training for the mine sweep flotillas. I had done this with the help of the local army units, since I expected enemy raids, which later occurred at Saint-Nazaire and Dieppe. This training had continued, and was accepted by all the officers with whom I discussed the issue. However, others were not so enthusiastic. Commander von Blanc, commander of the approximately 1,000-man-strong 2d Mine Sweep Flotilla, stationed in Benodet seventy kilometers west of Lorient, learned about this. Before routine overhauls in dry dock for some of his boats were due, von Blanc had forwarded to Navy Group West, through channels, a request for close-combat training. At Navy Group West, the chief quartermaster received it and in turn sent it to the Paris branch of the 2d Admiral–North Sea, bureau of personnel. It took them only six weeks to reply that combat training for sea-going units was out of the question. But the commander of the flotilla, because he anticipated a similar reply, had already made provisions via another channel so his measures could be executed without interruption.

In the afternoon we visited Benodet, which in the meantime had been transformed into a flotilla base, with a small workshop for regular repairs and a pontoon as a pier for mine sweepers. One of these, M-9, was moored there, and it was a somewhat nostalgic feeling to stand once more on the deck of a mine sweeper, if only for a few minutes.

A light rain fell when we visited the Bay of Douarnenez, where offshore obstacles had been increased considerably. We spent the evening at Brest with sea commandant Rear Admiral Kähler, who had distinguished himself as captain of a raider. For dinner the three of us were alone and could combine eating and shop talk. We had to be careful, however, not to discuss matters in detail, since, as at the Benodet officers' quarters, a French girl served dinner. It must have been fun for those on the other side of the Channel to carry on their intelligence activities. The conditions which had developed during the four years of occupation in France were a gift for every intelligence officer working in France, and a nightmare to our own counterintelligence. After dinner we continued the conference with some staff members. Rommel's ideas were well received and understood, as everywhere else in the navy.

We left the next morning, March 20, at 0730. The weather was clear and very cold; there was a thick hoarfrost everywhere. Because we were in a hurry, we tried with the car to climb the highest peak on the main road to the east, the Menez Bre, a flat hill all of 302 meters high, but did not quite make it because soon we were stopped by a mine fence. Shadows of Rommel! But even from here, the view to the south to the Monts d'Arrée was rewarding.

General Straube welcomed us in Guingamp very cordially. His engineer officer, who happened to be present, reported on experiments in the Bay of Saint-Malo with ships against wooden beams which had been quite successful. In protected areas like Saint-Malo the wooden beams should last through the summer at least.

During this time some changes occurred in our staff. Prince Josias von Coburg, our adjutant, was replaced by army Captain Lang, a native of Württemberg and a panzer officer decorated with the Iron Cross, First Class. Soon all of us had good rapport with him. Several days later, Major General Diem joined our group. He had once been Rommel's superior; now he had the duties of special deputy for supply services and engineers, to look after things whenever Rommel could not be present personally.

Progress and Opposition

On March 21 Rommel returned from Führer Headquarters completely satisfied and, without delay, started work again. In the question of whether the fortress commander should become independent or remain under the orders of the local divisions, he was for keeping the existing arrangement, because no additional forces could be made available for the fortresses. Therefore he rejected the organization of fortress skeleton regiments, since they could only be formed at the expense of the more mobile divisions.

He ordered the subordinate commands to obstruct all level areas suitable for airborne landing inside the fortress areas and in the divisional combat zones by stakes, barbed wire, and similar obstacles. These measures had long been discussed and postponed because wood and labor were available only in limited quantities and emphasis came first on the more important offshore obstacles. But work on them made such good progress that obstacle installation in the rear areas could now be started.

Western Command ordered the construction of offshore obstacles using all available geologists and in cooperation with the naval agencies. OKW ordered the transfer of the 349th Infantry Division to the east and the withdrawal of five assault gun detachments.

From March 23 to 27 Rommel, accompanied by General Meise, Colonel Lattmann (artillery), Lieutenant Colonel von Tempelhoff, the operations officer, and myself, went on a five-day trip to the Netherlands. We started at 0630 on March 23; toward noon we arrived at Brussels at the

113

quarters of the military commander, General von Falkenhausen, who appeared both distinguished and wise. During dinner he spoke about, among other things, the consequences of power and quoted Confucius, somewhat modified, "Power corrupts; total power corrupts totally." After dinner Rommel and Falkenhausen talked in private. As I found out much later, it was the first time they made contact in order to find ways to end the war and to change political conditions in Germany.

From Brussels we drove to Utrecht to Major General Reinhardt, commanding 89th Corps; Admiral Förste, the commander in chief of the Navy High Command–North, and Vice-Admiral Kleikamp, the commanding admiral of the Netherlands, had already arrived. Reinhardt was well informed and gave a clear report on the work done in his sector. Flooding to protect the fortresses and positions with broad areas of water presented the main problem in this flat terrain. The work was in full progress, to be finished within three weeks. The entire 110,000 hectares would then be under water. The civilian authorities, understandably angry, protested against the loss of agrarian land and pastures. Rommel explained that "all interests, economic and otherwise, will have to be subordinated to the military requirements, since the improvement of the defense readiness will protect the Netherlands from destruction and enemy threat" (KTB). For this reason he demanded that the project be finished by the end of April because from then on the weather would be good and therefore the attack was to be expected. Rommel was not satisfied with the quantity of offshore obstacles. At the same time he demanded that the fortress areas take measures against airborne landings. Kleikamp remarked that good protection existed already through powerful naval antiaircraft units which covered the area in checkerboard fashion.

For Rommel, the units were still too far inland. With great vigor he advocated the creation of a fortified zone with its land front no more than five to eight kilometers from the coast. This zone should contain the entire infantry and artillery while the ship-training detachments would guard the rear. After lengthy discussion, the chief of staff of the Wehrmacht's commander included some places located farther inland that already had an all-around defense in the fortified zone, such as Alkmaar, ten kilometers from the coast.

Rommel protested against the practice of counting training units of 39,000 men as a fighting strength of only 20,000 because the rest were recruits. In his opinion, such recruits could, after some days of training, handle weapons and would then be able to occupy and defend prepared positions.

This was followed by the usual disagreement about the reserves. Rommel expressed the opinion that it was already too much to keep some battalions back as reserves. All men belonged in prepared positions.

Afterwards we drove to General Christiansen, the Wehrmacht commander, who received us very cordially. Undersecretary Wimmer, the Reich Governor's deputy, Admiral Förste, and Kleikamp came for dinner. After the busy day, we parted early.

On March 24 we started at 0700 for Den Helder, the major naval base in Holland. Flooding had considerably increased the strength of the good defenses. I continued the drive in Admiral Förste's car to use the time for discussion. Later all of us climbed the sand dunes, Rommel faster than most of the higher brass. In the soldiers' home at Bergen-op-Zee he conferred with Förste. In the afternoon we once more climbed numerous dunes and saw good offshore obstacles. In the rear area Rommel determined which depth the fortress sectors were not to exceed, and clearly demanded that even the division commanders had to live in them. On our way home we drove past some crocus fields in bloom.

In the meantime Rommel had reflected on the losses to agriculture which would result from flooding and mining the land. In the following discussion with Undersecretary Wimmer, he restricted his demands to a strip about one kilometer deep on the sea side and on the land side of the fortress, areas which were five to eight kilometers wide. The land in between was to be protected with stakes against airborne landings only and could otherwise be used for agriculture.

Wimmer agreed to stop the withdrawal of workers for the Sauckel action. General Christiansen proposed to bypass the labor agency and recruit labor for defense construction freely. Enough would come since the Wehrmacht not only paid well but also provided meals. In contrast, the Dutch workers did not like to go to the Organisation Todt because they feared a sudden transfer to Germany. In any case, Christiansen would refuse to surrender any more workers to Sauckel, because in the current situation offshore barriers were more important than munition workers. Wimmer eventually relinquished a number of motor pumps for the installation of the stakes. On the whole, Rommel achieved what he believed necessary without too much interference with the local economy.

We inspected the forward water position of the Amsterdam sector, then the port of IJmuiden with its motor torpedo boat bunker and powerful coast artillery. The officer commanding the sector reported on fighting targets at sea, on the combat orders for his batteries, on the command organization and tactical dispositions, without evoking protests or disagreements. Evidently, army and navy had cooperated locally in the question of the coast artillery.

Everywhere we saw floodings and positions of encouraging strength as well as good offshore barriers. At noon we listened to a report in Wassenaar, where we also took lunch. Rommel detected reserves which had been well hidden from him and he transferred them inexorably forward to the fortified sector.

The fortress commander of Scheveningen explained the construction effort and the plans for the defense in a very instructive way by using a model built-in sandbox. The construction work throughout the sector was superb, and Rommel expressed his approval to the division commander. Only the reserves were to be divided up and moved close to the coast. In the event of an alert, SS training units would move into the rear area. The final result noted in the TBR was: "Landing almost impossible. It will, however, be necessary to move the naval training detachments and the SS close to the coast."

We stayed overnight at Rotterdam's Park Hotel. The Field Marshal joined us at the crowded coffee shop for a late cup of coffee. From the room one had a good view of the busy street. All around us "rear area" activity abounded. General Wahle, a friendly Saxonian decorated with the Knight's Cross of the War Merit Cross, and the port commander, a successful First World War submarine commander, joined us for dinner at the naval officers' mess. The port commander had seen much of the world, and, between wars, for a time had organized Paraguay's navy. He was entertaining and a bit overwhelming, which was balanced by the fact that the representative of the local naval office did not say a word.

On March 26 we left at 0700 for Hoek van Holland to hear a report given by the fortress commander. Since February 1, 1944, 140,000 mines had been laid in his area, but now the supplies had stopped. To make up for it, a rumor had been started that accidents had occurred in the mine fields—fields which already had signboards but in reality contained no mines. Warnings and press notices were designed to increase the impression of their danger with the inhabitants and especially with the enemy, who would undoubtedly be informed through his intelligence channels.

In view of the relatively small difference in the tidal levels, the offshore barriers, consisting of eight rows of obstacles topped by numerous mines, were especially good. At the time, IJmuiden, which we had visited twenty-four hours earlier, was attacked by 300 bombers. However, the motor torpedo boat bunker, apparently the main target, was not seriously damaged. In the coastal defense sector Dordrecht, the division commander planned to increase the number of mines to 500,000 by May 1.

After the port commander's report on mining and port defense we visited the peninsula of De Beer and inspected the central fort and the heavy Rosendahl naval battery, both of which made a good impression. A division of Tartars from the Volga acted as the mobile reserves of the division. We crossed over to Voorne, where the flooding was especially good. The people, nevertheless, greeted us voluntarily and in a friendly way. Via the bridges of Moordijk and Willemstad we drove to Breda, where Rommel commended the commander of the 719th Infantry Division on the progress of the defense work and asked him to convey Rommel's thanks to the troops.

Then Rommel again outlined his opinion on defense and discussed with General Reinhardt and Admiral Kleikamp on moving the units forward. Unfortunately, Navy High Command had once more refused to use naval training detachments in the event of alert. The decision was both unfortunate and incomprehensible, for the navy could hardly continue with training while the Invasion battle raged a mere fifty kilometers away.

Rommel's arrival had apparently become known. At any rate a large crowd assembled in front of the hotel. This had been completely vacated for us, which had not at all been our intention. Double guards secured our floor constantly. They accompanied every wayfarer to the "place of seclusion," where they officiously turned on the light—well intentioned but a bit too much courtesy.

The first point on the agenda for March 27 was the report of the 89th Corps commanding general at his command post in Antwerp. His main concern was this big city with 104 units and establishments billeted there, which in case of an alert could muster only 13,000 men of limited fighting value. Therefore it was only possible to defend the edge of the city but not the old forts farther out. Only a few guards protected the large stores of food and ammunition there. The floodings in the city's northwest section eased the situation somewhat. For the protection and blocking of the Schelde, only dummy mines had so far been designated.

The next point on the agenda caused some annoyance, since the corps command had selected the wrong division for the inspection. The mixup was easily explained because for reasons of camouflaging the division number, only the total of the division number's digits was transmitted. That of the wrong division, the 48th, was synonymous with that of the intended division, the 165th Infantry Division. The victim, however, was the 712th Infantry Division which was inspected without advance warning. Although the sum of its total digits was different, it was located on the road to the 48th Infantry Division. With his characteristic sixth sense for weak points, Rommel at once made for a strip of beach which was covered with only a thin line of Belgian gates, and where, since his last visit in January, no progress had been made. The photographer to our regret did not dare to take pictures of Rommel giving a good dressing down to the responsible officer. Without mincing words, Rommel demanded that mined stakes be installed immediately along the entire coastal sector of the division. He did not accept the lack of wood as an excuse.

The 48th Infantry Division, adjoining to the west, was in better condition. The lunch break at the soldiers' mess in Adinkerque started with the report by sea commandant Rear Admiral Frisius on the tests conducted with landing craft on offshore barriers. This was followed by an officer of the 2d Security Division reporting on the successful laying of Czech hedgehogs from flat-bottomed craft. The Field Marshal liked Frisius and invited him to travel with him in his car.

At Calais work progressed satisfactorily as well. It must have been here that a later much-talked-about episode took place. Our cars had stopped on a side road and we had stepped out to listen to someone explain a resistance nest, when suddenly a fast-traveling motorcycle came into view, driven by a lance corporal with a very pretty young girl in the sidecar. Glancing at this sight, some faces turned stern, others showed unconcealed delight. The corporal grasped the situation with remarkable presence of mind. In a cloud of dust, he swiftly screeched to a halt, handed the motorcycle to the apparently well-trained girl, saluted smartly and happily reported to the Field Marshal: "Corporal Schmidt and the regiment's laundress on their way to work." Rommel returned the salute, highly amused, and with a merry gleam in his eyes. The corporal beamed at him admiringly, turned on his heel; he and the girl mounted with lightning speed and hurried off before anybody had time to analyze the situation and ask embarrassing questions.

Behind Abbeville, although the hour was late, the Field Marshal once more felt drawn to the beach. About 1900, in the Ault area west of the mouth of the Somme, in the sector of the unsuspecting 348th Infantry Division, Rommel again detected a beach void of any offshore obstacles. After making a note, he returned, satisfied, to La Roche-Guyon.

The most important event during our absence had been a telephone conversation between Gause and the aide-de-camp of the Wehrmacht operations staff on the evening of March 25. Referring to the structure and subordination of Panzer Group West ordered by Commander in Chief West, Gause pointed out that "this does not take into account the promise regarding the subordination of mobile units given by the Führer to the commander of the army group chief of staff. OKW is asked for decision" (KTB).

Two days later Gause talked to General Warlimont, as Jodl's deputy, in the same sense. Warlimont declared "the OKW is determined to regulate command relations in accord with the Führer's decision. The OKW has not yet received and is awaiting the Commander in Chief West's command regulation sent by courier" (KTB).

On March 31 Rommel conducted a telephone conversation with Jodl concerning the same subject. In it "he gave as reason for the necessity of putting the motorized units under Army Group B the unification of operational command in the Western Command area under one man. Commander OKW (Jodl) stated that the order from Western Command has not yet arrived and that upon examination of the document, in keeping with the commander's (Rommel's) personal discussion, the matter will at once be brought to the Führer's attention for decision" (KTB). With this, the command problem was back to its starting point.

Other telephone calls concerned the order from Western Command to transfer the 12th SS Panzer Division (Hitler Youth) to the boundary between the Seventh and the Fifteenth Armies, the creation of a replacement unit for the 155th and the 179th Reserve Panzer Divisions, and the transfer of the 21st Panzer Division into the area vacated by them.

The difficulties of the command organization were drastically demonstrated once more in a telephone call in which the operations officer of the Commander in Chief West informed the army group that Rommel's request for troop transfers in the Netherlands to the coast had been forwarded to OKW, which had been asked to obtain consent from the SS Main Leadership Office, the Replacement Training Command, the Luftwaffe, and the navy.

On March 29 the recently retired General Geyer visited the Field Marshal to say goodbye before leaving for Germany. He stayed for lunch and once more stimulated the discussion, which touched on Russian claims, especially those in the direction of the Mediterranean; the Italian fleet; the question of bases in the Mediterranean; Saint-George's day (the April 1918 raid on Zeebrügge); Admiral Gladisch; coastal defense, which both army and navy passed on to one another; and a lively Saint-Barbara festival in Ulm, for which the guests arrived in a Black Maria with a man impersonating a detective, who picked up the general at his house.

In the afternoon the adjutant of the senior officer of the 10th Mine Sweep Flotilla came from its base, Saint-Nazaire, to discuss with Captain Peters and me the close-combat training and weapons situation of the flotilla. At an earlier date the senior officer of the flotilla had directed the close-combat training of the flotillas stationed on the Belgian coast. Now he had instituted a close-combat training school, which was ready for the Field Marshal's inspection.

At the same time Rommel had invited the commanders of the engineers to impress on them the need for increased support for the tasks assigned to their sections. On the following day (March 30) he drove with Gause to the Bay of the Seine to check on the new construction of the foreshore barriers. He started with the 711th Infantry Division. "Several of the army group's orders have not come to the division's attention and therefore there is still ignorance of the concept of a land front. The foreshore had not yet been closed off with barriers" (KTB).

At the 716th Infantry Division's command post in Caen, a conference took place with General Marcks, followed by reports of the commanders of the 382d and 77th Infantry Divisions, about the state of their organization.

At 1900 Rommel met with Field Marshal von Rundstedt at the 81st Corps in Rouen, for a conference in which the chief of staff of the Fifteenth Army and General Kuntzen also participated. Unfortunately the minutes have not survived. Since Rommel's arrival in France, Rundstedt had undertaken very few trips to subordinate commands.

On March 31 Admiral Krancke and his chief of staff came for lunch. Preceding lunch Rommel discussed with them the sea-mine situation, the possibilities of laying mines, the question of the alert units, and the forward deployment of training units to the coast. Of great significance was the fact that the enemy had not mined the Bay of the Seine for quite some time, but currently was mining the narrow part of the English Channel.

In the afternoon Rommel, Gause and Tempelhoff discussed the following points with Blumentritt:

1. Protection from airborne landings in various areas, including those of the panzer and strike force divisions.
2. Strengthening of the Antwerp sector with naval units.
3. Manning of the second positions and the stopping of work where they cannot be manned.
4. More practical organization in the sector of the Nineteenth Army.
5. Increased mine production. Goal: For each meter of coast, one mine on the offshore obstacles.
6. Information on a current deception action of the Western Command requested.
7. The 3rd Parachute Rifle Division, still in the process of formation, has no artillery. Is to receive one or two batteries of 88mm anti-aircraft guns; however, 3rd Air Fleet refuses.
8. Suggestion to collect roll obstacles on airfields and to put them on the beach.
9. Suggestion to utilize the combat engineers battalion of the 9th Air Corps, stationed in the rear area, for work on the coast.
10. Military geologists to dam the Dives River (east of the Orne).
11. Shifting of the 12th SS Panzer Division and the 21st Panzer Division.
12. Acceleration of the rail transport Paris–Brittany, which currently requires three weeks.
13. Putting Panzer Group West under Army Group B. Blumentritt "in this connection emphasized the Western Command's willingness to fulfill the wishes of the commander–Army Group B, and conveyed the opinion of Western Command to transfer the fast mobile units near the coast" (KTB).
14. Current questions in reference to Führer Directive 40.

As early as the following day, OKW refused point 9, since the engineers battalion in question was directly subordinated to the Luftwaffe command. In the following weeks most of the other points were discussed many times.

During the morning of April 1, Rommel inspected the manufacture of reinforced concrete and the revolving concrete turret at the Paris engineer depot. He liked both, and he regretted not having known about them previously. The turret had even come through shelling by a 150mm gun without damage.

While we took a walk in the beautiful afternoon and unsuccessfully made attempts on the lives of rabbits, Gause conducted several telephone calls regarding the limited mobility of the stationary divisions. Horses were available, but not the men to take care of them.

In the evening I left for a two-week vacation at the mine sweepers' recreation home at Schwalbach in the Taunus hills. During this time, Captain Peters deputized for me. Life at headquarters continued in the same rhythm, determined by Rommel's travels, visitors, and memoranda.

Again and again the most important factor in pushing the work forward was the Field Marshal's personal influence on the people whom he visited. Without pathos, but by a sober description of the situation and their tasks, by praise and blame—but more praise than blame—and by his personality, he was able to inspire them to high performances. Many needed only a slight nudge to give their best, others were inadequate or possibly already used up. These he forced to work not with the slave-keeper's whip, but with his personal example, his frequent visits, his indefatigable working power, his quick comprehension of all problems brought to his attention and those which developed unexpectedly, and with his calmness and humor.

When necessary he knew how to act the Field Marshal. This had to be done very rarely when someone hinted that Rommel was outranking him unjustly or was just an old soldier who had struck it lucky. One of these treated Rommel very condescendingly when he had only the right to inspect, and continued to do so at the first conference after Rommel had been made commander in chief. The tension in the briefing room increased slightly during the reports, but Rommel remained outwardly calm. After the conference, while Rommel's group entered their cars— I rode in his car—he remained for a few minutes with the gentleman in question, who then, with a red face and a greatly changed demeanor, accompanied him to the car. Rommel bade him a friendly farewell, as if nothing had happened. But when the car drove off, he turned to me, winked, pointed to the rear and said: "He is a thoroughly rude fellow and has to be treated the same way." But once was enough. Rommel did not bear a grudge, and from then on the relationship between the two men was unpretentious and comradely. No doubt existed, however, as to who had the upper hand.

There was never any doubt that Rommel sat at the head of the table. He achieved this without obtrusiveness. I also believe that he never hurt the feelings of his co-workers. He always remained a human among humans, a man among men, and a soldier among soldiers.

For one who came from the navy, the immense number of telephone calls between the higher and the supreme army staffs concerning the most important matters seemed rather odd. After the First World War, the navy had found out that the enemy had read most of its wireless messages, which seriously affected Germany's conduct of the war. Because the navy had learned its lesson, and also because of the inherent danger of direction finding, it limited wireless traffic to a minimum. It had also introduced a totally secure code system with coding machines and had applied this experience to use of the telephone and transmitted urgent and secret information only through a teletype machine with a built-in code key. One could never be sure if a telephone call was monitored, illegally through wiretapping or legally through a second listener, as was often the custom in higher staffs, if only to preserve the results of a conference by a second person taking notes.

In the navy one had to learn to command without the telephone, by orders transmitted though couriers, or, if time was short, via teletype. So, for instance, the operations officer of Security Area West (equivalent to an operations officer in the army) became well-known for his teletype messages, which he learned to rattle off like an expert teletype operator. His counterparts in the security divisions also learned it quickly; now a completely secure way to communicate existed which made wiretapping impossible. In addition, there was an immediate typed copy at one's fingertips. No doubts would arise later about what actually had been discussed. The teletype also forced brevity, while the telephone encouraged lengthy conversation.

Probably the reasons for the army's use of the telephone in long-term and operational matters could be attributed to the bad example set by the OKW, and had its ultimate roots in the inadequate structure of the highest command. OKW wanted to keep the reins in its not-too-firm grip all the time and to give orders to all units, down to the battalion level. To do so, it had to know everything—which was only possible through the telephone.

It would have been much better if the subordinated commanders in chief and commanders, who had been trained to independence, had been allowed to act independently as much as possible. Then a few long-term directives would have been sufficient. This would have greatly reduced the number of orders and improved performance.

Applied to Rommel's task in the west, a more effective policy would have resulted in a directive giving him command over all the armed forces in his sector, and the command authority over at least those Luftwaffe and navy units which cooperated in tactical matters with the army. It went without saying that Rommel would not have interfered in the submarine war or in possible air operations against Britain. In an emergency, however, it was necessary that he be able to command the fighting power of the naval training detachments, the Luftwaffe engineers and the fast mobile units in his sector. The appointment of qualified officers to his staff would have obviated any danger of intrusion in the affairs of the other branches of the armed forces. Moreover, it would have assured deployment of fast mobile units in such a way that they could be quickly withdrawn should the OKW need them at another place. Actually, Führer Directive 40 should have been sufficient. Yet OKW could not make up its mind to create the indispensible clear command organization with correspondingly clear responsibilities.

The Anglo-Americans used a system of command in which each war theater had just one commander in chief, under whose command were all units of the three services, each under their own commanders. In the southwest Pacific, for instance, General MacArthur commanded the fleet through the fleet commander, who transmitted all orders to the naval forces and who also could categorically parry all meddling with the internal affairs of his units. Of course, the effectiveness of this system of command depended much on the trust between the commander in chief and the commanders of the subordinated units of the other services. In the final analysis it is human intelligence which decides; the organization should be an expression of it. Better organization on the German side would have all but eliminated the constant confusion over the panzer divisions and the deployment of the other defense forces, and would have considerably increased the strength of the German defense. Trust, which cannot be ordered, was assured through Rommel's personality.

A staff meeting at the army group on April 3 on artillery strongpoints showed that generally the Schelde and the Somme still were considered as particularly threatened. Navy Group West interpreted heavy enemy activity with light naval forces west and northwest of Cap Gris Nez two days later, as intensive mine sweeping in preparation for landing operations in the narrows of the English Channel. This was in keeping with the OKW's expectations. Firing at these ships was not possible because interference was too strong for German radar. The same occasionally happened to the Luftwaffe's radar.

The reason for this meeting was the experience at Nettuno, where enemy infantry did not dare to attack under reasonably heavy artillery fire. The artillery of the divisions was not very strong; in the narrow of the Channel they had:

18th Luftwaffe Division	1 battery for every 2,000 meters
47th Infantry Division	1 battery for every 1,200 meters
49th Infantry Division	1 battery for every 1,000 meters

Railroad batteries and the heavy naval batteries, however, increased the strength. The main concern was therefore directed towards the sectors joining to the south, on both sides of the Somme. Rommel visited them from April 3 to 5, starting with the 384th Infantry Division at Le Treport. Here the land front was too far away—twelve kilometers from the coast. Otherwise, good progress had been made, and the Field Marshal expressed his thanks to the troops.

About the subsequently inspected 344th Infantry Division, he noted in his daily report: "It is amazing what has been done here, thanks to the initiative of the commander."

In the 82d Army Corps' sector, thirty-seven guns had been already emplaced with another fifteen by May 1. Rommel wished them emplaced in such a way that guns which retained their wheels could be pulled out and used against an enemy attacking from the flanks or from the rear. He also immediately took steps for the construction of concrete revolving turrets.

At the 49th Infantry Division even Rommel found the plans for mining a bit too generous. He reduced their numbers, since the mines for the intended area would not be available for many months to come. Also, he demanded that all units of the division move into the now-reduced coastal strip, including the divisional staff from its hereditary staff quarters at Montreuil. At several places Rommel had concertinas and harmonicas distributed to especially efficient stake installers and mine layers.

Sixty Days before the Invasion

Rommel spent April 6 at headquarters conferring with the chief of staff and the engineer officer of the Nineteenth Army. On April 7 he drove to the 245th Infantry Division, located in the Dieppe area. He found "considerable progress, but still no ingenious work." Gun emplacement through the Organisation Todt progressed much too slowly. Rommel thanked the troops for their diligence.

A conference at Fifteenth Army followed. They received a research group consisting of one each botanist, zoologist, geologist, engineer, tank specialist, artillery specialist, and infantry specialist, who were to advise in the creation of artificial and natural camouflage. Moreover, the army received two more construction battalions, in addition to the two it already had.

With regard to submerged mines on offshore obstacles, I previously called attention to the danger that one mine could detonate a neighboring mine. Firing tests now showed that shells which exploded in the water caused the flat land mines in about a twenty-meter radius to explode as well. Thereupon the army group asked for a specialist from the navy to clarify the matter.

April 9. OKW informs that Hitler had earmarked only 1.3 million cubic meters of concrete for the construction of the Atlantic Wall.

With reference to troop transfers in the Netherlands, the OKW decided: "The army's fast mobile detachments can be transferred. Since in the case of alert the transfer of the Waffen SS training units is a foregone conclusion, the matter needs no special mention. For bringing forward parts of the Hermann Göring regiment, consent of the Reichsmarschall has still to be awaited." This by no means concluded the telephone calls and the teletype messages about the transfers in the Netherlands area.

At noon we had a conference with General Blumentritt about the deployment of fast mobile units in case of enemy airborne landings and the forward deployment of the 2d Panzer Division and the 12th SS Panzer Division. General Geyr von Schweppenburg came in the afternoon to talk with Rommel about the same subject, the forward deployment of the panzer units. No progress was made. "Strong differences of opinion prevented any results" (TBR).

On April 10 a massive air attack struck the heavy naval battery Octeville, north of Le Havre, which was still under construction. Of the three

380mm guns, one was put out of action for three to four weeks; another had a destroyed firing platform. Only the third remained undamaged, but was not yet ready for firing.

The intelligence officer of the army group kept current maps, one showing the daily air attacks, another sabotage activity. From them one could clearly see when the enemy concentrated on special places.

In the afternoon, Rommel and Gause drove to Rundstedt. Their topic: deployment of the panzer divisions.

April 11. The 1st SS Panzer Corps troops were transferred to the area of Beauvais (seventy kilometers north of Paris and ninety kilometers behind the coast). Rommel wanted them even farther forward. The navy suddenly transferred the 1,400-strong engineer battalion from Antwerp to Denmark. A strenuous search for a substitute began. A fake headquarters near Tours was introduced in the wireless, a part of the intelligence game.

From April 11 to 14 Rommel once more traveled in Brittany, starting east of Saint-Malo near Canale (April 11) where a bunker capable of firing inland only aroused his displeasure. He continued his tour via Le Val André (conference with General Straube), Brest, Lorient, Saint-Nazaire, Angers (engineers school), to Le Mans. In northern Brittany there was uncertainty about priming the stakes with mines. "Generally the Field Marshal declared that it was wrong to experiment over and again, and to listen to any kind of pessimistic talk. Rather the orders should be executed precisely as given by the army group" (KTB).

In the Brest sector (344th Infantry Division) and that of Lorient (265th Infantry Division), the impression was "that the defense work had been tackled with much energy." General Farnbacher (25th Army Corps) reported in Brittany that acts of sabotage and assaults on soldiers had taken on such dimensions that one could well speak of Russian conditions. For days no freight train had reached Brest; rear-area troops and the *Sicherheitsdienst* (Security Service–SS) were not up to the task. During the next days, the matter of sabotage was repeatedly discussed and it was determined that the troops should not act against the population. In Normandy, before and even during the Invasion battle, there was hardly a case of sabotage.

Near Brest a new offshore mine was demonstrated. Its charge was detonated when a ship touched a lever extending from a concrete block. The mine was good, provided that it could withstand the sea.

Five tetrahedron factories worked in the sector of the corps. So far they had completed 6,000 pieces, partly of a new, improved design. New landing obstacles were also demonstrated. Thirty-four kilometers of offshore obstacles had been completed, and 10,000 land mines had been laid in ten days.

The question of attacks by low-flying planes with rockets on the large embrasures of the casemates was discussed. The sea commandant proposed makeshift protection through torpedo nets made from small wire rings, which seemed both flexible and resistant. It was a pity that this method could not be tested immediately.

On April 13 Rommel inspected the railroad battery 4/264 on the Bay of Quiberon. It consisted of four older 340mm guns of French origin, with a firing range of thirty kilometers and a spread of 1,000 meters. Momentarily one of the guns was in Germany for testing purposes.

Work had progressed well in Saint-Nazaire, the land front had been shortened in order to man it sufficiently with the available 7,500 men (including 4,500 antiaircraft personnel). The obstacles on the beach of La Baule had been completed, and their considerable depth impressed us. Rommel's quarters in La Baule were heavily guarded, since information had been received about a possible raid.

On April 14 Rommel inspected the defense installations in Nantes and was pleased "that an energetic field commander had successfully engaged himself for the defense of the town" (KTB). After Rommel had inspected the Engineers School in Angers, the commanding general of the 10th Air Corps reported on the combat-readiness of his troops.

At headquarters the telephone calls about the transfers in the Netherlands and the deployment of the panzer units continued. On April 13 Hitler stopped the transfer of the motorized units, and in a telephone conversation with Gause on the same day, Blumentritt emphasized "that complete agreement exists in the opinions of the two commanders in chief and that there can be no question of any strategic intentions in the year 1944; that as before the enemy will still have to be defeated on the beaches and that all counterattacks can only be purely tactical measures" (KTB).

April 16. In the morning Captain Peters awaited me at the railway station in Paris and, during the drive to La Roche-Guyon, filled me in on what had happened there during my vacation. Of special importance was the matter of mine detonations caused by the explosion of the next one. Navy Group West had proposed to install the flat land mines in concrete on the beaches. It was expected that the concrete would absorb the brief shock of a close detonation without exploding the mine itself. A ship running on it would break the concrete and explode the mine. This was again a good idea, and would most likely have come up earlier had the measures against a landing been worked through systematically. The same held true for the lever mines, called "nutcracker mines," of which several samples had been built and tested.

Rommel had suggested the utilization of coastal sailors for the transport of construction material along the coast of Brittany. The question about whose allotment would furnish the concrete for the naval batteries had not been answered and aroused tempers.

No progress had been made in the question of the employment of the naval training detachments in the occupied areas.

The enemy had become more active, in the air as well as with mines. In the last few days aircraft had attacked an army coast battery (155mm) near Nieuport, not under concrete, rendering two of the four guns inoperative. Attacks in the same area on radar installations and on an unprotected 170mm army coast battery near Dieppe were unsuccessful. A stronger air attack on Le Havre's port installations had caused no substantial damage. Ground mines had been laid off Le Havre, Zeebrügge (i.e., off the Schelde) and north of Walcheren. Altogether this could mean that the enemy intended to land at the Somme or on the narrow part of the Channel and that now, as a preparation, he intended to put the ports on the flank and single batteries out of action. The mining, however, did not eliminate the Bay of the Seine as a possible landing area.

We reached the staff quarters towards noon. I reported to the Field Marshal, who was very pleasant but, on the whole, most serious. He talked about the grave situation in the east, where Field Marshals von Manstein and von Kleist had been relieved of their duties on short notice. Rommel believed that we were in a crisis of confidence, but that the situation could only be mastered through mutual trust. In the west Hitler's verbal promises had not been confirmed in writing, and some had not been kept. The evacuation of the Crimea had apparently become a catastrophe.

Then I welcomed our new chief of staff, Major General Dr. Hans Speidel. He took over from Gause, who was to take command of a division, although Rommel was sorry to see him depart. I knew and valued Speidel from 1941–42 when he was the military commander's chief of staff in France. I had occasionally listened there to lectures or given some myself and had always felt very comfortable in this stimulating circle. After the *Sicherheitsdienst* in 1942 took over the judicial power in the territory of the military commander in France, Speidel requested transfer to the east (Russia). As a corps chief of staff he played a decisive part in the successful breakout from the Russian encirclement at Tscherkassy. Rommel had personally asked for him as Gause's successor. We understood each other at once, in service matters as well as personally.

In the afternoon Rommel, Meise and I went on an "armed" stroll. We saw pheasants and rabbits, but did not harm them. On our return we found annoying news from the navy. The Wehrmacht Commander-Netherlands reported that he had just received orders for the transfer of Naval Training Detachment 24 to Germany. This, of course, disturbed the efforts to improve the defense.

Major Friedel from the Wehrmacht operations staff had visited Naval Training Detachment 20. In answer to his question as to "how they envisioned their commitment, the officers answered unanimously that this was only conceivable in completely finished positions in the 'forward water position.' They considered any other procedure inexpedient . . ." (KTB). These officers apparently did not expect useful results from either the mine defense of their own garrisons or from a more mobile employment. This totally corresponded with Rommel's intentions for these detachments. They were to man the second line of defense or the land front. Here they could free army troops and protect the rear of the coastal defense.

Fifty Days before the Invasion

From April 17 to 19 the Field Marshal, Speidel and I visited the coastline between the Somme and the Schelde. We drove in three cars; the third one was filled with war correspondents and concertinas. Lutz Koch, Ertel, Podewils and Baron von Esebeck were the correspondents who, most of the time and in changing numbers, accompanied us on our tours. Five to ten minutes before departure we would gather in the courtyard of the castle and tell stories until the Field Marshal appeared. He would then quickly greet each of us and the cars would pull out without losing any more time. Rommel deliberately used propaganda to impress the enemy and perhaps in this manner delay the invasion a bit longer.

Our first destination was Ault (April 17), where we met with General Sinnhuber, commander of the 67th Army Corps, and Major General

Seiffert, commander of the 348th Infantry Division. The offshore was riddled with many different types of obstacles, a pleasant surprise after the fiasco three weeks before. Rommel was very satisfied and gave three concertinas to the working men.

Inspecting several strongpoints, we drove along the flat coast via Cayeux to Saint-Valéry-sur-Somme. Here we ate a field kitchen meal, and immediately afterwards we continued further north to the 344th Infantry Division where we inspected both the land front and the coast, and then to the 49th Infantry Division. A flustered guard addressed the Field Marshal as "Herr Major," which Rommel took with composure.

Here not everything had progressed as well as it had further to the south. The stakes lacked mines, and staked obstacles were only thinly distributed at several points. Rommel noted in the TBR: "The difference in the progress of the divisions in the completion of the offshore obstacles is astonishing and depends on the division commander's initiative." Overnight we stayed in Le Touquet. The next morning (April 18) we continued to the 331st Infantry Division, which stood in the second line of defense. After the commander's report, Rommel briefly outlined his ideas, and declared that the position would be ideal if no movement was necessary for twenty-four hours.

We then continued on to Boulogne, past Cap Gris Nez, to the sector of the 47th Infantry Division. The offshore mainly had tetrahedrons, since driving stakes was too difficult in this terrain. The division ran a concrete factory with forty workers. Beyond Calais we saw good artificial swamp areas. Then it was the turn of the 18th Luftwaffe Field Division. Here the inhabitants had already been evacuated to such an extent that there was a labor shortage. The remaining Frenchmen did good work, for which they were fed and paid at once.

At Dunkirk we were just in time for an air attack on the town and port. We stopped outside the town and watched how wave after wave approached under heavy antiaircraft fire, not very high, approximately at 3,000 to 4,000 meters. When a close formation of eighteen bombers came directly towards us, we ducked into a ditch. General Sinnhuber unfortunately landed on a pile of broken glass, Speidel and I in the stinging nettles, and only Rommel, with his sharp eyes, found a spot of soft clean grass. The bombs fell far away. Two planes of the next wave were shot down and crashed into the sea. Some of the crew members bailed out with their parachutes, and a harbor patrol boat steamed out to them.

Parts of the 18th Luftwaffe Field Division's sectors still looked rather thin, but the adjoining 712th Infantry Division had progressed well after their last scare. The crew of an artillery position, who had labored heavily to gather and install especially thick tree trunks, received the first concertina. The TBR remarked: "One gets the impression that not all unit commanders are aware of their responsibilities. One cannot repeat often enough that the war will be decided in the west. . . . In the 712th Infantry Division's sector an astonishing increase of performance and enjoyment of the work was noticed."

In Breskens I was billeted in the home of an apparently very musical family (April 18 and 19). I did not expect that Breskens would play any particular part in the invasion, and I hoped that my kind hosts would safely get through the war. I fear, however, that the house did not survive the later fight for the little town.

On April 19 we assembled at the port of Breskens at 0700, where General von Gilsa, the commanding general of the 89th Corps, and sea commandant Captain Aschmann joined our group. We were to come in the flagship of the harbor patrol flotilla, a heavily armed yacht named "Sarah," alleged to have formerly belonged to Chamberlain. But a frigid east wind had pushed the water out of the Schelde and the proud ship could not enter the port of Breskens on account of her draft. We therefore took the normal ferry to Vlissingen. "Sarah" and three harbor patrol boats protected our crossing. At Vlissingen our first conference took place with the sea commandant who, while not being prepared for the conference, knew his subject well and gave a good report. Then the commander of the 165th Reserve Division described his affairs and reported, among other details, that of 500 bunkers, 283 had so far been completed. During an attack each of his men could fire from a battle station. "Rommel explained his principles once more with great lucidity and touching patience" (PAV).

Here the installation of "nutcracker" mines had already started. Offshore obstacles and minings had not progressed satisfactorily around the naval batteries. The extremely slow commander of an army artillery detachment heard some well-deserved straight talk.

In beautiful weather we returned on the "Sarah" to Breskens at 1100. High in the air an enemy reconnaissance plane surveyed us constantly, and I was glad when the Field Marshal was safely on the other side. In beautiful spring weather we drove to Brügge for a conference with the commander of the 48th Infantry Division and for lunch at the soldiers' mess. In the afternoon Rommel visited General von Salmuth, who lay ill with flu in his bunk. Near Hazebrouck, a local unit had blocked the main road for the purpose of conducting some drills. The guard had never heard of Field Marshal Rommel and therefore did not want to let us pass, an incident which caused some annoyance.

The overall evaluation of this inspection tour was: "The tour has shown that, compared to January, an extraordinary amount has been accomplished. However, the commanders of all units must use their strength of personality, common sense, and some imagination since much must still be done to strengthen defense readiness and complete the coastal defense with offshore obstacles" (KTB).

We arrived at staff quarters shortly after 2000. I discussed the results of the trip with Peters and later on joined Gause and Speidel. Gause told us how in November 1942, after the Allied landing in northwest Africa, he took possession of the fortress Biserta with 350 men, one "Tiger," three armored combat cars, and nine fighter bombers.

April 20. The day was taken up with tetrahedrons, "nutcracker" mines, stakes, the transfer of divisions, and the completion of much paperwork. In the evening we held a farewell party for Gause. The youngest La Roche Foucauld, somewhat timid, clad in his nice sailor suit, came to see me in the afternoon. Some sweets, designed to elicit the reason for his visit, were ineffective. But finally it became apparent that his mother had sent him to see if I was available. She arrived with a beautiful bouquet of lilacs and several bottles of a most delightful wine for Gause's farewell party. With his quiet, pleasant, and considerate manner, Gause was well liked by our hosts.

The Field Marshal gave a lengthy speech in honor of his departing chief of staff, with a few serious introductory words on the occasion of Hitler's birthday. Then he spoke about Gause's and his mutual experiences in Africa and France, describing the situations very vividly and at times bitterly. Gause answered adroitly and, in an especially nice way, mentioned the representatives of the Luftwaffe and the navy and emphasized the idea of the unity of the Wehrmacht. Von Tempelhoff, the operations officer, concluded the official part of the celebration. As the first function of the unofficial part, we elected Gause as tetrarch of the tetragoner, riding on a roll obstacle, with permission to wear two bristling Czech hedgehogs on a dark blue "swamp ribbon." We talked for the rest of the evening and parted at 0200, a truly unaccustomed hour for our staff.

April 21. After an early, rather low-keyed breakfast, Gause left at 0730 to catch the train in Paris. At the same time I started off in the same direction to join Rommel at the fortress engineers depot, where he watched an exercise and inspected the various new products from Hoyer's factory. Among other improvements, Hoyer demonstrated new types of nutcracker mines which seemed to be quite good. A naval construction official and a naval first lieutenant talked about anchoring buoys and mines. An explosion test with a T-mine against a barge had hardly caused any damage to the barge, which had disappointed the organizers, but could have been foreseen if the test had been calculated through in advance. The distance simply had been too great for the small explosive charge.

It was to be welcomed that everywhere experiments with makeshift solutions were made, for time was short. On the other hand, fundamental technical knowledge and group cooperation were insufficient in many places, not from bad intentions but rather from insufficient familiarity with the subject. This resulted in a large amount of unnecessary work. Yet according to the old principle, it was better to initiate something imperfect than to do nothing at all. In any case, the attempts helped us learn something. It was, however, important that the troops did not get any false impressions about effectiveness and ineffectiveness.

Long condensation trails appeared on the blue spring sky. The air raid warning was given, but nothing serious happened. Again and again one had to realize the danger for us and the advantage for the enemy which accrued from the current and perfect air surveillance of our whole defensive system in France.

I drove to the command quarters of Security Area West for a conference on the coastal mine A, still lagging in manufacture and installation. After lunch I went to Navy Group West and talked with the chief of staff and the supply officer about questions involving the coastal mine A, alert units, additional batteries, etc.

Western Command permitted the transfer of the 77th Infantry Division to the coast near Saint-Malo and Saint-Brieuc and the transfer of the 21st Panzer Division to the line Flers-Argentan, i.e., about sixty kilometers southeast of the Bay of the Seine. "Since the final decision for moving the panzer units forward has not yet been made, Western Command will report the transfer to OKW operations staff as completed fact in order to save time" (KTB).

How much consideration for the inhabitants was still exercised was shown by a string of telephone conversations between our staff and that of Western Command. Rommel finally intervened personally. He had allegedly ordered that all women up to fifty years of age should be utilized for defense work. This could not be done without express orders from Western Command "since this contravened the armistice conditions" (KTB). In a telephone talk with Blumentritt, Rommel finally clarified the situation: "Stake installations against airborne landings have progressed well in the 348th Infantry Division's sector. There the division has utilized the work of women who have participated voluntarily and for pay. Army group commander (Rommel) had recommended this measure to the commanding generals and the division commanders. The commander of the 165th Reserve Division seems to have misunderstood it. No intention exists to force all women up to fifty years to work" (KTB).

The Fifteenth Army complained about the lack of concrete, barbed wire, and fuel. The artillery general protested against releasing tractors for work on the obstacles. Overly zealous soldiers searching for stakes had to be stopped when they started to cut down trees which served as camouflage for the shelters for the V1 rockets. South of Le Touquet-Paris-Plage, an army coast battery was hit by twenty-one bombs; one gun suffered slight damage but could be repaired on the spot.

Forty-five Days before the Invasion

April 22. In the morning, rain. At noon, General Kanzler came and reported on mine production; in the afternoon beautiful sunshine. All together it was a quiet day without special events, almost without telephone calls; a quiet respite before the storm which, although becoming more threatening every day, did not seem to be immediately imminent. At dusk one of our few reconnaissance planes sighted a group of enemy vessels five kilometers east of Dover, consisting of thirteen landing craft and approximately the same number of escorts, apparently a landing exercise by the enemy.

April 23. Another quiet day. Captain Peters drove to Paris on navy matters. He took special pains to clarify the orders for the coastal artillery.

April 24. On April 24 and 25 inspection of troops and position on both sides of the Seine. Rommel drove in the first car with Colonel Freiberg; a war correspondent and I in the second car. We separated in Rouen, heavily bombed since I had seen it the last time. I visited Vice-Admiral

Rieve while Rommel inspected the 84th Reserve Division near Yvetot. Rommel requested as a most important point that the units, including the artillery, should move away from the villages.

All morning long I discussed new orders for the artillery missions in case of an enemy landing, the matter of fake positions, and more with Rieve and his artillery experts. Rieve was optimistic, since everywhere the work had progressed well.

At noon I rejoined Rommel's group at Crasville. After lunch at a regimental command post, we drove west along the rough coastline towards Le Havre. In Army Coast Battery 2/1253 an air attack had damaged three of the six 150mm guns. One had already been repaired. A lack of stake installations in the rear area and the thin offshore obstacles evoked some harsh words. In places the subsoil was very unfavorable—gravel or quicksand. Discovering broken pieces of numerous tetrahedrons did not improve the Field Marshal's mood. To save hard work, the soldiers had thrown them thirty to forty meters from embankments onto the beach. Not even the best reinforced concrete could stand such treatment. When it turned out that not much had been done in the ravines and a cold fog rolled in, the inspection of this division ended in trouble.

In Le Havre we inspected the fortifications, the port, concrete bunker, and the motor mine sweepers; everything made a good and clear impression. The sea commandant and the new port commander, formerly commander of Helgoland, participated in the inspection. With one salvo of 305mm shrapnel he had shot down four airplanes from an approaching bomber formation.

Rommel's annoyance quickly abated. We had a peaceful dinner, seasoned with shop talk, at the enlisted men's mess together with the naval commander and the port captain. As usual, the Field Marshal retired early.

April 25. The next morning there was sunny weather again—in every respect. During breakfast Rommel joked about the preceding day's "fog." With regard to the ravines we had arrived at the same solution, putting in antitank or similar obstacles. Further up, they could always be defended against infantry without panzer support. I warned against wasting labor and good iron rails on the quicksand.

At 0700 we drove in the rear area to the 346th Infantry Division at Bolbec. The stake installations against airborne landings had progressed well, and the division made a good impression.

Following the commander's report, Rommel explained his opinions on the defense against airborne landings. Sitting in the back, I took down the essential ideas in shorthand without regard to the style. They record only the content but cannot recapture the strong impression of the fluid and convincing address. He said:

> We will have to think very modern; the commanders will have to keep in step with technical developments. What can we do? We will have to shape the terrain in such a way as to inflict defeat on the enemy during the landing phase. The artillery represents only a coarse tool for striking. Unfortunately cooperation with the early warning service is still imperfect. We have to expect that the enemy will use the most advanced methods against us—for example, an airborne landing at night, as in Burma—and yet we will still win. Like a cunning hunter we will have to lay in wait for the wild birds descending from the air.
>
> Utilize the labor power of the population. Pay them at once for work rendered. Use your personal prestige as general. Sell them on the idea that there will be less chance of an enemy landing where much work has been done. Take trees from the villages. The troops will move out of the villages anyway. Wire is scarce; utilize fence wire, and replace it with later supplies. Of greatest importance is that everything is paid at once, not after weeks and months. The farmer is glad if he has money in his coffers. No forced recruitment, only indirect recruiting. Have the workers sing on their way to work. Do convince them that the work assures their own security.
>
> The enemy will have a confoundedly difficult time getting out of the water. Then the moment will come when he tries to attack from the rear. No counterthrust without artillery support! Otherwise the losses will be heavy. Fire! Fire!
>
> Make the officers versatile for fighting against airborne troops and panzer troops. An officer will have to know all that. Experience has shown that carpet bombing destroys the field positions. Dugouts are useless. The best solution is to place the men in widely spaced Hube holes [the expression was first used for individual dugout positions used to fight against tanks; shortly before General Hube had died in an accident]. Do not dig in along the periphery, but dig widely dispersed positions in the open fields. A regimental commander will have to be with his troops in the field. Envision swarms of locusts falling from the moonlit sky.

Altogether, Rommel's speech again boosted the men's morale. A good exercise of the antitank unit with self-propelled guns followed; then we drove through the division's sector. Everything was in good order, except that not enough attention had been given to camouflaging new construction. But Rommel was satisfied and distributed two concertinas.

During dinner the Field Marshal reminisced about his experiences in the same area during the summer of 1940. As division commander, he, with a tank reconnaissance detachment driving northward, broke through a French division marching on Fécamp from the east. Rommel gave orders to shoot in all directions, broke through, and turned toward the right and left. Near Petit Dalles he surprised the French artillery commander in his bath, and took him prisoner along with a bowlful of freshly fried chicken. When the attack from the east on Fécamp failed because destroyers interfered from the sea with their artillery, Rommel called it off and took the town the next day from the south. The following fight for Saint-Valéry-en-Caux was bitter; he won it by concentrating his firepower. The enemy sought protection behind the steep cliffs; the following morning 8,000 men surrendered.

At 1230 we drove onto the ferry over the Seine to Quilleboeuf. While crossing the already full river, I talked about the Mascaret, the flood wave, which, in spring and fall during the flood tide, reaches a height of one to two meters and moves upriver like a seething wall of water at a speed of approximately fifteen kilometers an hour. This led to a discussion of the possible, but not yet implemented, utilization of the tidal currents in Norwegian fjords and in Brittany. Rommel asked me: "What do you think I would like best to do after the war?" Of course I did not know and he replied, "I would like to be manager of Europe's power systems and reorganize them for the whole of Europe according to modern centralized principles." In my diary I noted, "I would much prefer him to become the man who becomes the director of everything." This thought, however, I kept to myself. It came from my constantly growing impression that Rommel was not only an excellent soldier with special capacities for leadership and technical comprehension, but that he also possessed an extraordinary talent and much instinct for political matters. I believed that with his fine reputation inside and outside Germany he would be the man to lead the reconstruction.

As already discussed with the troops and at the table, we then talked about cooperation with the French—not just for the moment but for the long term, to achieve a sensible rebuilding of Europe. Now they should be put in charge of the antiaircraft defense of their own towns. Our discussion finally turned to forms of addressing people. Rommel shared my dislike for addressing people in the third person and, above all, rejected it completely for real conversations.

On the southern bank of the Seine we took a beautiful shortcut which gave us a view of the wide river valley and the chalk cliffs on the other side. Major General Reichert awaited us at Honfleur to guide us through the sector of his 711th Infantry Division. He reported about several air attacks on battery positions. On two occasions the enemy had severely bombed dummy positions while leaving the well-camouflaged batteries, only a few hundred meters' distant, unmolested. First we inspected the emplaced army coast battery on Mont Canisy. The supports of the guns had remained undamaged, but one mount had become severely twisted through a bomb which had entered the ground at an angle and had exploded under it. Some roofs had received hits, but all guns had remained ready for firing. The battery, however, was not combat-ready, since the terrain around the gun positions was so severely torn-up that the transport of ammunition from the ammunition depots some distance away to the guns was not possible.

This bomb damage clearly decided the question about the best type of emplacement in favor of the navy. Generally it built its gun emplacements a bit larger than the army, with ammunition space and an approximately one-meter-thick protective shield surrounding the whole construction. This required more concrete, but ammunition was always within reach and the protective shield prevented the tilting of the entire gun emplacement from an oblique hit. Unfortunately it was now too late to utilize this experience effectively.

Near the shell-pitted ground of a fake battery—completely plowed under—a corporal described very graphically how he had been peacefully bicycling when the attack had surprised him. He had thrown himself into the road ditch, had experienced the incredible force of the carpet bombing from the closest distance and, a bit dazed but without injury, had continued his cycling. The ditch was a measured distance of eight meters away from the nearest bomb crater.

We finally inspected the floodings of the Dives and sections of the beach. Everything was in good order, and Rommel, highly pleased, donated three concertinas. From Cabourg we returned via Vernon. I sat in Rommel's car and he spoke with me very frankly.

At first he talked about his method of leadership. He believed that sometimes roughness was the shortest and the most painless way to reach the necessary goal. The result of good peacetime training was a tendency to be very careful in executing an order precisely as instructed. Nowadays, however, orders were often not carried out. The SS had never had peacetime training. With bitterness he then talked about personal envy and the tremendous amount of interference. Subsequently he discussed camouflage, mobility, and ingenuity of the troops. He greatly regretted Hube's death, who died in an airplane accident while on his way to Führer Heaquarters. One should not call such men for reporting but instead send somebody for them.

Changing to lighter subjects, he talked, among other things, about how he became a hunter. When he was put in charge of the Goslar Jäger battalion, he found that none of the officers knew how to hunt. He arranged that they learn how to hunt, and tried to be a good example. As his first achievement, however, he shot the wrong buck. As penance, he allowed himself to shoot only a buck with deformed antlers, then one with antlers like screws, and only then did he deserve a good six-pointer. Near Goslar he hunted for stags. He shot a fine eight-pointer; then he was promised an even better one. After long stalking however, he sighted only smaller stags. While returning home with the gamekeeper, Rommel unexpectedly saw the proper stag in the woods. When he pulled the trigger, nothing happened, because the safety was still partially engaged. He wondered whether the rifle would fire if he completely released the safety. He held the rifle tightly and released the safety completely, but nothing happened. Cocking the rifle would have been too noisy, and the stag would not have waited much longer. Thereon the gamekeeper handed his rifle to Rommel and the stag fell. Afterwards he shot several more.

Finally he related how he had begun to teach his then six-year-old son to ride. At the riding track Rommel held the horse on a guide rope. The sound of a steam siren frightened the horse, it bolted, the boy fell and got caught in the stirrup. Fortunately everything went well. Father Rommel, however, had received a severe scare. Relieved, he gave the boy five marks, didn't tell his wife, and stopped the lessons.

Rommel then became more serious and talked about the wear and tear on individuals, especially of military leaders in war. What during the early war years had still been easy was often no longer possible in the fifth year of the war.

Shortly after 1900 we arrived at staff quarters. Meise introduced dinner with a bang as loud as it was unexpected, by throwing a new glass fuse for land mines to the floor. He was greatly delighted that the device functioned so well.

The 2d Panzer Division was to be transferred to the Somme. Western Command wanted the division stationed in the area of Amiens; Rommel at once requested Amiens–Abbeville to move at least parts of the division closer to the coast.

April 26. High-pressure weather with sun and a cool northeast wind. A reconnaissance airplane reported many ships at Spithead roadstead, outside Southhampton and Portsmouth. The beginning of the invasion? Unfortunately our reconnaissance did not often penetrate to the enemy's concentration areas, and thus we were never safe from surprises.

Speidel drove to Western Command for a conference of chiefs of staff on the situation. The Fifteenth Army wanted to sandwich parts of the 12th SS Panzer Division in the sector of the 711th Infantry Division. Rommel immediately rejected the request. True, he wanted the panzer divisions so far forward that they could reach the beaches with the artillery of the foremost units. They were to be placed to the rear of the infantry divisions so that they could be moved as a whole without difficulty. This would not have been possible if they had been wedged in between the infantry.

The commander–Netherlands pointed out the weakness of the defenses in the west Frisian sector and asked for unlimited utilization of the naval training units in case of a landing and simultaneously the transfer of a reinforced grenadier regiment each from the Corps Districts VI and X. The approved request was forwarded (KTB).

Rommel ordered the immediate construction of at least one dummy position for each battery in the main combat area and the installation of numerous individual foxholes in a 100-meter circle around the real guns. He wanted deployment of the eastern battalions on less endangered spots only and then always between two German units.

In the afternoon, enemy aircraft bombarded the bridges at Mantes. The sky showed many condensation trails, the noise was great, but the bridges remained undamaged.

Rommel, who to his dismay was gaining weight, had started to ride. A white horse was given to him, a beautiful animal but without temperament. He said afterward, "The horse has so little temperament that I get quite jittery. I also do not like boring people. You most likely have already noted that."

He did not agree with the press coverage. An article he had discussed with one of our war correspondents had appeared in the "Brüsseler Zeitung" several days earlier but not yet in France. In this connection, he told the reporters: "You can write about me whatever you wish as long as it gains us another eight days' time." Towards evening Peters and I went for a walk. I found a land turtle and took it back to the castle.

During dinner we talked about which important people had to be invited. Somebody proposed to feed a whole group at a time. But Rommel replied: "No, this will only lead to superficial discussions. I want to work on everybody individually; only this will bring results."

On our way back from the movie that played twice or three times a week in a cave, he spoke sharply about the people who wanted to prevent him from carrying out his plans. "The panzer units will be deployed forward" (PAV).

Forty Days before the Invasion

April 27. Beautiful weather again. The British took advantage of it and, for the first time, attacked from the air offshore obstacles on both sides of Boulogne. Of late we had been receiving good situation reports from Navy Group West. This time they contained a thorough report about the sinking of torpedo boat T29. During the night of April 25 to 26, it had engaged in a fight with superior British forces off the coast of northern Brittany. The crew had behaved exceedingly well.

On Hitler's orders, the staffs of the 2d Parachute Rifle Corps and the 5th Parachute Rifle Division were to be moved to Brittany immediately since he feared a landing there. Rommel requested them to be moved in the area of Rennes from where they could operate in the direction of Saint-Malo as well as of Lorient.

I drove to Paris, first to the fortress engineers to question them about the protective plate for concrete emplacements. It turned out that it was prescribed, but often had not been included in order to save concrete. It was admitted without hesitation that the naval construction was more practical, although it required more concrete.

Then I drove to Admiral Krancke. He was very cordial. The matter of my personal subordination was no longer mentioned. Without my asking, he repeated his justification for not laying mines and his reasons for the so-called "lightning barriers." The material for them was stored at various ports, prepared in such a way that they could be laid very quickly in case of an alert. I was of a different opinion, since I doubted that they could be laid in time at the point of attack, where they would be needed most urgently. Once more I pleaded for the mining of the Bay of the Seine and for the laying of coastal mine A.

Krancke and I then talked about batteries. Krancke regretted the conservative attitude of the engineers, who only knew about and built according to their standard building methods. Construction of the revolving concrete turrets could have started two years ago. Now it was too late. We finally discussed matters of camouflage and the fight of the T29.

For lunch I was the guest of Field Marshal Sperrle and did not need to starve. He was amiable and overwhelming as always and scolded the navy a bit because, at an earlier date, they had been unable to reach an agreement about the manning of the sea rescue boats.

I ordered the mandatory field-gray field uniform and drove via Maisons Le Fitte, crossing the Seine on a narrow bridge near Meulan, since I did not trust the situation in Mantes. On this route we remained unbombed despite the extensive air activity above. Shortly after Meulan I picked up three officer aspirants of the Army Antiaircraft Corps. They had much luggage and stood somewhat lost on the roadside. They simply had orders to go to a village whose name they did not know eight kilometers past Meulan.

During the night enemy planes passed overhead endlessly. The ratio between the German and the enemy air force is humiliating.

April 28. In the morning I finished my mail and my paperwork, an endurable task since most of the smaller problems had been solved and not much could be done about the larger ones. I finished my income tax declaration, which in comparison to the overall situation seemed rather unimportant.

Peters drove to Paris to convince the navy group of his idea to let the coastal artillery fire only with a lateral observer, as far as possible.

I reported to Rommel on the results of my Paris trip—lightning barriers, camouflage, and protective plates. In the anteroom I introduced the turtle to the young dog, who was frightened at first but finally started to bark with great courage. This lured the chief of staff from his desk, then also the commander in chief, and, for a few minutes, the seriousness of the situation was forgotten. In the afternoon I finished more mail and paperwork and read a book on Charles XII. "Surprising parallels with Hitler. Obviously, bullheadedness alone is not enough" (PAV).

At 1700 General Geyr von Schweppenburg arrived for a meeting with Speidel; Guderian came at 1800 and the discussion continued with Rommel. Subject: fundamental questions of tactical employment, especially the use of the panzer divisions.

At 1900, the commanding general of the 11th Air Corps visited us to recommend that the 5th Parachute Division (5,000 volunteers from the signal corps and antiaircraft units with no heavy arms, only 1,500 rifles) be retained a few weeks longer in the area of Chalons-sur-Marne because half their equipment was available there. The ordered transfer to the area of Rennes would slow down training considerably. Rommel declined; he was anxious to get forces near western Normandy.

Guderian was very lively and entertaining during dinner. He spoke about the development of self-propelled artillery mounts and assault guns. The artillery specialists did not want them, for guns had to be drawn with the muzzle pointing to the rear, as had been done for a few centuries. The "Tiger Tank Primer" was once more reviewed and quoted. Another instruction booklet in rhyme was already available but was still too long. Guderian's and Rommel's unaffected manner of discussion and several remarks gave me the impression that Guderian neither rejected nor fought Rommel's plans. It was to be hoped that the commitment of the panzer units would soon be decided in Rommel's favor, thereby strengthening the defense decisively.

Final Measures

Ten weeks had passed since Rommel had taken command. During this time much noticeable progress had been made despite many difficulties and some resistance. The measures ordered by Rommel had been started everywhere, although some with considerable delay.

The enemy had not been idle either. His preparations in southern England had also progressed considerably according to all news that seeped through. The intelligence picture indicated that the enemy had made forces ready in the Mediterranean too, possibly for an operation against southern France, perhaps southwestern France. Therefore, Rommel once more visited the Mediterranean and the southern part of the Bay of Biscay to check the progress of the defenses in accordance with his inspection orders.

We started on April 29 at 0600, and on that first day covered a distance of 780 kilometers. At 1100 we made our first stop at Nantes, received the usual reports, and lunched at the soldiers' mess. Two Frenchwomen, apparently unaccustomed to the task, served lunch at a snail's pace. They constantly offered the food from the right-hand side, began several places from the Field Marshal, and gave most of their attention to the younger men. One looked rather German; the other was well made-up and emitted a lovely fragrance.

In the afternoon we drove along the coast from the Loire to the Gironde (Pornic, Saint-Jean-de-Monts, Saint-Gilles-sur-Vie, Les Sables d'Olonne, Rochefort, Pointe de La Coubre with the 80th Corps, 158th

Reserve Division, 700th Infantry Division, 17th SS Panzer Grenadier Division to the rear). We arrived at Royan at 2045. I lodged with the sea commandant, Captain Michahelles, with whom I got along well. At 2115, dinner at the officers' quarters. Subsequently the navy met at the Golf Hotel. I knew most of the participants.

The main problem at headquarters was the battalion of military geologists which was placed at the disposal of Army Group B by SS Lieutenant General Jüttner, the question being was it guaranteed that the battalion would be used only as one unit.

April 30. Early in the morning we crossed the Gironde in a harbor patrol boat. We circled the destroyer Z37 in an honor round; the crew paraded, and Rommel was visibly pleased. On our way to Bordeaux we inspected several positions. A major forest fire had destroyed 10,000 mines of 200,000 already laid. The area was thinly manned; Rommel forced himself not to criticize, since it was not under his command. At the headquarters of First Army (General Blaskowitz) we had a conference with the immediate staff. Rommel and Blaskowitz talked about their war experiences during the refreshingly simple lunch. Rommel related how, before the breakthrough at El Alamein, British tanks had systematically destroyed fifty of his seventy 88mm antiaircraft guns. Before the anticipated breakthrough, Rommel had prepared for mobile warfare and pulled back his supply trains. Orders from OKW, however, forced him to send them to the front. Despite this the British took few German prisoners. They dominated the sea and the road along the coast, but the Africa Corps marched through the desert parallel to the coast, bringing back 70,000 of its 80,000 men.

At 1300 we continued to Arcachon. A bunker near the water caught our attention, because its firing field was directed only toward land. Farther south we found much sand, and my car developed problems. I could not keep pace with the column, and drove directly to Biarritz, our destination, through wonderful Sunday peace in a sunlit landscape with light and deep green, pine groves, stone oaks, brooks, flat-roofed Basque houses, old men absorbed in some game, girls in Basque dresses, and horses in harness with double wooden collars.

At 2045 at the Biarritz soldiers' mess, we had dinner, served on Basque china made in the Saar by Villeroy & Boch. Subject of the conversation was what we had seen on that day, and then Rommel's first African retreat, his dispute with General Bastico. A major from the mountain troops recalled how, despite strong Italian resistance, they occupied the Greek islands in 1943.

The soldiers had come in large numbers to see the Field Marshal and to give him a spontaneous ovation, which pleased him. Among them was a boatswain's mate with the Iron Cross First Class from the naval anti-aircraft gunners. He had stood his position with a handful of Germans at Castellamare near Naples in September 1943, and had made his surviving adversaries prisoners.

May 1. We started at 0600. From an anonymous admirer the Field Marshal received a bunch of lillies of the valley. We drove to the Mediterranean. The weather was at first foggy, then it cleared, and finally the sun broke through in all its glory allowing us a beautiful view of the Pyrenées.

At 1330 we arrived at Perpignan. Policemen cordoned off the streets. Rommel was surprised to find that it was done for his protection. The population showed much interest in him.

We lunched at General Petersen's, the commander of the Luftwaffe Field Corps. Besides the other generals present was Rear Admiral Schulte-Mönting, the sea commandant–Provence. Until Grand Admiral Raeder's retirement, Schulte-Mönting had been his chief of staff. His was a superior personality, quick in comprehending and deciding, with a gift of intuition for people and interrelations. During dinner we discussed with the local division commander whether it would be possible for the navy to take charge of the defense of the ports. We agreed that older naval officers should be able to do so. Later La Rochelle (Vice-Admiral Schirlitz), Royan (Captain Michahelles), and Dunkirk (Rear Admiral Frisius) proved us correct.

After dinner the division commander reported on his sector and on the progress of the defense work. Subsequently we drove to Port-Vendres, the Portus Veneris of antiquity near the Spanish border. An antiaircraft corvette lay in the harbor. We drove along the coast towards the northeast enjoying the beautiful view of the sea and the Pyrenées behind us. We inspected several resistance nests tunnelled into the rock. Tetrahedrons stood in the water where a sandy beach made small-scale landings possible.

So far, 237,000 mines had been laid in the sector of the 277th Infantry Division, 99,000 in April alone. In Sète we visited the fire control station high on the hill that dominated town and harbor. The road was stony, and cost us time. On top the commander of the 271st Infantry Division gave his report. According to the KTB: "They work here in an organized and diligent manner." Subsequently we drove a bit to the east and then back again.

On the whole trip we frequently had to get out for short inspections. We usually continued rather quickly, and Schulte-Mönting was not quite used to the pace. During the drive he told much that was interesting about the internal naval history of recent years. Particularly revealing to me was that Hitler knew about Italy's negotiations with the western Allies shortly after Mussolini's fall, but did not inform Kesselring.

We arrived at Montpellier at 2130. For once the Field Marshal remained in his high boots. It took me twelve minutes to change and I made it just in time for the dinner given by the commander of the 271st Infantry Division at a manor house outside the town. General Kaliebe related how during a visit he had introduced himself to the commander of a naval battery and received as an answer: "127mm," because the commander believed Kaliebe to have asked for the gun's caliber.

Important matters at headquarters on this day: The advance parties of the 2d Parachute Corps and the 5th Parachute Division started to move to the Seventh Army on April 30. On May 2 the 91st Parachute Division leaves for the Cotentin Peninsula. The transfer of the 2d Panzer Division will be completed by May 3.

OKW via Western Command requests a short situation evaluation to be used in a report to the Führer. Subject: the defensive ability of the 84th Army Corps sector, with special consideration given to our comparative force strength with regard to enemy attacks from the sea and airborne landings. On the same day Western Command receives a corresponding report from Seventh Army and a situation evaluation of Army Group B. Navy Group West decides to lay a number of lightning barriers now (by torpedo boats), most of them between Le Havre and Boulogne.

Thirty-five Days before the Invasion

May 2. In beautiful weather we started at 0630 to the 388th, 244th and 242d Infantry Divisions. First we drove through La Camargue to the old town of Aigues-Mortes with its completely preserved town wall. From here Louis IX in 1248 put to sea for Tunis for the 7th Crusade. On the beach near Le Grau-du-Roi we saw offshore obstacles and rows of wooden stakes. Continuing to Port Saint-Louis, we passed a trench plow which plowed up the flat countryside as precaution against airborne landings.

We joked about the fine protective trenches which this method created for enemy parachutists. Near Fos Plage the offshore obstacles consisted of mine-topped wooden stakes supplemented by four-meter-wide wooden floats, topped by mines and anchored to concrete blocks. They would hold through the summer, but most likely could not withstand a winter storm.

Farther inland in the completely flat lagoon area we passed many fields covered with stone cairns approximately one and one-half meters in height, obstacles against airborne landings; they changed the appearance of the countryside considerably.

On an atrocious road through stony terrain with a beautiful view to the sea, we drove south of Port-de-Bouc in the direction of Marseille to the boundary of the division behind Couronne. On a hill with the sea in the background, the Field Marshal gave an impressive speech to the assembled officers.

Starting from his experience in Africa, he described the combat methods and the toughness of the British and emphasized their use of the most modern equipment. He pointed out that it was perfectly understandable to prefer using one's own experience rather than those of others under pressure. However, time had run out for us. The clock stood at five minutes to twelve, and we could no longer gather our own experience; therefore his mission.

He asserted that after the original idea to repel the landed enemy in a counterattack had been discarded in favor of defeating the enemy at the main battle line on the beaches, the plan at hand corresponded with the actual reality. The fight would be hard. All available technical resources would have to be utilized to balance the lack of manpower. The work done so far represented a good start. Rommel mentioned that he had been here before and that he was especially pleased to find that his suggestions had been accepted and further developed so excellently. Nobody should, however, believe that the goal had been reached. This would only be the case once each company had its own concrete factory to manufacture offshore obstacles of all types. The ultimate aim for the obstacles zone on the beach would be a width of at least 300 meters.

Three goals:
pre-coastal "coral reef;"
large mine fields with land front;
installation of stakes against airborne landings.

The "coral reef "needed to have a destructive effect. In order to achieve this, not only would it be necessary for every engineer to cooperate mentally, but every officer and soldier would also have to be imbued with the desire to construct offshore barriers and to strengthen them. The bulk of the division would have to be deployed in such a way as to be able to effectively control the beach with its weapons. Much had been accomplished with the mining; still the result was not yet satisfactory, since momentarily each coastal meter contained three mines, while the target was 100. There remained 800 square kilometers to be mined in the division sector.

The rear area was of great importance as well and would have to be strengthened with all available technical means. Since we would have to expect the enemy to use superbly equipped air landing troops, the best protection here would be the mine fields too. Conclusions drawn from the experiences in Africa showed the best defense solution to be the installation of resistance nests within the mine fields. In these nests even the last man from the supply companies would have to be placed.

The war would continue for some time. The large-scale enemy attack was unquestionably imminent. It was quite possible that the attack would start in the south. The enemy was reputed to say: "Kill the Germans wherever you encounter them." Such behavior is alien to us. We fought as respectable soldiers—though just as tough as the others. The crushing defeat of the enemy attack at the coast of France would be our contribution to vengeance.

The speech conveyed the same fundamental ideas as always, but in an especially effective manner. Afterward we drove past Marseille to Toulon. At the hill near Fort Le Rove a large crowd of officers awaited us, among them Vice-Admiral Wever, the commanding admiral of southern France, and Lieutenant Commander (Reserve) Polenz, the chief of the 6th Security Flotilla. From above we had a good view of the harbor. The commander of the 244th Infantry Division explained his right sector; later at the command post at Aubagne he explained the left sector which contained the bays at La Ciotat and Bandol. In the division's area 127,000 mines had so far been installed.

During lunch at the soldiers' mess in Aubagne we were seated strictly according to rank which unfortunately separated me from my navy friends. Only the toast was noteworthy: "To the Field Marshal's most distinguished well-being." After lunch we inspected, east of La Ciotat, a factory for tetrahedrons and a new type of Czech hedgehog which measured two meters in height and had a concrete block in the middle. We drove to Hyères, inspecting the artificial swamps and mine fields. There we finished the inspection around 1700. On our way back we drove through the town of Aix, where the citizens promenaded peacefully under the sycamores of one of the town's squares. We reached Avignon at 1930.

At General Sodenstern's we received—not unexpectedly—a fine dinner together with stimulating conversation which by no means dealt solely with our immediate tasks, although they certainly played a major role. The host quite candidly told me that he now understood what Rommel wanted, and that he believed Rommel's plans to be correct. He was just a bit displeased with himself for not reaching the conclusion on his own.

One of the guests, a colonel of the mountain troops, had taken part in the Narvik campaign and had not become a special friend of sea travel. Rommel talked about mobile tactics in Africa. At 2300 the Field Marshal drove to his quarters. Under the moonlit sky, his staff went to the Palace of the Popes and afterwards sat in the hotel bar to get a glimpse of the smart set. This consisted of two somewhat embarrassed officers and two mediocre girls, who were not in the least self-conscious.

On May 3 we started shortly after 0700, driving up the Rhone Valley. Except for the sighting of some *German* airplanes, nothing special happened. We took lunch at the soldiers' quarters at Chalon-sur-Saône. The reservation had been made in general terms for a certain number of men with the remark that the gentlemen might possibly wear civilian clothing. The astonishment and the joy was great when it was discovered who the main guest was.

New ideas were discussed during dinner. Rommel considered the possibility of illuminating the forefield to distract and mislead the enemy during night landings. The cables and the energy sources presented difficulties. At the start of our trip I had given him a memorandum on a novel use of mines. He agreed with it; the new, quite simple method was used, but too late to be of any consequence.

Rommel then pleaded for cooperation among the services, the ministries, and the other administrative bodies. There was too much working at cross-purposes. He came out sharply against ambition, envy, ill-will, and selfishness. He intended to invite noncommissioned officers from all the services in the near future in order to speak to them. Our trip continued via Avalon and Auxerre to Fontainebleau. The last car had a light collision, but could follow. At 1930 we were back at La Roche-Guyon.

The mood during dinner was cheerful. After dinner we watched a movie. The plot: old farmer vs. young farmer; well acted. Then I accompanied Meise home. We talked about mines.

General Blaskowitz had been put in charge of Army Group G, which consisted of the First and the Nineteenth Armies. General Diem had visited the Cherbourg area and had noticed that mining and staking were still very inadequate (KTB).

May 4. A moderate amount of paperwork; fighter plane attack on the bridges at Mantes. From the grand hall of the castle we watched their approach. In the afternoon I visited General Gehrcke, our staff signal communications officer. When I asked a soldier for directions, I noticed that he was Russian. With an uncanny Swabian inflection in his German he answered: "General Gehrcke, here he is."

During dinner Rommel recounted happy events from his days as a lieutenant. He expressed his satisfaction with the Nineteenth Army.

Western Command wanted to place the 7th Smoke Launcher Brigade in the area of Beauvais, approximately eighty kilometers behind the coast, and Seventh Army's 101st Smoke Launcher Regiment approximately equally far behind, between Flers and Alencon. Army Group B, however, wanted to place the latter on the Cotentin Peninsula. It was typical that while Rommel's defense plan was accepted in principle, the higher staffs especially could not bring themselves to act accordingly.

On May 5, except for conferences with the different staffs in Paris, we remained at La Roche-Guyon.

KTB: Speidel conferred with the artillery commander of the 309th about the employment of the 7th and 101st Launcher Brigades. The Navy High Command had authorized the deployment of naval training units 14 and 15 forward and on the rear water front in Holland. Rommel rejected a Fifteenth Army proposal to have Luftwaffe personnel inspect the airborne landing obstacles. As with the offshore obstacles, Rommel knew only too well that they were not ideal, but he counted also on their psychological effect. The morale of the German troops would have been impaired by the probably negative verdict of the Luftwaffe experts. He wanted to prevent this.

May 6. Light drizzle; cool. Speidel had a conference with the chiefs of staff of the armies and with the military commanders, which continued with Krancke, Stülpnagel and the chief of staff of the 3rd Air Fleet.

Reorganization in the navy. Navy Group North was to be dissolved. Dönitz requested me; Rommel declined.

The 2d Parachute Division is available from the east, which is to be deployed with the 21st Panzer Division.

At 1630 State Secretary Ganzenmüller from the Reich Ministry of Transport came for a conference with Rommel at tea time. "He could also not report much that was encouraging. At the moment of the invasion only small transport movements could be expected" (TBR).

The Seventh Army wants to pull out the staff of the 74th Army Corps. Rommel did not agree.

The chief of Western Command telephoned because Hitler considered the area of Cherbourg very threatened and he desired that appropriate countermeasures be taken.

> The Führer is of the opinion that an invasion along a 500-kilometer-wide strip is unlikely; that, however, attacks will occur primarily at Normandy and to a lesser degree at Brittany. The most recent information once more points in this direction. Simultaneously OKW is concerned about the 243rd Infantry Division's supply of horses. OKW apparently has not considered strengthening the northern half of the Cotentin Peninsula with a larger unit, but instead contemplates the deployment of numerous smaller units. According to the OKW's point of view the utilization of the reserves is for the time being out of the question (KTB).

Since the OKW transmitted Hitler's opinions regarding the coming invasion's possible landing point with such emphasized haste and since it supported them with further information, it seemed to follow that it was no longer against forming a troop concentration in Normandy as Rommel had requested. Instead of the fast panzer units, however, OKW thought of only one infantry division. Therefore the tiresome making of applications and the search for substitutes continued.

This necessitated, first of all, numerous talks with the Seventh Army, according to which the 700th Training Unit, 206th Panzer Battalion and the Assault Battalion came into question for the Cotentin Peninsula. The 243rd Infantry Division's units were utilized, until May 16, for the completion of coastal barriers.

During the night, air attacks on the bridges at Mantes. Considerable noise.

Thirty Days before the Invasion

May 7 (Sunday). Cool. During lunch, air attacks on Mantes and Vernon.

Seventh Army made the following proposals for strengthening the Normandy sector:

a. Moving the 243rd Infantry Division to the northwest, north of the line Saint-Saveur-le-Vicomte/Barneville.
b. One regiment of the 243rd Infantry Division reinforced by the 206th Panzer Battalion to the sector Cap de la Hague–Cap de Carteret.
c. The 342d Tank Destroyer Battalion to remain in the division's present sector and to occupy the dominating hills.
d. Transfer of the Assault Battalion of the Seventh Army into the area around La Haye-du-Puits.
e. Movement of the 2d Luftwaffe Division into the 243rd Infantry Division's present area.
f. Deployment of the 100th Panzer Reserve and Training Battalion in the interior of the Cotentin Peninsula.

The army group promised the respective orders and deception instructions.

Telephone conversation with the Netherlands: commander of the Netherlands' Waffen SS stated that he could not take over the left sector of the 16th Luftwaffe Field Division without express orders from the chief of the SS. Therefore, no other alternative remains presently but to wait until the matter is clarified (KTB).

Formation of the 9th, 11th and 116th Panzer Divisions utilizing and dissolving the 155th, 179th and 273rd Panzer Reserve Divisions.

May 8. No special events at headquarters; air raid alert. Went shortly to Speidel to inform him about the reorganization of the fleet command and the disbandment of Navy Group North; asked him to restrain the commander in chief a bit in his technical requests. Instead of the 2d Luftwaffe Division, the 91st Air Landing Division is transferred into the 243rd Infantry Division's present sector. The decision was reached within two hours. The increase of sabotage on the railroads endangers the supply line of the Seventh Army.

Basic Order Number 38–Commander in Chief West arrived. It rearranged the command structure in the area of Western Command and was to take effect at noon of May 12. New for Army Group B (Rommel) was only that the line dividing the combat command between Army Group B and the newly formed Army Group G (Blaskowitz) ran from Tours to the east along the old line of demarcation down to the Swiss border near Geneva. The new command structure was on the whole unsatisfactory, since with regard to the command of the fast panzer units, it changed nothing. As previously, Army Group B still had only tactical command of the 2d, 116th and 21st Panzer Divisions, and was not authorized to move them and so form a concentration. The 2d SS Panzer Division and the newly formed 9th and 11th Panzer Divisions stood in the sector of Army Group G, to which they were subordinated in the same limited way. The 1st SS Panzer Corps, with the 1st and 12th SS Panzer Divisions, the 17th SS Panzer Grenadier Division and the approaching Panzer Lehr Division (panzer instructional division) remained as OKW reserves. Therefore, Rommel could neither move them closer to the coast nor could he, in case of an enemy alert, directly command them without their release by OKW.

Panzer Group West (Geyr von Schweppenburg) remained under the immediate command of the Commander in Chief West (von Rundstedt) and was at his disposal as command staff in case of an enemy alert. It was still responsible for the training of all panzer units stationed in the west and for possible new formations of units.

Navy Group West and the 3rd Air Fleet were asked to continue working in close cooperation with Western Command and the commander in chief west-subordinated Army Group B and Army Group G.

The "Basic Order," although it was absolutely clear, did nothing, however, to change the inadequate command structure, which prevented the commanders in the west from using the forces in their sectors uniformly and without delay.

In the afternoon Rommel drove to Paris for a meeting at Field Marshal von Rundstedt's with Sperrle, Blaskowitz, Geyr von Schweppenburg, Krancke, and their chiefs of staff.

May 9. "Drive to the Cotentin Peninsula, which seems to become the focal point of the invasion" (TBR).

At 0700 via Vernon (bridge destroyed; took ferry) to Houlgate; good offshore obstacles. While we walked on the moist sand, inspecting the obstacles, the tide returned. On this beach it rises three meters in an hour, so we had to leave the beach in a hurry. We inspected the battery at Houlgate, not emplaced under concrete, pretty much roughed up by air attacks. The floodings at Dives had receded due to the dry weather. Before entering Caen we waited for an air raid alert to pass. At first, the Field Marshal consulted privately with General Marcks while the rest of us waited in the sun. Then General Marcks gave his report. Heavy enemy air reconnaissance, especially on both sides of the Orne and over the Cotentin; air attacks on artillery positions on the east coast, on thorough-fares in the area of Carentan, and on road crossings. The commander made his intentions known to increase the troop strength on the Cotentin Peninsula, in part to protect the flanks from any western threat. In view of the narrowness of the peninsula (approximately thirty-five kilometers; from Carentan to Lessay, twenty-five kilometers) and the good protection which the hedgerows gave against observation from the air, each unit stationed in the interior could quickly take part in the defense of either the east or the west coast. He expressed his concern about the defense of the Channel Islands. Marcks considered a landing on Guernsey not possible due to the powerful fortifications. An airborne landing on Jersey was possible; a landing from the sea very difficult. The Organisation Todt had not received any deliveries of cement by train since May 1. Cement was now supposed to be delivered by boats from Le Havre.

The commanding general had changed over to wood for as much of the work to be done as possible, especially the offshore obstacles. Eighty kil-ometers of offshore obstacles had been completed; 170,000 stakes had been installed as obstacles against airborne landings.

A briefing by the fortress commander of Cherbourg followed. The city was well fortified, facing the sea. The land front still needed some work (KTB, very optimistic).

A briefing by the commander of the 21st Panzer Division followed. The commander in chief requested from him a precise reconnaissance of all roads suitable for troop transport and of all readiness areas for a combat group on Cotentin. In the event of moving there, all five crossings over the Vire were to be used. The commander figured four hours to Cher-bourg for wheeled units and twenty-four hours for tracked units. The division should also be prepared for combat in an area not suitable for panzer warfare.

After dinner Rommel inspected the 716th Infantry Division's sector west of the Orne. The Riva Bella battery had been hit by carpet bombing which the concrete had withstood. The staking along the coast was quite good.

The Naval Battery Longues (four 150mm) in the rear area near Bayeux made a good impression. Rear Admiral Hennecke joined us here. We inspected the ports of Grandcamp and Isigny, where too many gun car-riers were placed too close to each other for my liking. We reached Saint-

Lô around 2000. Stimulating dinner at General Marcks'. Subsequently Colonel Lattmann, Captain (Army) Behr and I took the half-hour walk to the guest cottage. "Nobody was concerned about partisans."

Bombing attack on battery 1/725 (Sangatte) by fifty bombers. Result: two wounded, insignificant damage. Four wounded at railroad battery 765 (Frethune); railroad battery 710 (Calais) tracks destroyed, all batteries ready to fire.

Heavy bombing attacks on the Marcouf battery (twenty-one centimeters, not completed); damage slight, since the guns were already under concrete. In the open battery Morsalines (four 155mm), however, one gun was totally destroyed as well as the mount of another.

"The bombing attacks have shown that only fortress-like construction will be of any value" (TBR).

May 10. Left at 0700 and drove through light fog via Carentan to the east coast of the Cotentin Peninsula. The British propaganda radio station opposite Calais had already announced Rommel's proposed visit to Cherbourg. Therefore the program was changed. Near La Pernelle we had a beautiful view of the sea and the shore. A brief address given by Rommel was recorded on tape. Subsequently we attended a briefing at Saint-Pierre-Eglise.

In the afternoon Rommel inspected the combined command post for the sea commandant, the fortress commander, the naval communications officer, the commander of the motor torpedo boats, and the radar center completely tunnelled into the rock. It was very practical to put all command posts under one roof. We then drove to Cap de la Hague and south on the western coast along the bays of Vauville and Sciotat. Progress had been made here also with the offshore obstacles and the batteries. In the evening we were back at Saint-Lô at General Marcks'.

Information from OKW about possible enemy attack arrived at headquarters. It read as follows:

1. OKW expects the enemy attack to begin in the middle of May. Especially May 18 seems a potentially favorable day. Irrefutable documentary proof is, of course, not available. Point of concentration first and foremost: Normandy; secondly: Brittany.

   It is to be expected that the enemy will attempt to destroy the ground troops in the interior and on the coast with air attacks in successive waves on narrow areas with large-sized bombs and with a simultaneous attack and heavy shelling from the sea. The use of new weapons is not impossible. Very heavy airborne landings might perhaps even be executed during darkness.

2. Therefore it is also important to deploy the troops in a cleverly camouflaged and dispersed manner and to dig in everything not protected by concrete. In the peninsula's interior special attention should be given to airborne landing troops. Sky observation!

Except for the date, this estimate of the situation corresponded with the later facts. However, it also failed to induce the formation of the constantly requested points of concentration. In the meantime, the panzer divisions' bridge-building columns were eagerly discussed on the telephone. They were scarce, and because of this, additional building material and ferries were to be stored at possible river crossings.

May 11. 0700, started via Caen to Falaise where, in an unannounced visit, Rommel surprised the panzer regiment of Colonel von Oppeln-Bronikowski (well-known tournament horseman; winner of the Olympic gold medal; decorated with the Knight's Cross; survived three times the destruction of his tank by enemy fire). He arrived after us, had apparently celebrated on the previous evening, and uttered without much emotion: "Catastrophe." Rommel noticed at once that Oppeln-Bronikowski was an excellent soldier, refrained from making any angry remarks, and learned all he wanted to know. The unit made a good impression.

At a drill ground, the staff of the 21st Panzer Division demonstrated mortars and *Nebelwerfer* rocket launchers which were to disperse tactical smoke. This was accompanied by the most atrocious noise, and in the process managed to ignite a small forest fire. Originally the 21st Panzer Division had been an infantry division. With captured French tanks General Feuchtinger, a good organizer, had elevated them to panzer division status. His staff included some people from "Rheinmetall" (a manufacturer of arms), a circumstance that benefited his supply of equipment. After the demonstration we had lunch at his staff quarters at Saint-Pierre-sur-Dives and later a brief discussion in the garden, while waves of heavy bombers passed overhead.

Sixty-five thousand of Organisation Todt's workmen were presently needed in France to repair railways and roads.

The subordinated units received orders to quickly construct mock tanks in order to simulate fast mobile units and, as with dummy batteries, divert the enemy.

Rommel planned to transfer the reconnaissance unit of the 21st Panzer Division to the area of Carentan.

Twenty-five Days before the Invasion

May 12. As a result of the trip, Rommel informed General Jodl that the southern half of the Cotentin Peninsula was still empty and that the 12th SS Division (Hitler Youth) should be transferred there. The air attacks had become massive; the damage reported by the troops, however, was quite often exaggerated. Installations without proper emplacements were a waste of cement. According to the view of the parachutists, the terrain with its many hedgerows and folds was well suited for airborne landings, contrary to the presently held opinion, since the landing troops could find cover at once and would be difficult to reach with defending fire.

All day long continuous attacks on batteries, bridges and airfields. Early in the morning I drove via Mantes, where the bridge still stood, to Paris to discuss at the command quarters of Security Area West the dispersal of the gun carriers, and with the chief of staff of Navy Group West the results of the inspections. Grand Admiral Dönitz had been there the day before. On our way back the car had a flat tire at Mantes. We just made it across the still-intact bridge and repaired the flat in haste and under some tension.

In the evening General Wagner, the general quartermaster of the Army High Command, joined us at dinner, after a meeting with the Field Marshal.

May 13. Fog. We started at 0700 in the direction of the Somme. The inspections began with the 2d Panzer Division at Courselles. The whole division was quartered in the fields and especially in the woods, none in the villages. Except for the lack of antiaircraft guns, training and equipment were good. The whole area from Boulogne to Dieppe had been scouted for combat routes. The Somme could represent a considerable obstacle. Two bridges had already been destroyed. Rommel proposed to build bridges below the water level and insert the middle part only when the need arose. He told the tank crews: "When the enemy approaches don't engage in operational maneuvers, but open fire immediately."

We then continued via Abbeville to the 85th Infantry Division in the second line of defense. The command post was at Crécy, the location of the famous battle between the British and the French. Above all there was a lack of machine guns. Rommel said: "When the airborne enemy touches ground, seize his weapons." The division was to be deployed in such a way as to be able to defend itself immediately. For that purpose it was to take an additional ammunition issue up front. Everything was well staked; the firing plan was well thought out.

Then followed the inspection of the 348th Infantry Division sector in the forward line with good strongpoints along the beach. Two hundred thirty stakes had been installed. The tetrahedron plant in Cayeaux produced a different design which Rommel did not like. "I want to have the most modern and the best model." When, for the first time, nutcracker mines (explosion charge ignited through a leverage) were demonstrated, he was content again. Several waves of bombers passed overhead while we drove to Le Touquet, where we stayed overnight once again at the soldiers' quarters.

May 14. A light rain fell when our trip continued at 0645. One was always grateful for bad weather, which made the enemy's decision to jump off more difficult. We drove first to the 326th Infantry Division in the second line of defense. They were well prepared for an attack on the possible beachheads. Rommel smiled, even though the prohibited word "counterattack" was heard. One bicycle-equipped regiment was fully mobile; of the other two, only one company each. The division had constructed fake batteries and installed close to 100,000 stakes, a task in which the populace had participated well.

Rommel proposed a sort of *Richtfest* (builder's celebration), a type of folk festival, and generally recommended concern for the local inhabitants and agriculture.

With great patience he explained several times his fundamental orders for foxholes as protection against tanks, dispersal of supplies, and taking cover from air attacks. At the same time he inconspicuously inspired his listeners with courage.

At Montreuil, General Macholtz (191st Reserve Division) gave a briefing and showed an interesting map on which all air attacks had been entered. In a battery south of Le Touquet, Rommel spoke to delegations from several units. Near Hardelot Plage we inspected the holes made by air attacks; on the sand the effect was not as pronounced as it was on clay or on quarry stone.

At noon, one-pot stew was shared with soldiers and workers at a special installation for V-weapons near Le Chatel in a tunnel-like vault deep in the hill. General von Salmuth (Western Command) spoke with the Field Marshal with genuine affection. It was gratifying that the two men had found each other. Later on, Rommel distributed concertinas. The first man who received one, a young Luftwaffe soldier, could even play the instrument, and started, what else, but the "Nordseewellen" (North Sea waves). The other recipients, including those from the navy, were not as talented. Although one combat engineer declared that: "Nothing was impossible with the combat engineers," he did not venture a try.

In the afternoon we visited the 331st Infantry Division. So far they had installed 98,000 stakes. We then continued on to the 182d (training) Infantry Division, which had only 182 officers and seven battalions and was poorly equipped with weapons; only four guns for four infantry gun companies. The artillery had only two issues of ammunition; the small arms only one. Four of the seven battalions had been transferred to other divisions; only six companies were in training.

At 1700 conference at the 82d Army Corps, General Sinnhuber. Rommel expressed his appreciation for the fine achievements in the corps area (for instance, the installation of 900,000 stakes against airborne landings). We returned via Beauvais and arrived at headquarters at 2030.

May 15. The Field Marshal called for me early in the morning to discuss the possible pullback of the army coast batteries' guns which were unprotected by concrete gun emplacements. He shared my view that in the vicinity of the beach, guns without concrete emplacements stood no chance of surviving the first shelling. Events later confirmed this opinion. I talked about the unusual weather situation, for there had been no gales in April and May; about the utilization of the landing flotillas for the transport of concrete, since overland transport had stopped; about the lack of information with regard to the preparations in southern Britain, especially in and around the harbors, since our air reconnaissance had completely failed; about stopping the destruction of small ports in Seventh Army, since it was not worthwhile and annoyed the population; and about the preparation for rendering large ports, especially Cherbourg, unusable.

While I repeated these points to Speidel, a phone call came from Hitler who talked with Rommel about the multiple rocket launchers. Rommel had ruled that such calls, on principle, be continuously monitored by the chief of staff in order to have a witness, since Rommel had had bad experiences with the OKW interpretation of such calls. For a short while, Speidel handed me the second receiver. It was a peculiar feeling to hear the somewhat hoarse voice of Hitler.

In the afternoon I drove to Admiral Kranke, where I was able to push my points through. He especially agreed to pull back the army coast batteries which were not protected by concrete emplacements, and to use the landing flotillas for the transport of cement. He talked about difficulties with the fortress engineers and related that the 3rd Air Fleet had attempted to attack Bristol, although the navy had demanded attacks on the ports along the crucially important southern coast. Moreover, thanks to the clever British jamming efforts, the attack had evidently missed the target.

At the mouth of the Schelde a mine detonation sank a Siebel ferry which had been put at the army's disposal; 20,000 aerial bombs and numerous old shells were reported as available for improvised mines. All staffs, from division staff upward, were now housed in completed command posts.

Navy High Command wanted to recall me; however, in this tug-of-war, the commander in chief remained victorious.

May 16. Ambassador Abetz came for dinner. Otherwise, no special events, which did not mean idleness. Quiet days like this provided a welcome opportunity for the completion of numerous minor chores and for the thorough discussion of particular issues.

Twenty Days before the Invasion

May 17. At 0700 departure via Caen in direction of the Cotentin Peninsula. Occasional rain, finally. The guide who awaited us east of Carentan to lead us to the newly deployed 91st Airlanding Division lost his way several times. Finally at 1100 we arrived at the division staff (Major General Falley). The local Organisation Todt leader and the engineer officer reported that they had an insufficient supply of cement and gravel because the trains were sabotaged too often. This was a task for the navy. Rommel recommended the creation of supply trails beside the roads by cutting through the hedges. In addition he suggested underwater bridges through the artificial swamps and the creation of smoke screens from available resources. We ate lunch at the division's staff quarters; a large room with beautifully painted walls which were supposed to look like marble, a promise they did not quite fulfill.

In the afternoon we drove through the Cotentin Peninsula, climbed several heather-covered hills, and inspected positions. During a talk to the men, the Field Marshal prophetically told them not to expect the enemy during good weather or during the day. They would have to be prepared for the enemy to come with clouds and storm, and after midnight. This was exactly what happened during the night of the Invasion and it also happened in the same area.

Shortly after 2000 we reached Val André, where the SS military geologists had constructed fine offshore obstacles. After dinner, during low tide, Rommel walked through his "forest." During dinner he had talked about the French campaign and a captured French general who had patted him on the shoulder and said: "You are much too fast."

At headquarters: Army Group B recommended to the armies to take the unprotected army coast batteries to concealed positions a bit farther back, according to the experience gained in the air attacks of the past weeks.

Western Command informed us that Marshal Petain had declined to participate in the proposed trip along the coast, since he considered it unwise to put himself in the limelight at this time.

Further topics: crop damage; mines; reserve ammunition; and the manufacture of multiple rocket launchers for which OKW now showed interest.

May 18. The commander of the 77th Infantry Division started his briefing at 0700. Rommel spoke strongly for cooperation with the French. Every soldier would have to work towards this objective. We then inspected the section of the division reaching from the Bay of Mont-Saint-Michel to the west. We saw glass mines and inspected three plants for nutcracker mines. The division made a good impression, especially Captain Sörensen who commanded a battalion of Tartars evidently in an exemplary fashion.

West of Saint-Malo, Rommel spoke to officers assembled there. At Quintin, the command post of the 2d Parachute Rifle Corps (General Meindl), General Dollmann and the higher commanders of the units deployed in the northwestern part of Brittany awaited us. Rommel spoke first to the assembled officers. We discussed offshore obstacles; airborne landing obstacles; artificial smoke screens and local makeshift measures; increases in the scale of rations for young troops; instruction given by German officers in French schools; antipartisan fighting by the Russian cavalry regiment; and the forward movement of combat-ready units. Rommel strongly emphasized that French cooperation should be sought through good treatment and prompt payment of wages and should in no way ever be forced, especially with regard to women.

When one of the generals made some derogatory remarks about the navy's "mammoth constructions" alluding to the U-boat bunkers with their tremendous need for concrete, Rommel spoke warmly about the close cooperation with the navy and the understanding that he had found there. "We receive many advantages from the navy, such as the artillery fire control positions. The navy is the branch you are sitting on; don't saw it off." Coastal mine A had already been installed in Brittany; in the sector of Corps Farnbacher, 129,000 stakes and 35,000 tetrahedrons.

Rommel told the officers of the 5th Parachute Rifle Division, "We officers must be able to cope with all difficulties. There will always be ways and means. We will have to be optimistic at all times. Even when things don't go right the first time, there will always be a way out. The main thing is to perfect training and to use every means to strengthen the defense."

On our way back we made a detour to the staff of the 21st Panzer Division with whom Rommel talked about the manufacture of multiple rocket launchers. He demanded 1,000 pieces, which seemed a bit much to them.

In the Falaise area we drove carefully, since the roads were endangered by low-flying aircraft. At 2130 we were at home again and at once held the concluding discussion about our tour in the officers' mess which had been cleared for this purpose. Dinner was only incidental.

May 19. After the third and, for the time being, last vaccination, we worked at headquarters throughout the morning to evaluate the findings of the inspection tour. Particular problems were the manufacture in France of multiple rocket launchers, mines, smoke screens, obstacle material, and coal for it, but also the proper protocol for the possible visit of Petain to the coast. Captain Peters came to report his departure to the newly formed Army Group G at Toulouse. In the afternoon, I drove to Paris to talk first with the commander of Security Area West and then with Navy Group West about current matters, especially about getting on with the installation of coastal mine A in the Bay of the Seine.

May 20. In the morning, several air raid warnings; heavy waves of bombers droned overhead during the evening. A diversionary action, "Landgraf," under way with units from Military District 6.

The commander in chief asked State Party Leader Kaufmann for a personal conference about improving inland shipping on French canals to increase the amount of supplies.

Marshal Petain's trip was canceled for good. Field Marshal von Rundstedt came as guest for lunch. He was accompanied by his son (a lieutenant) and General Blumentritt. He was visibly pleased with the invitation. In addition to many service matters, we talked about Karl May and detective stories, which he liked to read. Finally our conversation turned to a thorough discussion of French internal politics.

In the afternoon, two British officers were brought to Rommel. They had been captured in the area of the Fifteenth Army while on a commando mission exploring the offshore barriers. According to the standing orders, Fifteenth Army should have turned them over to the *Sicherheitsdienst* (Security Service SS). Speidel, however, had given instructions to send them to La Roche-Guyon, and, with Rommel's consent, had them moved to a prisoner-of-war camp, which probably saved their lives. Rommel talked with them for some time. One of the officers asked Rommel if he believed a soldier capable of organizing a government. Rommel, who later told me of the incident during one of our "armed" walks, answered in the affirmative. The Englishman then told Rommel quite candidly that he considered him the right man for the reconstruction. The officer insisted on knowing where he was, so that after the war he could return to the location. When, for obvious reasons, neither the name nor location of the castle were divulged to him, he remarked that after the war he would search all of France until he found the spot.

May 21. Heavy overcast; little air activity. Admiral Rieve came around noon to discuss with the Field Marshal the pullback of army coast batteries and the artillery control on the coast. After lunch we went for a walk and discussed further matters. Rommel meanwhile discussed with Assistant Secretary Michel from the military administration the procurement of coal and electricity for valuable military production in France.

At 1600 Rommel, Meise, the two dogs and I started on a walk that lasted for nearly three hours. Talking about the situation we touched on the removal of several officers in the highest positions. Rommel remarked that sometimes he felt a bit uneasy about such actions.

Fifteen Days before the Invasion

Early on May 22. Rommel inspected our alternate command post at Le Vernon. He took along the reporter Lutz Koch in order to get an article in the press that would divert attention from our command post at La Roche-Guyon.

General von Salmuth came for lunch and for conferences. He did not want to part with his last Siebel ferry.

May 23. At noon, conference with State Party Leader Kaufmann about increased transports on inland waterways. Numerous air raid warnings in the afternoon. In between, we played table tennis. Lengthy telephone calls became necessary to get the release of transports from Germany which were held up at a frontier train depot for a considerable time for delousing.

May 24. During the morning Rommel inspected, at the army ordnance depot, a machine gun with periscope designed to be fired from defilade, and, at a factory, the production of an improvised smoke screen device.

In the afternoon I drove to Paris about artillery questions and to "liberate" concrete for gun emplacements. On our way back we had to take a detour since a bridge was bombed and numerous fighters flew overhead.

The army group attempted to obtain from 3rd Air Fleet three antiaircraft detachments for the coast.

The navy is to take command of the Ameland and Schiermonnikoog islands.

May 25. The chief of staff of the 47th Panzer Corps came around noon. Beautiful weather. At 1600 we left to hunt rabbits in the lovely, hilly countryside where they abounded, but without success. Subsequently Rommel discussed with the chief of propaganda at Western Command pertinent questions. French rumors filtered in that our staff had left La Roche-Guyon. The installation of coastal mine A barriers was now finally to start.

May 26. At noon General Pickert (3rd Antiaircraft Corps) reported at La Roche-Guyon; in the afternoon Lieutenant General Student (1st Parachute Rifle Corps), and the commanding general of the 47th Panzer Corps. Telephone call with State Secretary Ganzenmüller who complained that State Party Leader Kaufmann was drawn into transport matters, and asked to leave such matters to the appropriate administrative railroad offices. For Rommel, however, it was a question of receiving "additional" transport space from Kaufmann.

I drove to the command quarters of Security Area West and the navy group at Paris, to advance our affairs. Among others, I met Herr Willesen, the radar expert. The radar installations had been repeatedly attacked by planes in the last few weeks. He could, however, tell me that ten of the eleven damaged instruments were already operational again.

Ten Days before the Invasion

May 25 (Whitsun Saturday). Beautiful, hot weather with little wind. In the morning, the Field Marshal drove to the artificial smoke factory; during the afternoon we went hunting for rabbit—this time with ferrets— but with little success. Most of the rabbits were too small for shooting and the ferrets preferred a rest in the rabbit burrows to hunting the animals. They finally had to be dug out, which took much time.

The 3rd Antiaircraft Corps was to be deployed as a mobile unit; two of its regiments at Fifteenth Army and one at Seventh Army.

May 28 (Whitsun). Beautiful weather. General astonishment and joy that the enemy did not take advantage of it. We played tennis and table tennis.

May 29. Generals Buhle and Jakob came in the evening to discuss the manufacture of multiple rocket launchers.

May 30. At 0630 we drove in several cars to a demonstration of multiple rocket launchers and smoke projectors. The bridges at Mantes were still standing despite the heavy bombing of the island between the bridges. Numerous aircraft were above us, none of them German. The demonstration took place near Riva Bella. Much high brass—Salmuth, Dollmann, Krancke, Kuntzen, Marcks, Baron von Funk, and others. The demonstration made a strong impression. General Buhle promised to send all the smoke projectors available in Germany to France. Subsequently, however, he withdrew the promise much to our regret.

The demonstration was followed by a lunch from the field kitchen, served under the trees of a park. Rommel, together with Buhle and Jakob, then inspected positions along the coast. Meise, Diem, Lattmann and I drove in two cars towards the Seine bridge at Gaillon, which, in the morning, had still been standing. When we reached it, there was an air raid alert. The first bombs had already fallen, but we hurriedly crossed. One hour later the bridge was gone as was the one at Mantes. During the day all the bridges over the Seine between Elboeuf and Paris were destroyed. This was inconvenient, although in several places a ferry service had been established. Returning to his headquarters, the commander took a boat to cross over to La Roche-Guyon.

May 31. During the morning, Rommel inspected the destroyed bridges at Mantes, Vernon and Gaillon.

Early in the morning I drove to Paris to the commander of Security Area West about the coastal mine A. No progress had been made. Many airplanes overhead. Guderian's son (a major) came for lunch. Lieutenant General (SS) Sepp Dietrich came in the afternoon for a conference; a thunderstorm in the evening. Lengthy phone calls regarding the transfer of 100 men from the 100th Panzer Reserve and Training Unit.

Five Days before the Invasion

June 1. During the morning the commander in chief discussed with Assistant Secretary Bernd from the Propaganda Ministry several matters, especially how to influence the enemy at the moment of invasion. In the afternoon he inspected the fortress at Dieppe and the coastal areas of the 245th and the 348th Infantry Divisions. The 170mm battery at Ault was bombed twice from the air. Rommel ordered it pulled back to the rear until the completion of the concrete gun emplacements.

Tempelhoff was promoted to colonel. Behr became a member of the general staff. There was a mild celebration in the evening together with the farewell dinner for Colonel Heckel and the other officers from our dissolved quartermaster staff.

June 2. The beautiful weather continues although it is a bit cooler. The Commander in Chief West (following Hitler's "wish") issued an order granting extensive powers of command to the fortress commanders responsible for the defense during the time of preparation (KTB).

Battue during the afternoon with approximately a dozen hunters. I had taken a place rather on the side where I had a lovely view of the Seine Valley. As for game, I saw only a tiny squirrel, but continuous air attacks on the Seine bridges.

Three Days before the Invasion

June 3. Once more the highest staffs debated about the battalion of military geologists which the Reichsführer SS wanted to pull out. Telephone calls about smoke candles and acid for producing smoke.

General Leeb and General Schneider promised the commander the manufacture of multiple rocket launchers and inspected them at Feuchtinger.

The army group ordered that the construction of the offshore barriers be continued, especially the extension towards the sea, by taking advan-

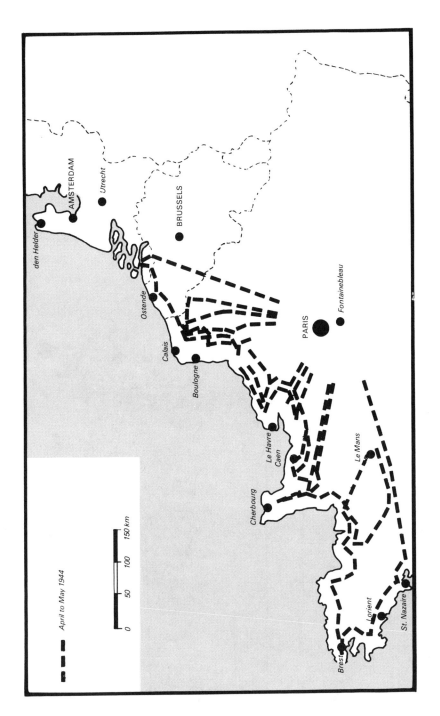

Field Marshal Rommel's inspection tours

April to May 1944

0   50   100   150 km

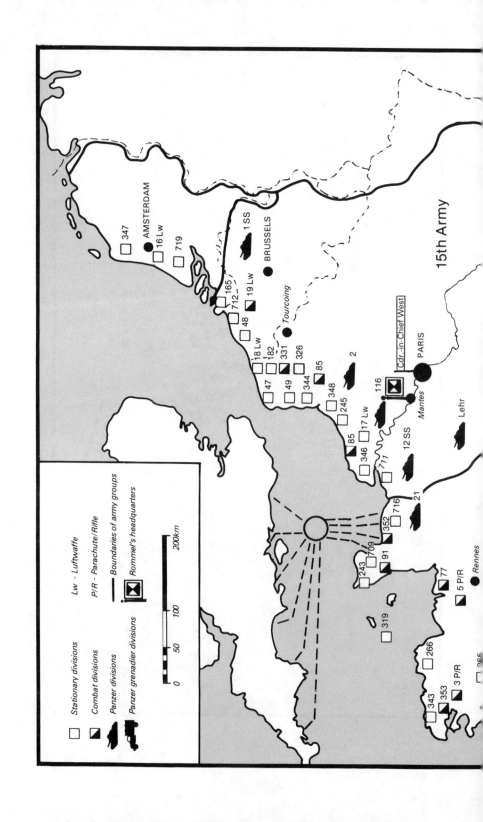

Lw - Luftwaffe
P/R - Parachute/Rifle

Stationary divisions
Combat divisions
Panzer divisions
Panzer grenadier divisions
Boundaries of army groups
Rommel's headquarters

0   50   100   200km

AMSTERDAM
347
16 Lw
719
1 SS
BRUSSELS
165
712
19 Lw
48
Tourcoing
18 Lw
182   331   326
47
49   344   85
2
348
245
Cdr.-in-Chief West
PARIS
116
85   17 Lw   Mantes
346   711   12 SS   Lehr
352   716   21
709   91
243   77   5 P/R
319   Rennes
266
343   353   3 P/R

15th Army

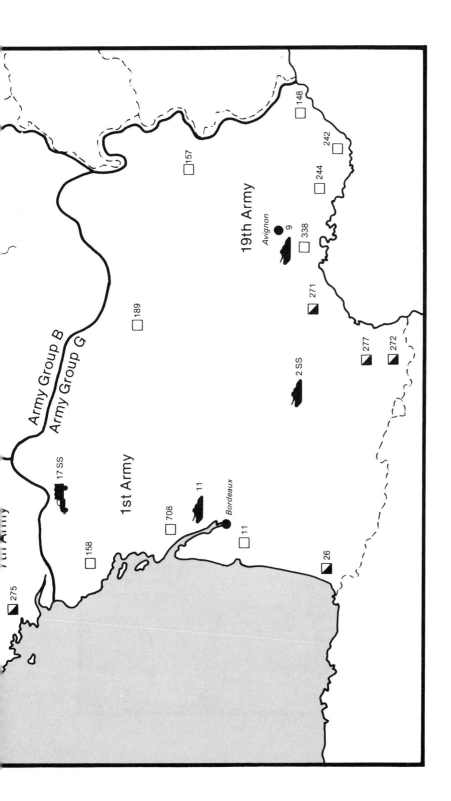

Deployment of German divisions on the day of the Invasion

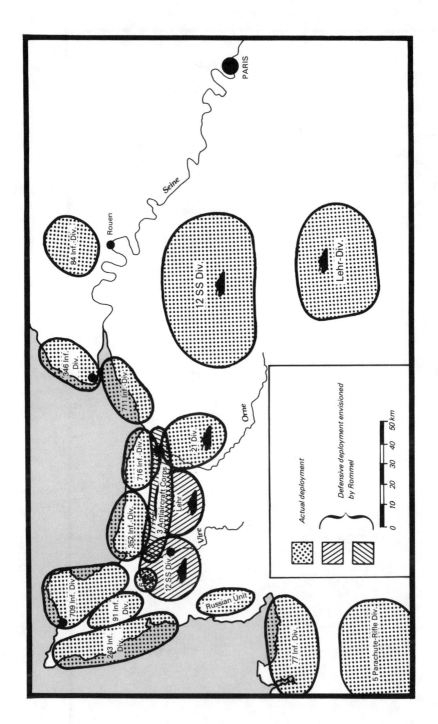

German deployment in Normandy on the day of the Invasion

Map labels:

PARIS

Seine

Rouen

84 Inf.-Div.

12 SS Div.

Lehr-Div.

346 Inf. Div.

711 Inf.-Div.

716 Inf.-Div.

21 Div.

Orne

3 Antiaircraft Corps

Lehr

352 Inf.-Div.

12 SS Div.

Vire

709 Inf.-Div.

91 Inf. Div.

243 Inf. Div.

Russian Unit

77 Inf. Div.

5 Parachute-Rifle Div.

Legend:

Actual deployment

Defensive deployment envisioned by Rommel

0 10 20 30 40 50 km

tage of the spring low tide. In addition the army group requested mine laying from the air in the navigation channels on both sides of the Isle of Wight.

The 84th Army Corps reports that due to unsatisfactory supplies and inadequate power supply they have fallen behind in the coastal construction.

This prompted Army Group B to request Western Command to decide that, vis-à-vis all special construction measures, highest priority be given to coastal construction.

The army group was informed to expect the immediate withdrawal of the 19th Luftwaffe Field Division and its transfer to Southwestern Command.

In the afternoon Rommel went to Rundstedt to discuss with him his intention of driving to Germany to stay there from June 5 to June 8. "Rommel above all wanted to go to the *Obersalzberg* and speak with Hitler personally . . . and to ask for the transfer to Normandy of two additional panzer divisions, one antiaircraft corps, and one mortar brigade" (TBR). While talking with Rommel, Major General Kramer, exchanged from a British prisoner-of-war camp, supposed that the main thrust of the impending attack would be on both sides of the Somme.

On June 4 the weather changed to rain and stormy westerlies. Several telephone calls dealt with the problem of activating the inland shipping. Early, at 0600, Rommel left for Germany. At the time of his departure he said: "There were all the less doubts that an invasion might happen in the meantime as the tides were very unfavorable in the following days and no air reconnaissance of any kind had given any hints of an imminent landing" (TBR). Moreover, he had thoroughly discussed with Speidel the measures to be taken in the case of an attack.

Plans for alerting the troops and the staffs had been carefully prepared. During the five and one-half months of his presence in the west, the defense had been considerably strengthened; still it was not complete. Mining, for instance, was still in progress; the construction of offshore barriers effective at low tide had at many places hardly been started. The weakest point in the overall defense structure was still the fact that the panzer divisions had not pulled up close enough to the "Rommelbelt" to allow them to participate immediately in the attack, thereby giving the infantry the urgently needed support.

The Landing

*N*othing indicated on the morning of June 5, 1944, that on the other side of the Channel the decision for the attack had been made, and that a giant armada was on its way to storm Fortress Europe. At the headquarters of Army Group B everybody did his work as on other quiet days. It rained as I drove to Navy Group West to prod them about the mines.

The 2d Mine Sweeper Flotilla, which was to be transferred from the west coast to Le Havre to serve as mine layers, had, during transit, received such heavy damage through bombings and in night combat that only one ship got through. The purpose of the measure was not quite clear since Le Havre had enough torpedo boats, motor torpedo boats, and motor mine sweepers, all suitable for laying mines. In 1942 we had used motor mine sweepers to lay a considerable number of barriers in the middle of the eastern part of the Channel. Because they had a low silhouette and were built of wood, they offered poor targets for the enemy's coastal radar.

Speidel had invited an interesting group for dinner: the writer Ernst Jünger, who served as captain with the military governor; Consul-General Pfeiffer, who after 1926 spent several years in Russia, 1940 in Italy, 1942 in Algiers where he was interned, and who had recently returned from the U.S.A.; Colonel List, who had been with Army High Command and was later severely wounded in Russia; the war correspondent Ritter von Schramm; Speidel's brother-in-law Dr. Horst, who worked for the military administration; and Fifteenth Army's naval liaison officer. The

171

highly animated discussion dealt with Italy, Russia, French-oriented politics, the French navy, the insufficient development of Hitler's future plans, conditions in the United States, and much more. After dinner, we took a quick stroll through the park and then continued our discussion. The Fifteenth Army's liaison officer left early in the evening; Pfeiffer and Jünger left around midnight.

June 6. Colonel List then dominated the conversation with interesting stories about Brauchitsch, Halder, the old Mackensen, and others. At 0135 Seventh Army reported parachute drops on the east coast of the Cotentin Peninsula. Fifteenth Army likewise reported parachute drops in the sector from east of Caen to Deauville. In addition, we received information about the approach of large aircraft formations.

During the following hours reports of parachute drops increased. With the break of dawn came reports of numerous vessels at sea. Landings along the coast had started. Only during the morning, however, did it become apparent to us that this was not a diversionary action, but a major attack instead, directed against the entire front from somewhat east of the Orne to northwest of the mouth of the Vire. I did not go to bed, although there was little I could do. "What a pity that the coastal mine A installations have not progressed further . . . the endless tug-of-war about the 12th SS Panzer Division command, which was OKW reserve and placed too far back. Very disadvantageous that the panzer divisions were not positioned as the commander in chief had requested over and again, and that, except for two regiments, the antiaircraft corps was not put into the front line. The area where the attack takes place is very weak" (PAV).

Unfortunately Rommel was still waiting in Germany to persuade Hitler once and for all about the deployment forward of the panzer divisions. Over the telephone, Speidel alerted him and the commanders of the fast mobile units stationed in the vicinity of the invasion area. Simultaneously, he activated all steps and measures which he had discussed with the Field Marshal before his departure. He informed Rommel before he started the return trip and again when he called while underway. When Rommel arrived at La Roche-Guyon in the evening, he was very pleased about Speidel's quick and appropriate action and approved of it completely. Speidel also tried to move the 12th SS Panzer Division, over which Army Group B had no power of command, in the direction of the battlefield—albeit without success.

At 0245, the Fifteenth Army had already requested the alert of the 12th SS Panzer Division; Army Group B had instructed Panzer Group West to move the division to both sides of Lisieux at 0550. OKW stopped all these movements at 0940. It is questionable if Rommel could have changed the situation had he been present at headquarters.

Hitler's decision on the deployment forward of the Panzer Lehr Division into the area around Flers was also still pending. Not until 1432 was permission given for the release of the 12th SS Panzer Division at Seventh Army, and at 1507 the 1st SS Panzer Corps (Sepp Dietrich) was given command over the 12th SS Panzer Division and the Panzer Lehr Division. Since both divisions were still far from the battlefield, they could not participate in the fighting on that day. Only parts of the 12th SS Panzer Division were at hand on the evening of June 7 because of obstructions and heavy losses caused by air attacks and the destruction of roads. Both divisions, together with remnants of the 21st Panzer Division, could begin the counterattack only on June 9. By that time, the enemy had already moved masses of men and materiel onto the beachhead and had firmly established his defenses.

In contrast, the 21st Panzer Division, which stood under the immediate command of Army Group B, was able to launch an attack on the day of the Invasion, but this did not stand under a lucky star. The division had assembled farther off the coast, counter to Rommel's clear orders. As it turned out later (and I was witness to the discussion), the division commander had misunderstood an order given to him in April. He apparently had followed Rommel's thoughts less closely than those of Geyr von Schweppenburg. In the morning of June 6, the division had started to attack British paratroopers east of the Orne; was recalled by the 84th Army Corps (General Marcks); marched with casualties through Caen; in the afternoon attacked west of the Orne in the direction of Riva Bella; *and, even then, with its foremost units* (Colonel von Oppeln-Bronikowski), *almost reached the sea.*

The British landing of additional airborne troops on both sides of the Orne "prompted the local decision to break off the attack and to free the rear units. A momentous service was done to the enemy by not utilizing the initial success" (Speidel, *Invasion 1944*).

On June 7, Rommel drove immediately to Geyr von Schweppenburg who was put under Rommel's command. Too late! The 12th SS Panzer Division had to march 120 kilometers; the Panzer Lehr Division, 180 kilometers. Both did not arrive as organized units and immediately had to fill gaps in the front. Their counterattack, launched on June 9, did not succeed; Geyr's headquarters was bombed out on June 10, which further increased the command difficulty. It was an irony of fate that he in particular should be so severely hit by the weight of the superior enemy air force. That conventional panzer operations, which had been so effective in Russia, did not apply to France, was a lesson that came too late.

After the counterattack had fizzled out by June 9, it was apparent that the enemy could hold firmly to his beachhead, and unmolested, out of reach of the German artillery, could continuously land reinforcements of men and materiel. The beachhead also had sufficient depth for the construction of fighter landing strips; in short, the beachhead was completely suited to serve as a starting point for a major land offensive. In addition, it extended far enough into the southeastern half of the Cotentin Peninsula to promise an early capture of Cherbourg, the major port that, in the long run, the Allies needed despite an artificial harbor which, utilizing prefabricated parts, they had swiftly erected at Arromanches. The northeast storm of June 19–21 destroyed the second artificial harbor on the eastern bank of the Cotentin Peninsula before it was completed.

With the successful landings and the creation of a beachhead suitable for the preparation of a large breakout operation, the enemy had reached his first and second objectives. It now became the main task of Army Group B to prevent the breakout, should the attempt to crush the beachhead fail. The forces available at this point were, at best, sufficient to form a somewhat cohesive defense front. Rommel devoted all his energy to this task. It was understandable, however, that he—to draw lessons for the fighting now following, not only on account of the mistrust noticeably coming from Führer Headquarters again and again—occupied himself with the reasons which had made the great success of the enemy possible.

In his observations of July 3, 1944, he listed the reasons and stated as the most important factors:

1. Superannuated divisions, insufficiently equipped; construction of fortifications in arrears; unsatisfactory supply situation.
2. 12th SS Panzer Division too far back.
3. Panzer Lehr Division stationed too far back.
4. 3rd Antiaircraft Corps not between the Orne and the Vire.
5. The mortar brigade not in the Carentan area as proposed.
6. Bay of the Seine not mined.

7. Air support less than promised.
8. Naval support less than promised. On the night of the Invasion, the Bay of the Seine was not protected by patrol boats.
9. No organic quartermaster for supplies.
10. Command relations insufficiently regulated.

Not much could have been done about points 1, 7 and 8; all of Hitler's and Göring's promises could not procure more aircraft than were at hand. The number of combat-ready aircraft was temporarily increased from 160 to 500 at the start of the Invasion, which flew up to 700 missions against 11,000 enemy missions on June 6.

The navy, forced by circumstances into a one-sided concentration on submarine warfare with its few destroyers, torpedo boats, motor torpedo boats and outdated submarines, lacked the means to help effectively. The small assault craft, which during the first few days could have been very effective, arrived a bit too late and the enemy was quickly able to adjust to them. After some initial successes, they suffered heavy losses without attaining anything. It became quickly apparent that a large operation could not be decisively influenced by auxiliary and opportunistic weapons.

With regard to "mine laying" the navy had held back too much. Navy Group West did not think much of the coastal mine A and had not allowed the laying of as many mines as was possible.

According to their war diary they did not give priority to defense against an invasion over the submarine war. At that time the effect of submarine warfare was slight, while, in light of the basic situation, an invasion in France would decide the war.

We know from British reports (*Operation Neptune*, p. 126) that the few moored mines which lay in the mine barriers in the middle of the English Channel caused problems to the twelve large Anglo-American mine sweeping units. Even if no doubts existed that moored mines were not too difficult to sweep, it would have been possible to strengthen the old barriers on their southern side with many explosive "grab" obstacles* between the mines. Vessels for laying mines were always available, since all our torpedo boats, motor mine sweepers and motor torpedo boats were equipped for mine laying.

---

*Small conical buoy with a device that "grabs" the sweep rope and cuts it by detonation of an explosive charge, thus delaying the mine sweeping process.

In more shallow water, ground mines with several types of remote fuses were needed, and in the shallowest water, the coastal mine A. It is absurd that installation of these mines had started south of the Gironde where Army Group B had never wanted them, while the Bay of the Seine, for which Army Group B had constantly demanded mines, had been completely neglected.

In this connection, a fact which has never been completely clarified, yet one which had considerable influence on the Invasion, should be mentioned. On June 5, Anglo-American mine sweeping units from the assembly area near the Isle of Wight searched ten routes towards the south. In the process they removed a small number of mines from the old German barriers. Two of these units approached the French coast during daylight. According to British reports (*Operation Neptune*), the 14th Mine Sweeper Flotilla was in sight of land near Grandcamp for three hours and approached so closely that houses and other details could be seen with the naked eye. The 16th Mine Sweeper Flotilla sighted the coast at eighteen nautical miles and approached during daylight to eleven nautical miles.

According to British opinion, both units could not escape detection by any lookout with normal vision. As far as could be ascertained, news of this occurrence was never passed on the German side. In any case, nothing penetrated to the staff of Army Group B, and, evidently, not to Navy Group West. No explanation is necessary to realize that the information of these ship movements would have aroused suspicion, and would possibly have led to reconnaissance flights. Above all, patrol boats would have been sent out and during the night they would have made contact with the approaching enemy landing units. This would have compensated for the disadvantage which lay in the fact that on the German side the weather situation could not be known because of a lack of weather observation in the Atlantic. Sandwiched between a series of lows which approached with strong winds from the west was an intermediate high which brought a weather improvement from June 6 to 7 for about thirty-six hours.

The Allied weather service, with its better data, recognized this condition. On the strength of it, Eisenhower came to the decision on June 4 at 2015 to set the large operation in motion. The decision was not made at his headquarters, but at Southwick Park, the headquarters of Admiral Burrough, the commander in chief of the participating naval forces. Located in the hilly countryside of Hampshire County approximately ten kilometers north of Portsmouth, Southwick Park is now used by the Royal Navy as a navigation school. The officers' mess still shows the three maps which touched off the Invasion. Had Eisenhower decided to postpone the attack, the next date with favorable tide and moon conditions would have been fourteen days later. Then the decision for the operation would have been made during completely suitable weather. The landing, however, would have been surprised by a storm from the northeast, which blew quite unexpectedly from June 19 to 21, and drove approximately 800 landing vehicles onto the beach and destroyed one of the artificial harbors. It is not probable that under these circumstances the Invasion would have succeeded; especially if, in the meantime, several German divisions had been moved forward as planned by Rommel.

This shows that situations could happen which, despite an enemy's materiel superiority, can prevent formation of the necessary large beachhead. In view of later speculation that, with their limited means, the Germans could under no circumstances have prevented the Invasion, or that a defensive victory with Rommel's plans would have been impossible, it seems only fair to examine the validity of these views. Because of the incredible effort made by the troops before the attack, and the bravery and tenacity with which they fought, they, as well as the men who commanded them, and whom they venerated, are entitled to an objective analysis of this problem.

How would the situation have developed if, under otherwise similar circumstances, the OKW had complied with Rommel's demands? It would have meant: more mines in the Bay of the Seine and consequently, for parts of the landing forces, ship losses and delay; the 12th SS Panzer Division standing ready at the Vire and in the southern part of the Cotentin Peninsula; the Panzer Lehr Division, the antiaircraft corps and the launcher brigade positioned between the Vire and the Orne. In the area of Bayeaux this would have put the 915th Grenadier Regiment and the 84th Army Corps Reserve considerably more forward, closer than the twenty kilometers from the beach where it finally stood in readiness, contrary to Rommel's orders. On the morning of June 6, following the orders of the 84th Army Corps, it moved west, received a counterorder, and in the evening joined the battle just a few kilometers from the original point of departure.

This regiment kept in readiness more forward, the 21st Panzer Division, the two strong panzer divisions, the antiaircraft corps, and the launcher brigade closely behind—all this would possibly have been enough to completely smash the airborne landings and to limit the sea-borne landings to a few shallow beachheads between the Orne and the Vire. Proof: The conditions at the 352d Infantry Division, a combat-experienced division, which defended the section between Orne and Vire. Although neither panzers nor antiaircraft guns stood behind it, it managed to limit the American gains on the first day of the Invasion to a small beachhead. With strong reserves behind it, this division would have made it still more difficult for the enemy. By attacking the 716th Infantry Division, a less combat-experienced stationary division, the British achieved deep penetrations of up to fifteen kilometers on the first day of the Invasion.

This could not have succeeded against infantry supported by panzers and antiaircraft guns. This is proved by the success of 21st Panzer Division, which came into action west of the Orne very late. If towards evening it could have penetrated almost to the beach, there can be no doubt that the British would not have come far had they been confronted by the excellent Panzer Lehr Division in the first hours after their landing in the area of Bayeaux–Caen.

The 21st Panzer Division could then have attacked east of the Orne and certainly would have destroyed the British paratroopers, since they lacked heavy arms and were connected with their own beachhead only via a bridge over the Orne and not directly with the sea. This bridge could have been destroyed as will be explained later.

The 12th SS Panzer Division, most possibly, would have done the same to the American paratroopers, for these jumped over a large area and came together only slowly.

Of course, no complete proof can be given for this theory. However, a corroboration lies in the following disembarkation figures which *Cross Channel Attack* gives (p.351):

Until the evening of June 7,	Planned:	Achieved:	Achieved by June 18:
Soldiers	107,000	87,000	619,000
Vehicles	14,000	7,000	95,000
Materiel (in tons)	14,500	3,500	218,000

This shortage of some twenty percent of manpower, fifty percent of vehicles, and seventy-five percent of materiel on the first two days was the result of Rommel's methods—the offshore obstacles, the resistance nests, and the heavy land mining. About the offshore obstacles, *Operation Neptune* states it forced the first landings to take place during daylight and low tide and even then the obstacles caused the most unpleasant difficulties and the heaviest losses. The major part of the 291 landing craft sunk or damaged on June 6 was credited to the offshore obstacles.

In summary, it can be said that, applying the aggregate of Rommel's measures, good chances existed to prevent the enemy from forming deep beachheads. Whether the enemy could have continued the operation or whether we could have thrown them completely back into the sea is another question. It is certain, however, that events would have been considerably different and more favorable for the Germans had Rommel been given complete freedom of action in December 1943. The poor command structure, divided responsibilities, and the insufficient freedom of action of the commander responsible on the spot are the main reasons why he could not become fully effective. Ambiguities in the command structure enabled willful commanders to dodge Rommel's directives and for their own units to enforce their own ideas over those of Rommel. This was most harmful in the case of Panzer Group West, which was not under Rommel's command and whose commander he never could convince. In the December 1949 issue of the journal "The Irish Defence," General Geyr von Schweppenburg writes:

> The only solution existed in taking advantage of the singular German superiority—the more skillful and flexible leadership of the superbly trained panzer units decidedly our trump card—holding heavy operational reserves consisting of five or six panzer divisions outside the reach of naval artillery and camouflaged from air detection in the woods northwest or south of Paris, from where they could develop their assault after the enemy had already penetrated deeply into the countryside. General Guderian, Hitler's advisor for panzer tactics, fully agreed with this proposal, however, without success. Rommel's plan prevailed.
>
> The result of Rommel's plan was that one panzer division after the other was deployed forward to the coast. Aside from the fatal strategic results of this decision, the incongruities inherent in these two schools of thought could not be hidden and had a harmful effect on the morale of subordinates. I held such decidedly strong views against Rommel's plan that I asked for permission to present them to the OKW at Berchtesgaden. Hitler yielded sufficiently to order the retention of the four panzer divisions: *Leibstandarte*, *Hitlerjugend*, Panzer "Lehr," and Götz von Berlichingen as strategic OKW reserves. On the first day of the Invasion, however, this plan was discarded despite Guderian's support of my point of view.

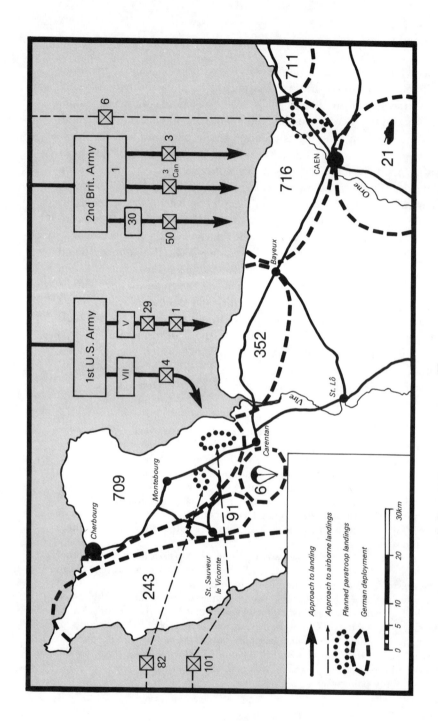

Approach routes, areas of landings, and potential airborne landings of the Allies

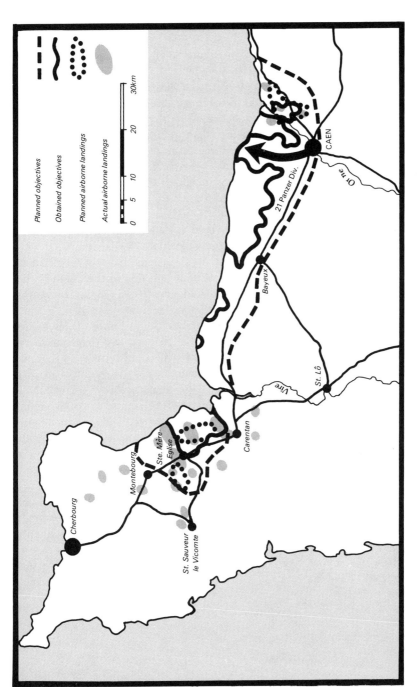

Planned objectives

Obtained objectives

Planned airborne landings

Actual airborne landings

0   5   10   20   30km

Cherbourg

St. Sauveur
le Vicomte

Montebourg

Ste. Mère-
Église

Carentan

St. Lô

Vire

Bayeux

21 Panzer Div.

CAEN

Orne

Situation on the evening of D-day. Shown are the remarkable penetration of the 21st Panzer Division and the scant American success.

This shows that Geyr saw no possibility at all to parry the landing itself, and that he wanted to destroy the invader with the panzer divisions alone. In contrast, Rommel saw in all clarity what an excessive burden an additional European front would mean to our already over-extended Wehrmacht. From this he concluded that the only possibility for a tolerable end of the war would be to beat off the landing. For this purpose he planned to integrate all available forces of the three Wehrmacht services for the defense. Events then proved very impressively that fluid operations as Geyr von Schweppenburg imagined them were entirely impossible under the pressure of the Allied air force which was many times superior.

Rommel's plan, in comparison, held certain possibilities for success. This was confirmed by, among others, Liddell Hart when, in the July 1946 issue of *Strand* magazine, he wrote: "It is possible that the Germans' only hope was to stop the Invasion at once and that in the event of their waiting, the planned counterattack would have been completely smashed by the Allies' overwhelming air supremacy."

It has always been good military practice that a junior officer express his opinion unequivocally in such a situation even if it differs from that of his superior. Good military practice, however, also decreed that once a decision had been made, every soldier loyally assisted the accepted plan. General Geyr von Schweppenburg was not a direct subordinate of Field Marshal Rommel. But Rommel was the senior officer who commanded the troops on the prospective invasion front and who, in all probability, would have to command the defensive battle. Hitler had decided in favor of Rommel's plan to beat the enemy at the beaches. Geyr assumed a heavy responsibility when he took steps to thwart an essential part of Rommel's plan.

With this decision, he deprived Rommel's concept of a large part of its effectiveness, without achieving the divisions' deployment according to Geyr's plan. The only thing he achieved fully was that the decisive battle of the Invasion was fought following two diametrically opposed plans thereby destroying, from the outset, any chances of success the Germans might still have had.

The Loss of Cherbourg

*J*une 9. The air superiority of the enemy is having the effect the Field Marshal had expected and predicted: our movements are extremely slow; supplies hardly get through; any deployment of tactical units is becoming impossible; the artillery cannot move to its firing positions anymore. Precisely the same thing is happening on land here as happened at sea in the Tunisian campaign (PAV).

The staff knew at this time that the Invasion had succeeded; that the situation depicted above left no chance to crush and eliminate the large beachhead and that, on the contrary, the enemy's strength increased constantly. It was feared that he would capture Cherbourg and with superior forces subsequently break through towards Paris. The army group had the task of preventing this breakthrough. Rommel's primary objective was to attack and to destroy the obviously not-too-strong enemy forces west of the Vire on the southeast coast of the Cotentin Peninsula and thus avert the danger to Cherbourg. OKW, however, ordered the forces concentrated in the Caen area.

Life at headquarters acquired a different tone. Rommel drove almost daily to the front or to higher commanders. On these trips he was, of course, primarily accompanied by army officers. With regard to navy matters, not much was left to do for the navy liaison officer after the weak naval forces had been destroyed, some in battle and some by air attacks on the ports.

Another task, however, developed; i.e., to get the supply traffic on the Seine going. Moreover, the Field Marshal felt the need to talk about the situation and its problems. He liked to do this with Speidel and me or with me alone during short strolls in the park of the castle or in the vicinity. He now carried an especially heavy emotional burden, since he felt responsible not only for the military situation in Normandy but also for the fate of the whole nation. He had predicted that with a successful invasion, the war would be unalterably lost. Now he sought to clarify the ways and means which perhaps existed to end a senseless war. He played a difficult dual part; that of the soldier who with all the skills of his leadership tried to put off the disaster of the enemy breakthrough as long as possible, and that of a man who felt himself responsible for the whole nation and waited for the propitious moment of political action. For the latter part he tried to sort out his ideas and conceptions during conversations in the smallest circle. This happened mostly in theoretical discussions. He never discussed his connections—handled by Speidel—with the groups preparing for the 20th of July, doubtless in the conviction that it was important to have as few confidants as possible. Speidel had given me several hints without, however, giving me a complete picture of the project.

The course of the fighting has been treated several times by competent authors who, with a retrospective view, analyzed the events in detail. They will therefore only be noted briefly as they appeared to us at the time and as they provide a necessary background. With regard to the diary notes, it may be mentioned that they could, of course, not be exhaustive and that, for understandable reasons, they had to be reticent on several points. They nevertheless give a useful picture of Rommel's thoughts during the most difficult time of his life.

June 10. The commander drove to Panzer Group West (Geyr von Schweppenburg). Enemy air activity was so heavy that en route he had to seek cover about thirty times, although he always traveled on secondary roads. Enemy aircraft made it impossible to reach the 1st SS Panzer Corps (Sepp Dietrich). Several hours after Rommel's visit, the command post of Panzer Group West was heavily damaged by an air attack. The chief of staff, the operations officer, and other officers were killed; the uniform command of the panzer units was temporarily disrupted.

June 11. The enemy used this day to move supplies into penetration areas; local attacks could not achieve any appreciable territorial gains. A few limited counterattacks in the area southeast of Bayeux and near Montebourg were locally successful; the battle for Carentan was fought in hand-to-hand combat. Because of weather conditions, the enemy was less active in the air, although low-flying attacks, especially on deployments and batteries, continued without interruption (KTB, version abbreviated).

In the morning Rommel drove to Rundstedt to discuss, above all else, the supply questions, since railroad transport had hopelessly collapsed under the enemy air force's blows. The specter of an additional landing at either the narrows of the English Channel or in Brittany still haunted the OKW. Concern about these not-yet-attacked coastal sectors prevented energetic measures to strengthen the heavily struggling front. OKW still did not release any of the divisions standing in double rows along the narrows of the English Channel. Only the advance vanguards of the 77th Infantry Division, the 17th SS Panzer Grenadier Division, and the 2d Parachute Rifle Corps advanced through western Normandy. This was very little compared to the approximately 50,000 men which, together with ample supplies, the enemy moved daily into his beachhead. In the afternoon, the Field Marshal took me along on his walk through the garden. It developed into a two-hour conversation during which we walked up and down the hill behind the castle, to and fro in the garden and at times just stood around and talked. Rommel discussed almost all questions arising from the situation, among them several which I had continually thought about.

In his opinion, the best solution to the immediate situation was to stop the war while Germany still held some territory for bargaining. He believed that the antagonism between the Americans and Russians still strengthened our position for the time being. American strength was so overwhelming that the Russians could not consider moving against them. Hitler, however, had no intention of negotiating—with him, it was not possible anyway. He wanted to fight to the last house. He had remarked several times that he did not know what would happen, but he was firmly convinced that it would end well. Rommel believed that the nation came before the individual. Justice was the foundation of the state. Unfortunately, Hitler's hands were not clean. The butcheries were a heavy guilt; the conduct of the war had been amateurish. Our own lives were not secure. After previously having had to endure interference in every petty detail, the highest military leaders were now being blamed for the turn the situation had taken.

He, Rommel, had, as a matter of principle, always conducted a clean war. In 1942, Hitler had wanted to replace Ribbentrop with Neurath, in the belief that this would settle everything. During reconstruction the cities would have to receive priority; all the old officers would have to be used in this work. The SS would have to be completely abolished; the Hitler Youth would have to be replaced with something like the *Wandervogel* (German Youth Association).

I told Rommel that during the reconstruction period he would have to play a major part and that, in my opinion, of all the military leaders, he was the only suitable man for the job.

A long and censorious inquiry arrived from the OKW, because the British had reported that they had surprised a few German soldiers in their underpants.

June 12. The enemy filled his beachhead with the men and materiel. His air force constantly attacked our troops in the front line. Armored enemy reconnaissance advanced through the gap between the 1st SS Panzer Corps and the 84th Army Corps to south of Caumont (KTB, version abbreviated).

With all energy, the vanguards of the approaching panzer divisions were directed into this gap. General Marcks, the commander of the 84th Army Corps, was killed during an attack by low-flying aircraft on the Cotentin Peninsula.

The commander in chief visited the 116th Panzer Division which still stood on both sides of the Somme. General Geyr von Schweppenburg came to dinner. He was greatly impressed by the events.

Repeated air alerts. Those of the immediate staff who did not accompany Rommel played some table tennis. Otherwise we sat around and discussed the situation. General Meise recalled that somebody had taken a shot at him. He did not seem much impressed by it; neither was anybody else. At the castle the tapestries and pictures were put into caves for safekeeping.

At Führer Headquarters, Göring made the statement that the antiaircraft corps had covered 600 kilometers in two days almost without interference from enemy aircraft. This expedient lie aroused general anger.

June 13. The enemy limited himself to local advances. Ten kilometers southwest of Saint-Mère-Eglise he achieved deep penetration. We closed the gap in the Carentan area. Continuous reinforcements into the penetration areas. The opening of large-scale attacks is expected (KTB, abbreviated).

Rommel drove to the 84th Army Corps command post. The companies of the 346th Infantry Division had only from thirty-five to sixty men left.

The 711th Infantry Division had committed its last reserves. Lack of fuel put 7th Rocket Launcher Brigade temporarily out of action. The 3rd Air Fleet offered to fly in twenty cubic meters of fuel with twenty-two planes; then, however, they put sixty tons of transport space at our disposal instead. A counterattack against the British positions east of the Orne was planned.

The motor torpedo boats suffered heavy damage during an attempt to attack ship concentrations off the landing areas.

June 14. In his beachhead, the enemy now has closed up with twenty-three to twenty-five divisions and numerous army troops of all kinds, in a uniform beachhead from the Orne to Montebourg. The enemy brings in more forces and, with respect to supplies, especially ammunition, seems to be superbly equipped. On June 14, the enemy launched an attack in the Tilly-sur-Seulles to Montebourg area with three specific points of concentration:

a. From the area north of Caumont towards the east to encircle the front sector of Caen. Attack repulsed in bloody battle and with the destruction of thirty-two enemy tanks by the Panzer Lehr Division and the 2d Panzer Division which fought splendidly and even recaptured some ground.
b. Breakthrough astride the road from Bayeux to Saint-Lô using paratroopers. With especially heavy losses repulsed everywhere.
c. From the Carentan area in a west-southwest direction with the objective to cut off the Cotentin. Heavy losses. Our forces melt away under the ceaseless fire of the ship and land artillery and the continuous waves of air attacks (KTB, abbreviated).

Very early in the morning I drove to Navy Group West. After Meulan we had a breakdown which took a long time to fix, since the car which the driver had taken over the previous evening carried insufficient tools. This gave us the opportunity to watch air-to-air combat and the downing of several planes. Some of the spent ammunition hit the road.

The commander in chief of Navy Group West saw the situation clearly, but he did not go into the consequences and the conclusions to be drawn. I did not pursue the subject since he wanted to drive to Rommel where he would also meet Rundstedt.

I took part in a situation briefing at Navy Group West. The 6th and 24th Mine Sweeper Flotillas had suffered heavy losses, one during the attempt to drop mines west of Cherbourg, the other while transporting supplies to Cherbourg. The provisions in the so-called fortress were insufficient; the supply of torpedoes for the motor torpedo boats became difficult.

On my way back I drove to the military hospital at Eaubonne for treatment; on the way I finally saw some of our own fighters who had downed several Englishmen. The fleet surgeon, Dr. Heim, showed me through what had until recently been a recreation hall. He had turned it into a collection point for the wounded with approximately 100 beds and a practical Italian vehicle for surgery. In return I gave him advice on the most efficient method to install slit trenches. Noteworthy was the physician's opinion that the morale of the men was much better now than it had been two years earlier.

In the evening a teletype arrived from Navy Group West protesting the transfer of the army's coast batteries from Saint-Vaast to the land front of Cherbourg. I lodged an appropriate complaint with Speidel, but to no avail. In view of the overall situation it would not have been effective anyway, for the land front was extremely threatened.

We had almost finished dinner when the Field Marshal returned from the front, very serious and deeply affected. He had visited the 1st SS Panzer Corps (Sepp Dietrich), the 47th Panzer Corps (Baron von Funk), and the 2d Panzer Division, under heavy air activity. OKW had requested immediate direct reports about the air situation from the general commands. Rommel was indignant over the mistrust of Western Command and Army Group B implied in this action.

After dinner Speidel and I used a game of table tennis as camouflage for a conversation about the situation. We agreed completely in our opinions. Subsequently Rommel walked with me for an hour in the garden, accompanied by the dogs, which occasionally cheered him up. Once more he talked about everything—the troops' fine bearing, the lack of materiel, and especially the lack of air support.

June 15. A heavy air attack on Le Havre put the majority of the naval forces stationed there out of action—all four torpedo boats in addition to ten motor torpedo boats and fifteen mine sweepers and patrol boats.

At breakfast we again talked about reports and reporting. OKW is always too optimistic, but this cannot do much harm because the army corps do not mince words. (Sepp Dietrich had written that the statement about the undisturbed transit of the antiaircraft corps was a stinking lie.) Why does nobody from the OKW come for a visit? Why are the decision makers men who have never even served at the front? Utilization of the Anglo-American air force is the modern type of warfare, turning the flank not from the side but from above. The battle will soon be over if this continues, since supplies simply can no longer get through. The situation in several areas is most unclear.

Admiral Krancke came towards noon. For three-quarters of an hour he was completely alone with the Field Marshal who informed him of the situation with complete honesty, which, in the previous afternoon, Rundstedt had apparently not done. After lunch Rommel, Speidel, Krancke and I took coffee together and continued the discussion. Rommel once more broached the subject of river transport, about which nothing had been done, despite clear requests from Army Group B. The bombed bridges blocked the navigable water; the transport craft could not move. All this was actually the responsibility of the military commander and the civilian transport authorities.

I proposed to use part of the crews from the vessels destroyed in Le Havre for the clearing away of the bridges and for the manning of the river craft. Krancke gave immediate permission. Subsequently I phoned in several directions to put these measures in force, without losing any time.

In the afternoon I had a lengthy discussion with Army Captain Lang, Rommel's aide, about the situation. Lieutenant Colonel Greif from the Luftwaffe High Command was present at dinner. He was deeply affected by the seriousness of the situation, yet he could not release more than 150 to 200 fighter planes against the 4,000 to 5,000 on the other side!

After dinner Rommel went for a walk with me. He talked about a proposal for an operation which Western Command had made to the OKW and which did not please him. Otherwise he talked about the situation and the options still open to us.

June 16. The carefully prepared attack executed with outstanding bravery by part of the 346th Infantry Division and the 21st Panzer Division east of the Orne had good initial success. In the afternoon, however, part of the recaptured ground had to be given up as a result of the devastating effect of the concentrated enemy ships' artillery. Our own casualties were high. Reconnaissance thrusts toward the western sector of the 1st SS Panzer Corps have been repulsed.

Heavy enemy attacks northeast of Saint-Lô and Saint-Mère-Eglise. Breakthrough near Saint-Sauveur-le-Vicomte on the Cotentin Peninsula has not yet been contained. Here concentrated enemy air activity (KTB, abbreviated).

"Every day one wonders how long it will last" (PAV). During the night a heavy air attack on Boulogne. The loss of navy craft was not as severe as at Le Havre.

A light rain fell, much needed against enemy aircraft. The Field Marshal left at 0830 and drove to the front of the Cotentin Peninsula, first to the 2d Antiaircraft Corps, then to the 84th Army Corps where he met General Farnbacher and General Meindl. Here, an order from Hitler arrived to the effect that no troops could be withdrawn from Cherbourg. After visiting the graveside of the fallen General Marcks, Rommel drove to Le Mans and General Dollmann. At 1430 he was back at headquarters.

The barge transport on the Seine was now begun. The commander of Security Area West provided as director Lieutenant Commander Homeyer, the recent chief of the 6th Motor Mine Sweeper Flotilla.

The Seventh Army requested sea transport of supplies from western France around Brittany to the ports of northern Brittany at least to Saint-Malo, possibly to Cherbourg. An attempt was to be made at any rate, although, in view of the enemy's sea superiority, the prospects looked dim. I suggested sending food supplies from the subterranean navy supply depot near Tours to the north and getting supplies from the south via the sea and river routes. A similar arrangement might also be possible for ammunition.

The Seventh Army caused an uproar because Rear Admiral Hennecke, the sea commandant of Cherbourg, had supposedly reported that the navy could not destroy that harbor. It had long been known that for the complete destruction of the giant installations, several thousand tons of explosives were needed which were simply not available. It was, however, completely possible to paralyze the harbor with the available means. During a conference I had proposed that Seventh Army dispatch its navy liaison officer (whom I never saw) to get the picture. This was rejected. Hennecke and I had discussed a very thorough mining of the harbor. As it turned out, the mining, in addition to the blasting of the most important installations, fulfilled the purpose to the extent that the harbor was out of order not for just a few days, as the Americans had expected, but for four weeks instead. The result of this was that Cherbourg could not be used as a disembarkation port for the breakout of the Allies out of their beachhead on July 31 and August 1.

June 17. Heaviest enemy attacks on Saint-Lô stopped after fierce fighting. West of the Orne, enemy attack on the 1st SS Panzer Corps' left sector. Stopped an enemy attack west of Saint-Sauveur-le-Vicomte. Only negligible recapture of territory east of the Orne. Since June 6, 511 enemy tanks and 161 airplanes destroyed (KTB, abbreviated).

Rundstedt, Rommel and Speidel drove to Soissons for a conference with Hitler and entourage. Speidel transmitted from there the following message: "The Führer has ordered: 'Fortress Cherbourg will have to be held under all circumstances. Permission granted for north group to fight its way back to Fortress Cherbourg while delaying the enemy advance. Retreat in one movement is not allowed. The secure retention of Cherbourg is decisive.' "

In the afternoon I drove to a meeting about river transport at the Naval Ministry where Rear Admiral Engineer Grube was in charge of the matter. He had gathered all the responsible officials and the participants; together they filled quite a large conference hall. The administrative authorities in charge of waterways had, until now, run their department according to a mild peacetime schedule. No traffic moved during the night or on Sundays and a complete three-day shutdown was in effect during Whitsun. The commander of Security Area West provided four officers, 200 men, and light antiaircraft weapons; the navy engineers took care of the bridges. After forty-five minutes complete agreement was reached; the assignments were distributed.

At Navy Group West I met with Admiral Krancke who was enraged about the events in Le Havre. Because a few German planes with new weapons (possibly glide bombs) passed Le Havre, the antiaircraft batteries had received orders to hold their fire. The British had apparently monitored the order because their bomber units approached at 1,800 meters. During the hours preceding the air attack, a desperate Krancke had telephoned in all directions to have the order rescinded, but to no avail. Thirty-one of the seventy-two warships which lay in the harbor were sunk, most of the rest damaged. To keep losses down they all had tied up singly on the long piers. Only four were double-berthed, and they were not even damaged.

For the destruction of the ports in Cherbourg, Krancke had released the mines still stored in the city. The destruction proceeded satisfactorily. I arrived at headquarters at about the same time as the Field Marshal. After dinner we went for a walk during which he told me details about his meeting with Hitler, who had had big plans for a counteroffensive.

Speidel had jotted down some of Hitler's remarks, for instance: "Don't call it a beachhead, but the last piece of French soil held by the enemy . . . the enemies require seven million tons of shipping space for the land (???) . . . the enemies cannot last longer than through summer." Rommel had relentlessly described the seriousness of the situation. Hitler was very optimistic and calm, judged the situation differently, and apparently influenced Rommel somewhat. "Must have an uncanny magnetism" (PAV).

June 18 (Sunday). Overcast, cool; mood no longer so good.

After heavy fighting the enemy broke through to the west coast of the Cotentin near Barneville. Own defensive front in process of being established. Otherwise only local fighting (KTB, abbreviated).

Cherbourg was now cut off. During the morning Rommel had conferences with Lieutenant General (SS) Hausser and General Obstfelder, subsequently with General Geyr von Schweppenburg and his new chief of staff, General Gause, who had not received a division after all. The four men stayed for lunch.

After a situation briefing in the afternoon I reported navy matters to the commander in chief, especially the mine situation and the loss of ships, and proposed to utilize the naval training units in the rear area as local defense against paratroopers. "When all is at stake, training can no longer continue" (PAV).

After dinner the Field Marshal went for a walk with me. He complained about the OKW, where they were apparently envious, feared for their own positions, and always claimed to know everything better. He no longer was in as good a mood as he had been shortly after his return from the meeting with Hitler. Still, he was optimistic since the situation on the front had generally stabilized and V1 rockets were now being launched against Britain. He then inquired about British and American conditions and talked about possible differences and likely inner weaknesses of the two nations. This did not change the fact that, with regard to materiel, we were inferior.

Then I went to see Speidel who told me some more details from Soissons. The Field Marshal dropped in and discussed several current matters. He was not very happy about the pace of the Seventh Army. The experiences of 1940 were no longer sufficient. It was similar with some gentlemen in the staff of Supreme Command West. Above all, the orders were too long, and there was no pressure behind them. In Africa Rommel had never transmitted any radio orders containing more than twelve words; if necessary he had sent several successively. He intended to adhere to this practice and keep his orders brief, and convey the rest personally to the commanders on the battlefield. It made leadership more difficult, but also more successful.

June 19. Small territorial gains east of the Orne. Repulsed heavy enemy attacks in the Tilly-sur-Seulles sector. Northwest of Carentan, the enemy makes territorial gains and also advances toward Cherbourg (KTB).

Light rain. Because the diaries show no notes about the northeast storm which, during these days, stranded 800 of the enemy's smaller craft and completely destroyed one of the two artificial harbors in the process of erection, this situation probably was not utilized particularly.

During breakfast we received news that Hitler, who had intended to visit our headquarters, had already returned to Berchtesgaden on the morning of June 18, because a misguided V1 had exploded near his quarters. Göring and Keitel had been against a trip so close to the front all along.

Rommel drove to the sector between the Seine and the Somme and to the area of the Fifteenth Army, which had not been attacked, apparently because OKW still expected a landing there. He returned quite satisfied with the results.

Using side roads I drove to Rouen to the admiral for the Channel Coast to discuss the situation. Rieve told me very graphically about a drive to Cabourg where he had observed a major part of the landing fleet. As an old hand in naval gunnery, he had passed on his experiences on firing at floating targets and, moreover, had obtained rangefinders. Long-range artillery was lacking; the unfinished 305mm battery near Le Havre could have been of great service. We agreed on the situation but not on what options were still open to us. I was of the opinion that political possibilities still existed. He did not see any way at all.

June 20. The enemy attempted a breakthrough to Cherbourg on both sides of Valognes. Our forces retreat fighting to the fortress. Otherwise only local encounters (KTB, abbreviated).

Lieutenant Colonel Ziervogel from Jodl's staff came in the morning for the briefing. He received a clear picture of the situation, especially of the supply difficulties.

On account of this visit we discussed, during breakfast, the problem of military command and considered how the command organization of the armed forces could be streamlined. "The many different squared charts and radio procedures were not as detrimental as the inadequate cooperation of the higher personalities" (PAV).

At 1130 the Field Marshal drove to the front east of the Orne. Air activity was so feeble that it seemed possible to move transport columns also by day.

After dinner Speidel and I went for a walk along the river. We talked about the enemy's fast advance southwest of Cherbourg, made possible by the late arrival of permission for General von Schlieben to conduct a coordinated fighting retreat. We talked about the so-called revenue weapons (V-weapons). We referred to them as "weapons au surprise," with no lasting value for our situation. The Field Marshal returned and was quite satisfied, except for the situation at Cherbourg. It had developed too rapidly; moreover, almost all leading men had been put out of action.

At 2130 Lieutenant Commander Homeyer came and reported on river shipping, which was now well underway. Lieutenant Prater, an old hand at mine sweeping, had received orders to run and protect the canal from Gent to Paris. This could have been done much earlier!

June 21. Little enemy activity: General von Schlieben tries to bring order into Cherbourg's defense (KTB, abbreviated).

Rommel drove to the 86th Army Corps, the 21st Panzer Division, and the 1st SS Panzer Corps. Good spirits there. Sepp Dietrich believed that he could withstand British pressure in any case.

In the evening the Field Marshal went with me for a walk; discussed supply problems, general troubles, and especially the difficult situation of Cherbourg which, although declared a fortress, was far from being one.

June 22. Summer solstice, beautiful weather; numerous incursions of enemy planes, strong antiaircraft fire.

On the front no important events; news from Cherbourg unpleasant since the garrison was a motley mixture, overaged and poorly equipped.

During breakfast, conversation about special weapons and the visors on navy caps. In the afternoon I telephoned the navy quartermaster about alert units; in theory the number was impressive, but in reality only 5,000 men had been moved into the French–Netherlands rear area, which seemed a bit skimpy. "Much silence during dinner" (TBR).

June 23. High pressure weather zone is abating. Heavy fighting for Cherbourg. On four points the enemy broke through the land front. East of the Orne heavy enemy shelling from ships' artillery and ships with rocket launchers. Otherwise no special events (KTB, abbreviated).

The OKW wondered whether a regiment should be flown into Cherbourg and a grenadier regiment be brought into the fortress via the sea route. Aside from the fact that, with forces of this size, the situation could not be reversed, the demand revealed a complete misjudgment of the situation in the air and at sea. Navy Group West then so clearly reported how slim the chances were to carry through larger movements across sea that the plan was discarded.

In sharp and pointed inquiries about troop distribution, preparations on the Cotentin Peninsula, provisioning of Cherbourg, etc., the OKW was clearly looking for somebody to blame. Nothing was gained by the action, it taxed communication channels and angered the commanders, who had better things to do.

In the evening Homeyer came and reported that river transport was completely ready, but that, however, not enough supplies came through to utilize the barges fully. This would need some organizing. I talked with the responsible people personally and on the phone, in very plain words.

June 24. Cherbourg's garrison fights bravely, but cannot prevent further advances of the superior enemy. Heavy artillery and air activity on the other front sectors (KTB, abbreviated).

At 0900 the Field Marshal drove to the command post of the 84th Army Corps northeast of Saint-Lô, where he discussed the tactical and supply situation. Because of heavy enemy air activity it took him six hours to cover the 230 kilometers. Returning via Vassy, he had a discussion at the 47th Panzer Corps, which was getting ready to attack but expected that the enemy would shortly attack also.

I telephoned about the alert units and river transport. Then I received detailed reports on the crippling of Cherbourg Harbor. Good work had been done, concentrated primarily on the unloading installations while taking deliberate care not to damage, for instance, the shipyards so that rebuilding could take place after the war. "It does not look good in Cherbourg. But we cannot expect this type of fortress to hold out for long. The harbor has been thoroughly wrecked and rendered unusable. It will be interesting to see how long it cannot be used" (PAV).

I showed a sergeant of the combat platoon who guarded us how, by cutting off some branches, he could open up an especially beautiful vista overlooking the Seine Valley for the Field Marshal's enjoyment. Read *Gone with the Wind;* endless parallels with our time. Talked with Lattmann about the situation. Off the mouth of the Orne stood a heavy formation of battleships, cruisers and destroyers. The Seventh Army wanted the navy to do something about that. Admiral Krancke called me about the matter. What could be done was done, but only small assault craft— a few motor torpedo boats and six snorkel U-boats—constituted the entire naval force in the Invasion sector. To send U-boats not equipped with snorkels made no sense, since they had to surface to charge their batteries and would be caught by the strong U-boat defenses of the enemy with dead certainty—in the strongest sense of the word. The snorkel U-boats had difficulty enough. They sank a few vessels but that was only a drop in the bucket.

I spent the evening at Speidel's together with Ernst Jünger, Speidel's brother-in-law and an important lawyer, a kind of refined Falstaff from the Rhine. Very stimulating and entertaining. After dinner we walked up the Donjon and looked down on the Seine which glistened like mother-of-pearl. Strange, to be able to enjoy such a beautiful evening so close to the edge of doom. Moreover, nobody had any delusions; we all knew the truth of the situation.

The conversation focused first on the American officers, who are rather good and remarkably young, at times almost Prussian. But then West Point is also organized in a very Prussian fashion. We then talked about the two British officers (prisoners) who were at the castle.

The Field Marshal returned around 2300. He was very serious since the losses of the infantry were extremely high. The enemy's superiority in materiel was just too overwhelming.

June 25. After a very heavy barrage, the enemy attacked early in the morning with overwhelming armored superiority on both sides of Tilly-sur-Seulles along a seven-kilometer-wide sector. Cut an approximately five-kilometer-wide and two-kilometer-deep breach between the 12th SS Panzer Division and the Panzer Lehr Division. The 1st SS Panzer Corps reported that a restoration of the previous situation could not be achieved with the available forces.

The battle for Cherbourg is nearing its end (KTB, abbreviated).

Rommel remained at headquarters. During breakfast we discussed our materiel inferiority. "We are always told to save ammunition, while the others save blood, which is right. And we believe to be able to decide the war with that puny amount of special weapons. Poor people should not fight a war" (PAV).

The discussion then turned to the Allied transport of supplies by sea from the U.S. to Soviet Russia, which, until 1942, those in the top command had not believed possible. For their tanks, the Russians now had almost exclusively new American equipment. OKW, however, did not want to admit this fact.

Very beautiful weather; very heavy incursions of enemy aircraft. At 1100 I gave a report to the Field Marshal on the harbor destructions in Cherbourg, the river traffic on the Seine, and the alert units. He made some very harsh remarks about the OKW order to carry out relief attacks for Cherbourg. In western Normandy the front units had been patched up with great difficulty and were totally incapable of launching an attack. The panzer divisions were assembled near Paris and could not be of any help. Of course, with regard to supplies, this was the better place for the tanks. Without mincing words, Rommel had reported the situation to OKW, but they did not draw the necessary conclusions. "They do not want to see that the war is going awry."

Field Marshal Sperrle came towards noon for a conference and stayed for lunch—enormous and breathing laboriously. With regard to pertinent matters, apparently no progress was made. He entertained the luncheon group with stories which, for the most part, were no longer news to us. Missing air support for Cherbourg could be explained without much trouble by the fact that the ratio of fighter planes was 4,000 to 300. Very heavy incursions of enemy aircraft; in the afternoon air alert and Stuka noises; bombings near Mantes.

Homeyer came in the afternoon and reported on the river traffic on the Seine. Rather unsatisfactory since, due to the overly complicated organization, nothing advanced. Too many departments were involved. The combat commander of Elbeuf, a practical major, made the best figure. He had already installed two supply depots, faultlessly guarded by French militia. The SS had discovered the fuel stored there and had busily transported it to the front line. The demand for potatoes, also stored there, was not so overwhelming.

Our chief quartermaster staff had unfortunately been dissolved. Together with Homeyer, I once more drove to the major in our staff, who more or less constituted the remaining chief quartermaster staff, and again discussed with him what was important. Homeyer wanted to go to Paris on the following day to make the rounds at all participating departments and report.

A quiet dinner again since the battle for Cherbourg was nearing its end. We only talked about the transport of supplies to Russia via East Asia, Persia, and the Arctic Ocean. OKW inquired after a battleship which was supposed to be stranded west of the mouth of the Orne. It turned out later that an old French battleship had been sunk as a break-water for the artificial harbor.

After dinner the Field Marshal went for a walk with me. He noticed that the view over the valley had been cleared, and rested for a while on the bench from which the view of the Seine was especially lovely.

He discussed the situation in great detail. He was upset that he had been ordered to launch relief attacks for Cherbourg when he felt fortunate that he had established some sort of defensive line at all. We then discussed if, in the event of total defeat, one should shoot oneself. Both of us rejected it as too negative a way out. I was of the opinion that we had to make peace and, since the enemy would not make peace with Hitler, if indeed he loved his people as much as he always asserted, he would have to commit suicide in order to open the way. "Aren't you the tough warrior," Rommel remarked. To which I replied: "One has to examine situations soberly and objectively; for years those on top have failed to do this." Rommel agreed and went into the matter very thoroughly. We talked about the time we lost during the second half of 1940, which I believed constituted the decisive loss of momentum, and about the good prospects an offensive in North Africa would have had at that time. He was apparently not quite aware of the advantage we would have gained had we captured Suez and Gibraltar and with it controlled the Mediterranean.

The situation was now hopeless due to the enemy's overwhelming materiel superiority. The average age of the men in our division was thirty-three years for the most part; in one case thirty-seven. Other divisions consisted mainly of very young lads. The Panzer Lehr Division had lost 2,600 men—one-third of its combat strength. A similar condition existed in the other units, in addition to lack of fuel and ammunition. Those on top tried to put the blame on Rommel. He believed that he could endure that. Hitler had a magnetic effect on all who surrounded him and lived constantly in some sort of euphoria. Now he would soon have to draw the conclusions, even though he had always evaded decisions. Nothing was gained by the redundant order "Hold out to the last man," since the troops would not stand for that in the long run. Caution had to be exercised with regard to commissars and the *Sicherheitsdienst*. Hitler's person was not unsoiled, since he had put himself above the universal code of ethics. This was proven by the case of the fifty British officers who had escaped from their prison camp and whom he had had shot following their recapture.

I talked about *Gone with the Wind* and the conclusion to be drawn from it that rebuilding after a total defeat was possible. Rommel told how in early 1943 he was given a vacation against his will. Then came his appointment as advisor at Führer Headquarters, a sort of deputy commander of the army. He was, however, not able to be effective since the participants at the situation briefings were too numerous and the problems were not approached in a clear-cut manner. It was dreadful to watch the approach of a collapse so clearly. Now it had happened for the third time (North Africa included). Wonder what the next weeks will bring.

June 26. In the Tilly area the enemy enlarged his penetration on the 12th SS Panzer Division's left flank by another five kilometers in width and three kilometers in depth. Apparently intends to wheel in an easterly direction with the tactical objective of cutting off the area of Caen and the ultimate goal of breaking through to Paris. In Cherbourg, fierce fighting. Successive waves of enemy air attacks render the movement of our panzer units difficult (KTB, abbreviated). Successful Soviet offensive in the middle section of the eastern front.

The Field Marshal remained at headquarters. Rundstedt and Blumentritt came in the afternoon, but I learned nothing about their discussion. A sudden cloudburst; little enemy aircraft activity; no evening walk.

During dinner the discussion first was about the fact-finding committee which the OKW had appointed to investigate the fall of Cherbourg. The committee consisted of one general and the chief judge of Western Command. We were generally indignant about these measures, although something similar had happened after the fall of Kharkov and on other occasions. In one case, the affair had successfully been brought to the border of the ridiculous, and as a result nothing more was heard of it.

The discussion then moved to the significance of fortresses. Tobruk had been superbly designed; everything subterranean and camouflaged. The British defended it with two well-equipped divisions which had at their disposal over a hundred tanks and received ample supplies over sea. Rommel believed that nowadays even very heavy fortifications could not be held without air support, because they would just be crushed. In Africa, Montgomery had fought in this fashion and had been victorious at El Alamein. Ever since that time, Rommel had worried that the same thing would occur in Europe. Now it had happened.

Rommel and General Marcks, 84th Army Corps, inspecting a camouflaged battery.

Rommel and Ruge crossing the Gironde from Le Verdon to Royan on 10 February 1944 with army and navy staff officers.

Rommel with General Dollmann and staff.

Inspecting the work on the coast.

Rommel conferring on defense plans with staff officers.

Rommel meeting Vice Admiral Wever on the south coast of France near Toulon, 2 May 1944.

Rommel and the author waiting for a ferry on the Seine River near Le Havre.

The Battle for Caen

*T*he enemy's natural objective was to break out of the beachhead and operate on the open field where they could take full advantage of their materiel superiority, mobility, and aerial superiority. The fall of Cherbourg had released considerable forces. Moreover, it was only a matter of days or weeks, independent of the weather, before large amounts of supplies could be unloaded there to feed the thrust south from the Cotentin Peninsula. Deployment for this purpose, however, would still take some time.

In the meantime, Montgomery had already started to storm Caen with British troops and to force the breakout from the eastern half of the beachhead. Rommel, acquainted with his old adversary's battle techniques, endeavored to parry the thrust by deploying his troops, especially the artillery, in deep echelons. The tanks were to cooperate closely with the infantry.

However, Rommel knew that in the long run he could not prevent the breakout of the enemy, who was vastly superior in materiel and would soon be so in manpower. Above all, he fought to gain time which could be of benefit to the political solution demanded by the situation.

June 27. On June 26, the 1st SS Panzer Corps, using its last reserves and with the ultimate exertion of all available forces, achieved a complete defensive success and destroyed over fifty tanks. Area of penetration blocked off at the fall of darkness. On June 27, after a heavy barrage and a preparation by formations of close-support aircraft, the enemy once more attacked and, amidst fierce fighting, crossed the Caen–Villers-Bocage road near Mondrainville in the evening hours. All available elements of the 2d SS Panzer Division and the 2d SS Panzer Corps are being directed against the area of penetration. In Cherbourg, fighting in some isolated resistance nests still continues. Enemy attacks at the Jobourg Peninsula have been repulsed (KTB).

At 0730 General Thomale, Guderian's chief of staff, who had visited the panzer units on the front, arrived. The Field Marshal discussed with him the commitment of the panzer divisions. Above all, he wanted Thomale to faithfully report his impressions to Führer Headquarters, especially the difficulties which resulted from the lack of a unified command. The Luftwaffe, for instance, had allegedly 19,000 tons of truck space in France at its disposal. This, however, could never be exactly established. The Luftwaffe was now supposed to release 1,000 tons, but neither Rommel nor Rundstedt were authorized to give the order. "One should not always have to beg. The revolutionary principle of the division of power is unfortunately also maintained in the conduct of war."

Subsequently Rommel drove to the command post of Panzer Group West and that of the 84th Army Corps.

After Rommel and Thomale left, the breakfast discussion centered once more on the fact-finding committee and later on the NSFO (National Socialist Political Officer) who would soon come and stay with us. From above came the request that he should be able to speak with the Field Marshal for at least one hour a day. "They have grasped the situation." In the evening Rommel gave a brief, cordial speech in honor of Lieutenant Colonel Olshausen who was being transferred after the quartermaster staff had been dissolved. "You are leaving us at a moment when your railroad has become very unreliable. Many of us would also like to leave and start all over again. That is, however, not possible and we shall weather the situation." We received propaganda instructions from above, not to mention the enemy's air superiority. This didn't help much either.

In the evening a phone call came from Western Command that Rundstedt and Rommel were to go to Berchtesgaden the following day. Flying was too unsafe in France, therefore they were to go by car.

June 28. The enemy enlarged his grand-scale attack in the Caen area to approximately twenty-five kilometers. Several penetrations, one especially deep near Baron, enabled the enemy, with reckless employment of men and equipment, to advance to the Caen–Evrecy road. Concentric counterattack of own panzer forces in progress; south of Tilly enemy attack carried forward in continuously new waves. In Cherbourg, isolated resistance nests are still fighting. The group of Lieutenant Colonel Keil, which allegedly had surrendered, continues to hold the Jobourg Peninsula (KTB, abbreviated).

At 1000 General Dollmann, the commander of the Seventh Army, suffered a fatal heart attack. Hitler appointed Lieutenant General (SS) Hausser as his successor. Field Marshal Rommel left for Germany at 1300. At 0715 I left for Paris to visit Navy Group West and to clarify several annoyances, especially the report of Battle Group Keil's alleged surrender, over which OKW had been so upset. It finally turned out that the report had come from Cherbourg's harbor captain, that it had been transmitted via Jobourg, Alderney, and Saint-Malo, and that a garbled version had arrived at Navy Group West. According to procedure, Navy Group West had transmitted the message to Western Command along with some theories of the possible meaning. Western Command, in turn, however, had passed on only one of the interpretations—unfortunately the version that just happened to be the least correct.

Following an order from OKW, Army Quartermaster West ordered Seventh Army to directly regulate the departures of the ships from Saint-Malo to the Channel Islands. The reason was that several days earlier a transport had not proceeded on schedule on account of storm and heavy seas. The shipping office at Saint-Malo had postponed the convoy of mostly small craft for twelve hours and quite rightly so. The station had done this sort of thing without criticism for the last four years. Thereupon the divisional commander–Channel Islands applied to Jodl directly. A typical example of inadequate reasoning from land into matters of the sea.

All other transports were on schedule; the changes in orders were later rescinded. None of the directly affected people would have followed them anyway since the battle commander of Saint-Malo, who would have had to arrange the convoy, had neither the equipment nor the experience.

I used one and a half hours of my time at Navy Group West with this and similar affairs and also attended the briefing. I found the participants to be rather nervous and sharp. Then I went to Security Area West to clarify more problems. They did not yet want to recognize the final consequences. Eventually I went to the Navy Ministry, where I arrived during the last part of a conference on river transport. This finally worked after the navy had also taken on the job of unloading and transporting from the unloading points. For this purpose it released 1,600 tons of transport space from its 10,000 tons. The rest was completely used up with the transport of ammunition for the coastal batteries, of torpedoes, assault craft, etc.

After dinner Speidel took me to the house of Monet, the famous painter, which was located a bit downstream in a beautiful flower garden. Monet's daughter-in-law, an elderly lady, looked after the place. Among the pictures, those of sea roses and irises were particularly impressive. The mood was dampened, however, by eyewitness accounts of unpleasant occurrences told by the war correspondent who accompanied us.

June 29. Grand-scale enemy attack for the possession of Caen with even increased intensity; heaviest artillery fire; heaviest fire from the ship artillery; continuous air attacks in successive waves. Successful counterattack by the 9th and 10th SS Panzer Divisions. Attacks in the Saint-Lô region repulsed. In Cherbourg individual resistance nests are still fighting. Jobourg also still holding (KTB, abbreviated).

Rommel arrived at Berchtesgaden at 1300. Conference with Hitler at 1800; preceded by one with Guderian. Our National Socialist Political Officer arrived in the afternoon, spent one and a half hours with Speidel; enthusiastic and impractical.

General Dietl was killed in an accident.

Thunderstorm in the evening. Passing through the main hall on my way from the briefing cave to my room I watched the lightning-illuminated landscape, when Speidel collected me for a nightcap with Tempelhoff and Staubwasser. Once more we discussed the dilettantism and the lack of organization. We especially stressed the idea that somebody who, like Hitler, had forced himself to the top of the state, carried much more responsibility than an individual who held this position by hereditary succession.

June 30. The 2d SS Panzer Corps' counterattack has come to a standstill. Heavy attacks at Saint-Lô have been repulsed. The battle for Cherbourg is over. Battle Group Keil is evidently making its last stand against overwhelming enemy superiority (KTB, abbreviated).

At 2300 the Field Marshal returned to headquarters. However, I did not see him. A short while before he returned I attended a meeting with Speidel. On the strength of a situation analysis by Panzer Group West, there were plans to evacuate the half-encircled town of Caen.

July 1. Due to combined fire from German artillery and mortars, the enemy, on the whole, kept quiet where he had broken in. The combined force of enemy airpower, land, and ships' artillery smashed the assembly area of the 2d SS Panzer Corps to the extent that an attack was out of the

question. We suffered considerable losses. In the Saint-Lô region, local
fighting; battle for Jobourg evidently over (KTB, abbreviated).

During breakfast the commander in chief mentioned very little about
his visit at Führer Headquarters. Hitler had told him that earlier he had
not quite believed his report about British battle techniques in North
Africa. A bit late for such realizations! Hitler was apparently very calm
and believed the situation not to be overly serious.

Lang was present at the conference during which many ifs and buts
were pronounced. Of the larger ships in the invasion sector, the navy
had only a single torpedo boat still ready for action.

Rommel soon drove to Panzer Group West's command post to discuss
the evacuation of the Caen beachhead. He was back in time for dinner.
Meise became the butt of our jokes when he was told that after the war
he would personally have to clear all the mines which had been laid at
his order. Rommel then talked about the situation and mentioned a remark of Montgomery which implied that the latter had pulled back his
leading units somewhat. Rommel pointed out that the destruction of our
own attack-ready units necessitated a new tactic, namely the smashing
of the enemy's assembly areas. Before the El Alamein breakthrough, he
had not been present in Africa. The lack of ammunition had persuaded
his deputy not to fire on the British assembly areas. When the British
began the attack, it was too late. It would have been much better to fire
earlier. In this way the striking power would be weakened, and time
would even be gained for ammunition resupply.

We began with the assembly of a map of the Atlantic Wall for OKW.
The news from Russia was very bad. During the afternoon and the evening, a tug-of-war via telephone over the evacuation of Caen. Rommel
had prepared the evacuation according to Hitler's instructions of June 29,
which included saving the combat-ready mobile units. Now Hitler himself rejected it. A surprising event was that around midnight Hitler's order was transmitted to relieve Geyr von Schweppenburg and to replace
him with General Eberbach.

July 2. Except for artillery fire, not much enemy action in the sectors
southwest of Caen and northeast of Saint-Lô. Increase of air activity; ammunition situation very tense (KTB, abbreviated).

The general mood during breakfast was very bad. OKW had ordered
not to inform General Geyr von Schweppenburg at that moment of his
relief since it was apparently believed that he would otherwise stop doing
anything. Army Group B was also informed that one of Hitler's aides

carrying a personal message from Hitler was on his way to Rundstedt expressing Hitler's concern about Rundstedt's health. Therefore, Rundstedt's relief could be expected also. Rommel drove to General Dollmann's funeral. I was with Speidel who told me about Berchtesgaden and said that the meetings had been essentially useless. Hitler had withdrawn his permission for a more flexible conduct of operations than he had given only fourteen days earlier, and ordered instead to hold every foot of territory. Always the same procedure since the Russian winter of 1941–42. At that time it might have been the right thing to do, not pressing on just before the winter. Another procedure Hitler liked was to dismiss all those who could not produce the success ordered. Field Marshal Busch had also been relieved. Without reserves a war cannot be conducted.

Over the telephone, I had several disputes with Navy Group West and the Navy High Command during the day, because of Rommel's request to have all Wehrmacht units present in the sector of Army Group B put under his command. This touched on the foundations of the current autonomy of the Wehrmacht's branches. They protested loudly, especially since their liaison officers had not been consulted for the draft of the text and because the wording was awkwardly phrased. In this matter, Rommel was completely correct, since it was absurd to have three branches of the Wehrmacht operate autonomously in such a strained situation. A good example had been the firing prohibition of the antiaircraft guns at Le Havre, which resulted in heavy losses for our naval forces.

During the Second World War, the Americans and the British had good results with their "theater commander in chief" approach, with one commander in chief for a whole theater of war (General Eisenhower for Northwest Europe, General MacArthur for the Pacific, Admiral Nimitz for the Mid-Pacific sector, Admiral Mountbatten for Burma). Prerequisite for good cooperation is, of course, the understanding that the commander in chief does not give direct orders to the branches of the armed forces or order petty details, but that he commands by directives to the subordinated commanders. Great caution must be exercised that the officers who represent the different branches at the commander in chief's staff act only as his advisors and don't begin to "rule" themselves. The temptation here is very great.

After dinner a light rain fell. At the window in the main hall, the Field Marshal talked with me for a long time. He suffered under the pressure of the situation and from the continuous mistrust. The letter of dismissal for Rundstedt had already arrived, and his successor, Field Marshal von Kluge, was already expected for the following day.

Reports from the panzer divisions clearly indicated that the enemy had smashed all our attack preparations. OKW, however, still did not want to admit that.

Rommel discussed whether one should attempt negotiating a way out with the Anglo-Americans or the Russians. He was for cooperation with the West. "It is, however, high time for the politicians to act as long as we still hold any kind of a trump." He was very serious and wished that the coming four weeks had already passed.

July 3. At and west of Saint-Lô, heavy American attacks resulted in several penetrations. In the Caen sector, artillery fire only. There, a concentration of our own artillery and mortars (KTB).

The situation in Russia was very bleak. Minsk had been bypassed on both sides. OKW gave orders to count the number of rounds fired by the enemy artillery, evidently since they believed the reports of enemy artillery strength to be exaggerated.

Rommel remarked: "They don't believe us; however, we are to believe (them)." He drove to the command post of the 84th Army Corps and to Panzer Group West. General Eberbach, Panzer Group West's new commander, arrived around noon. After lunch I discussed with Speidel the affair of the subordination of all branches of the Wehrmacht. Field Marshal von Kluge arrived in the afternoon, about the same time as Rommel. They had a long talk, at times privately. There was, evidently, a strong controversy. Later, however, they managed to agree to some extent. During dinner Rommel remarked: "I told Kluge that he had never fought against the British." Moreover, he told Kluge that, above all, he had to see to it that enough supplies came through. Kluge apparently had wanted to act with great vigor and fly to the front in a (Fieseler) Storch at once. But then he refrained from doing so.

After dinner Rommel talked with me for a while. He had to lend his name, but a name alone did not yet mean success. The enemy had such overwhelming superiority that they would with certainty break through on one of the three fronts. He, Rommel, had conducted the war with all possible energy. In the beginning, the discussion with Field Marshal von Kluge had been like an interrogation.

July 4. Grand-scale attack both sides of the Bayeux–Caen road, mostly repulsed. Heavy fighting with penetrations in the western half of the front (KTB, abbreviated).

During breakfast we discussed an inquiry from OKW about the penetrations in the Saint-Lô sector. There the situation had been made more difficult by the recent withdrawal of the 17th SS Panzer Grenadier Division, which had been ordered by OKW to form a reserve. Consequently only a thin line of defense existed, which the enemy broke through quickly. Rommel remarked: "They (OKW) cannot demand of me to hold the attack of three American divisions with one-quarter of a division."

Our own casualties are not being considered. Cherbourg is not even counted. No statistics! But the troops that have been taken prisoner there now are sorely missed on the front. The army is being treated like a machine without a soul. As Rommel put it: "And every once in a while they remove several wheels and replace them with some which do not fit well. But despite this an improvement is expected. Constantly it is run at maximum speed, not well oiled, and when it suddenly stops working or even falls apart they are surprised."

He asked me to go with him to Rouen to the 81st Army Corps' command post. Lang started to ponder over the seating arrangement in the car, a large, open cross-country vehicle, since, in addition to him and me, an aircraft lookout had to be seated as well. When we started Rommel seated himself with me in the rear of the car; the aircraft lookout was in the escort car. Under low clouds and occasional drizzling rain we made good progress.

The Field Marshal talked with me all the time—discussed the situation and the essential events of the previous week. The meeting with Kluge had been very stormy because Kluge had more or less declared that he was to make Rommel obey. When Rommel contradicted him at once, Kluge became more friendly, after he had sent the other officers away. He then requested that Rommel submit to him reports from the front, which Rommel declined to do.

Then we talked about the mistakes of the past, about the future and the tasks of the future, about the disregard of intellectual achievements, about the instigations of the young against their teachers, about similar attempts against officers as well, about the division of power, the selfish gains many had made, exaggerated ambitions, and the limitless goals. "If you talk this way in public they will put you up against a wall," said Rommel. "That's why I only tell you, *Herr Feldmarschall.*" Attempts are apparently made to have him shelved. "They have misused my name." Neither the army nor the navy have received enough supplies and despite this the Luftwaffe was not ready either. He had sent a report to General

Schmundt describing the things he (Rommel) had initiated and the things he had requested for which permission had been denied. With Schmundt, one was certain that he would transmit reports to the top level.

Once more we debated if the officer should shoot himself as expected by those above. We, however, agreed that it was wrong since it looked like the admission of guilt. Moreover, those in question would generally be needed later on. He spoke sharply against cliquism and remarked that the navy was better in that respect.

At 1030 we arrived at the 81st Corps. General Kuntzen reported on the defense of his sector, especially on the fortress Le Havre. Admiral Rieve talked about coastal artillery, mine barriers, and radar. At 1330 we were back at headquarters. I found a teletype message from the Naval War Staff waiting for me, pertaining to Rommel's request for a centralized command in his sector. The message showed that the meaning of his request had been completely misunderstood.

After dinner Rommel telephoned for some time. Afterwards he came to the mess for a short while and finally invited me for a walk. The sky had cleared and we enjoyed beautiful views of the lovely and peaceful countryside. Rommel once more unburdened himself about his conversation with Kluge. He had been especially angered by Kluge's remark that he, Rommel, had so far actually not commanded more than one division.

He was in a very serious mood because, in his opinion, the enemy could presumably no longer be stopped. We discussed the possible American and British attitude. During the discussion Rommel informed himself, as he had done on earlier occasions, by asking many pertinent questions. He remarked that the efforts of the soldiers had been in vain. I contradicted him and mentioned that in 1918 the overall situation had appeared to us hopeless also and that precisely the respect for the German soldier had made reconstruction easier. Respect existed this time as well, especially for him.

Then for the first time we spoke about personal matters; first about languages, starting with the examination for English interpreter. Back in 1915 as lieutenant in the Argonne front, Rommel had studied Turkish as I had done during the same time on the old battleship "Elsass." Neither of us, however, had ever reached Turkey. Then I described to him the scuttling of the High Seas Fleet at Scapa Flow.

All day long the staff of the Commander in Chief West telephoned our staff to inform themselves of several details. "Commander in Chief West states that he has absolutely no intention of interfering with the command of Army Group B as a matter of principle; that, however, should he deem certain matters necessary, he would clearly express them" (KTB, abbreviated).

July 5. Counterattack by our forces to recapture Carpiquet does not succeed; otherwise in the eastern sector of the front, artillery battles only. In the western sector, heavy enemy attacks with penetrations for which fighting is still taking place. The 2d Panzer Division—*Das Reich*—has been put under the 84th Army Corps (KTB, abbreviated).

Morning fog. At 0600 the Field Marshal drove to the panzer group and to the 2d Panzer Corps. The panzer group should be prepared to release two panzer divisions for use at the Seventh or Fifteenth Armies in the event of a second landing. The divisions were to be replaced by infantry divisions. The 271st Infantry Division was approaching; the 277th Infantry Division was to replace the 9th SS Panzer Division. In accord with Hitler's orders, "not a foot of territory would be given up" in the Caen sector. Panzer Group West prepared a second line, had orders to let the enemy run against our lines, and, above all, to take him under fire.

"Own larger movements are at the moment not possible during daytime. It is scandalous that the full extent of enemy air superiority is still not completely believed in high places" (KTB).

General impression from a telephone call with Seventh Army: Despite our own units' courageous fighting, the overall situation is decidedly strained due to enemy superiority and our exhaustion. The Americans are apparently more effective than the British and fight with lavish use of materiel. Air reconnaissance and prisoners' statements confirmed the existence of fifteen airfields in the beachhead.

Early in the morning I drove to Paris. On the way we observed air combats and bombings on Pontoise and, while stuck in a herd of cows, were sprayed with antiaircraft shell fragments.

Navy Group West was also against Rommel's request for subordination of all units from the other branches of the Wehrmacht deployed in his sector. I discussed with Willesen his radar situation. Clear and encouraging; unfortunately, the essential improvements came a bit too late. Two U-boats have returned from the English Channel. One had sunk two fully loaded landing ships, the other had fired a torpedo salvo at an American battleship from a good aiming position; the torpedoes, however, had detonated prematurely.

Shipping on the Seine functioned well. The traffic through the canal from northern France to Paris was constantly interrupted by sabotage. I spent noon at the command quarters of Security Area West. In the afternoon Rundstedt came to La Roche-Guyon to say goodby. Unfortunately, I was not present. During dinner we talked about Italy's reconstruction which, to a certain degree, will be easier than in Germany, since in Italy many things are not as technologically developed as they are in Germany. The climate is helpful since one does not need so much heating and clothing.

July 6. In the eastern sector of the front, slight disengagement by the enemy on two points. The 21st Panzer Division and the Panzer Lehr Division were pulled back from the front line without the bulk of the artillery. At the 84th Army Corps the heavy defensive battle continues. Despite the enemy's complete air supremacy and the heaviest use of men and material, our valiantly fighting troops were able to prevent a decisive breakthrough, partly with successful counterthrusts. Heaviest enemy airpower prevented the attack of the 2d SS Panzer Division north of Lessay. Seventh Army has now thrown all its available reserves into the battle. The combined forces of our own fighter planes were forced away before reaching the combat area by the enemy air force and, therefore, could not support the heavily committed troops (KTB, abbreviated).

Because the tide conditions were the same as it had been during the night of June 5 to 6, OKW expected another landing to take place, but it did not occur. The Field Marshal drove to Le Havre. Unfortunately, I found this out after he had already left.

An operations officer from a division stationed in the Crimea and a colonel of a propaganda battalion were our guests for the evening. The latter told us that effective propaganda was now very difficult as it was not permitted to saw off the branch on which the highest command was sitting. But they were doing a good job of sawing at this branch themselves. Questions received from the army troops were always the same, like: "Where is the Luftwaffe?", "What means do we have to still win the war?", "Why, with regard to decorations, do the Luftwaffe and the navy receive preferred treatment?" The attitude of the men was, however, still surprisingly good. The operations officer spoke very bitterly about the Crimea and the evacuation of Sebastopol, where teamwork was sorely lacking.

Homeyer came at 2200 and told us, quite satisfied, about the shipping traffic on the Seine, which the enemy had apparently not yet detected.

July 7. All quiet on the eastern sector of the front. In the sector south of Carentan, an American grand-scale offensive with deep penetrations and a bridgehead over the Vire. Further west after heavy fighting in counterattack reestablishment of a main battle line. Heavy attrition of own units (KTB, abbreviated).

Lengthy tug-of-war about the deployment forward of the 5th Parachute Rifle Division, which was finally cleared by Hitler's personal permission. In the afternoon Rommel went to Kluge's to discuss the supply situation and the current organization.

July 8. Grand-scale attack in the Caen sector, which achieved especially deep penetrations in the 16th Luftwaffe Division's sector. The 21st Panzer Division started a counterattack. Although fighting with exemplary bravery in heavy combat, the 12th SS Panzer Division had to give up several villages. Between the Vire and the Taute the enemy made further advances; farther west no longer any coherent attacks (KTB, abbreviated).

The Field Marshal drove to Panzer Group West, to the Seventh Army's forward command post, and to the 2d Parachute Rifle Corps.

General Diem and I started at 0500 to inspect the organization of the unloading phase of the Seine transport. Homeyer joined us at Louviers. At Elbeuf we found no barges; instead, however, large numbers of enemy airplanes overhead. There an Austrian major who made a good impression was in charge. His reasons for not using Elboeuf for unloading made sense but, despite his good reasons, the unloading points had to be utilized. In the woods we passed a large, nearly unguarded ammunition depot. The actual supply staff in charge was at Saint-Pierre-du-Vauvray on the Seine, five kilometers northeast of Louviers, which we reached after some delay due to air activity. The staff could have shown more initiative. At unloading point twelve an ammunition barge which leaked badly was being unloaded. Work was done with a hand crank operated by two men while twelve others watched. Therefore the output amounted to only ninety tons in sixteen hours, which was decidedly insufficient. Neither antiaircraft protection trenches nor any other camouflage had been installed. A nearby ferry station under construction was completely unprotected. General Diem expressed his opinion in no unclear terms to those in charge. Then, a quartermaster officer from Panzer Group West appeared, accompanied by an oversized commissariat officer who made a favorable impression. In the beginning he was tough on the navy, since he did not know the connections and because the supply staff tried to cover up its shortcomings with big speeches. After some well-chosen words had corrected the matter, the situation improved. The main complaint was that a barge with fuel had not yet arrived. Unfortunately nobody had previously mentioned that this ship was so urgently needed, and that they had put in the entire fuel supply for several days. The ten days lost in this way were to be greatly regretted. Two unloading piers were ready; ten more under construction.

Without rest we continued our drive, crossing the Seine at Port Joie on an engineer ferry. The countryside was beautiful. We enjoyed the view of the wide river with its islands, lovely tree groupings, and pretty summer cottages built in modern Norman style. These stood on a huge piece of land which the Renault company used as a vacation resort for its employees. We drove up a hill to get a wider view, detected an entrance leading to a park, drove in a bit, and left the car. We found a beautiful rose-lined path at the rim of the embankment, and at the end of the path a lookout point with comfortable wicker chairs. There we took a short rest. Soon a waiter appeared with a most promising coffee tray. It was not intended for us, however, but for a party of well-dressed French people seated nearby. A countryside exquisite and peaceful, possibly one of France's most beautiful spots. The sky turned cloudy; a thunderstorm threatened and some airplanes made the area unsafe, but our excellent airplane lookout, a lieutenant, detected them in time. In the evening Rommel went to see General Meindl; Speidel to Paris to see General von Stülpnagel.

July 9 (Sunday). At the sector of the 16th Luftwaffe Field Division, the enemy penetrated into the town of Caen. Amidst severe fighting the 12th SS Panzer Division was pushed back further; encircled groups defended themselves against overwhelming superiority. The 21st Panzer Division's counterattack did not succeed. The Americans enlarged their bridgehead between the Vire and the Taute. On all fronts, heavy losses of men and equipment (KTB, abbreviated).

The withdrawal into a shortened line south of Caen, which Rommel wanted to carry out a bit earlier in a well-organized fashion, had now to be executed under enemy pressure. Behind the line, Rommel now formed a deeply staggered defensive zone. He remained at headquarters. OKW sent instructions to penetrate to the enemy battery positions in night attacks. Rommel had discussed this previously with General

Meindl. It could be done in isolated cases with assault troops but not along a wide front. OKW ordered, in addition, the preparation of a proposal for an extensive operation to eliminate the enemy's beachhead. Rommel remarked that with a 1:5 ratio in artillery and 1:10 in ammunition, the OKW could, if they wished, dismiss a few more from the command; but the facts would not change. On the whole the order was received with gallow's humor. It was decided to draw up a beautiful plan with pretty arrows, with the sharpest points possible. Whether the plan could be realized was a different matter entirely. Rommel remarked that following the recent mixup in orders, we would most likely receive orders to attack the Americans, when he was just ready to attack at the eastern sector. This would mean regrouping and in the meantime everything would be different again. The Americans had announced that it would take some time and patience to make the port of Cherbourg serviceable again.

As to be expected, the 16th Luftwaffe Field Division had been smashed at Caen. Officers and noncoms were brave men, but they had been insufficiently trained for infantry combat. Parts of the 12th SS Panzer Division were cut off, the town had been evacuated, the losses were much higher than if this had been done a bit earlier and methodically.

After dinner Rommel, Speidel and I were invited by the owners of the castle for a visit.

July 10. The enemy did not continue his attack from Caen, but achieved a wide penetration farther southwest at the 10th SS Panzer Division which could be stopped after fierce fighting. The Americans made only negligible ground gains (KTB, abbreviated).

The Field Marshal drove with Lattmann to the 86th Army Corps, Panzer Group West, and the 1st SS Panzer Corps. At Panzer Group West, he drew attention to the Seine transport. "For transporting ammunition it is necessary to use the Seine. One freight barge can carry 250 tons of ammunition. If ten or more barges are used, several thousand tons can be transported to the front in two nights, whereas at least a month will be needed to transport the same amount by road or rail. The whole matter will have to be better organized" (Appendix, KTB).

The breakfast conversation dealt with the replacement officers who had been grouped incorrectly. In order to receive pay corresponding to their more mature age, they were promoted to a rank more advanced than their experience warranted. Appropriate pay without promotion would have been more practical.

Then we discussed how many units still used horses. We all agreed that for commanders, only the use of automobiles was practical. The battalion commanders, however, had not been allotted automobiles. Therefore, they often used the doctor's car or grabbed a motorcycle with side car. Rommel remarked on the idea of a battalion commander riding a horse at the battlefield of Caen.

In the evening we discussed the several types of divisions; especially the stationary divisions which were at once sent into battle and then did not function immediately. Effective young officers went mostly to Russia; and the local commanders were often not quite fully fit for field duty.

Stories were told about a high-ranking commander on the Russian front who had installed barrage fire behind his own lines and who held every artillery commander personally responsible that it was fired. Rommel replied that there were certain things which he just would not do and this measure was one of them. In the long run, such methods couldn't hold a line anyway. Moreover we also agreed that under these circumstances the men would retreat covertly and say nothing in order to avoid this additional menace. This situation in Russia, according to Rommel, was worse than here so that a decision might be reached there earlier. But which one?

July 11. In the Caen area some successful counterattacks; heavy losses. In the Tilly area heavy British attacks on the whole repulsed. American grand-scale attack in direction of Saint-Lô; successful attack by Panzer Lehr Division northwest of Saint-Lô, successful at first but made difficult later by U.S. counterattack. Farther west, heavy attacks with little success by the Americans (KTB, abbreviated).

Rommel remained at headquarters. His orderlies tried to get him accustomed to one fried egg in the morning, since he had rejected an increase in his butter ration. After breakfast he asked me about the unloading in the Elboeuf area. He had apparently received some one-sided reports. I described the situation as it was and he was satisfied. Then I heard that Speidel would drive to Le Havre. I accompanied him. We drove in drizzling rain and under a low cloud cover and, therefore, were not disturbed by airplanes. Speidel drove himself and I navigated, which was not very difficult since I knew the area well. Following the talk I had earlier with Rommel about the Seine transport, Speidel and I discussed the misunderstandings that had apparently developed. On the strength of incomplete records, Rommel had wanted to start a larger action at Western Command. Speidel, however, had dissuaded him from doing so. I once more described the situation. The navy had initiated the following:

- Cleared the river in three days with navy fortress engineers. Subsequently started construction of unloading ramps. So far, three completed.
- Provided Lieutenant Commander Homeyer with men and arms for duty and as guards for locks and unloading ramps.
- Provided crews for the barges which had been left by the French.
- Engaged a stevedore company for loading the barges.
- Provided a director for the unloading and three truck companies for transport.

Because of the existing command organization, the navy could not take over command since inland waterways were none of its business. The army quartermaster and the general in charge of transport had to take command. And they should have had a good organization a long time ago.

We discussed this subject until we were halfway to Rouen. Then we talked about the house and the car which each of us would like to have; of the four seasons, which one did not notice so much at sea as on land; of summer vacation in France in which even the small businesses and the craftsmen participated; and finally of the fact that two world wars were a bit much for one lifetime.

In Rouen we first visited Admiral Rieve, who requested, above all, more concrete to install more weapons. He clearly understood the seriousness of the situation and was of the opinion that the solution could only be a political one. He got on well with Speidel. It was a particular difficulty for him that he had no one he could talk to openly and frankly. This inner loneliness of many of those in the high and highest command during this period is a fact which in addition to their incredible tension has not been considered sufficiently in some later judgments about initiative and lack of initiative of the military.

Our trip took us then to the staff of the 81st Army Corps. General Kuntzen was not present. Continuing our drive we agreed that one could not speak as openly with many others as one could with Rieve, and that some commanders quarreled in every direction. In Bolbec we visited the commander of the 89th Infantry Division. He had just arrived from Norway and wanted to hear news from Speidel about the situation. Evidently, however, he did not trust me, and, a bit sad and without success, he returned to the affairs of his own division, which was very funny. The division was well trained.

The soldiers' mess in Le Havre had burned down, so the same staff had opened another one. There we had a bite to eat and then visited the fortress commander who was still in his area. His operations officer, in civilian life a Silesian lawyer who knew much about music, represented him well. We met the sea commandant, Rear Admiral von Tresckow, in front of his command bunker where, with good binoculars, we could see several ships and smoke screens off the mouth of the Orne. An explosion several days earlier, followed by a fire in the motor mine sweeper bunker, had apparently been due to neglect. Two hundred liters of gasoline improperly stored in the torpedo depot had caught fire.

Through open terrain we drove to Etretat to visit the 17th Luftwaffe Field Division, then via Fécamp to the fortress commander of Dieppe, then on side roads to Forges-les-Eaux, and from there on the heavily bombed main route to headquarters where we arrived at 2200.

As we ate our meatless dinner, Rommel joined us. Speidel was soon called to the telephone. In great earnest, Rommel talked about the situation. The left flank was threatened by the breakthrough; the troops were bled white. But, despite all this strain, he remained always amiable and, in his reserved manner, personable.

In the final analysis he had achieved more in the battle for Caen than was realized at the time, despite the loss of the town. The British had planned to occupy it on the first day of the Invasion, and they needed almost five weeks to take it. Despite strategic air support and the force of their combined tank units, they could not force the breakthrough. The tanks had suffered such heavy losses south of the town, especially in the last days, that they were operational only in a limited way. An American observer at British headquarters, Ralph Ingersoll, relates his own observations in his book *Top Secret*: "It was a defeat from which British arms on the continent never recovered. . . . He (Montgomery) was stopped just beyond Caen, after practically destroying the British Armored Corps by running his tanks in successive waves head on into German 88 fire. . . . His forces were exhausted."

The success would have even been greater had Rommel been allowed to carry out his evasive action in time. Therefore the losses were very high which, in view of the slow movements of reserves and supplies, was especially grave. The battle of attrition continued; the breakthrough was only a matter of time.

The Breakthrough

*J*uly 12. Quiet in the British sector; heavy American attack east of the Vire has been repulsed by the superb fighting riflemen of the 3rd Parachute Rifle Division. West of the Vire fierce fighting. Due to attack by the Panzer Lehr Division, American breakthrough attempt could not develop. Panzer Lehr attack, however, also without success. Farther west additional penetration through the main battle line (KTB, abbreviated).

The commander in chief drove to the 47th Panzer Corps and to Panzer Group West. The fuel and ammunition situation had improved slightly. The 12th SS Panzer Division had lost all its antitank guns, eighteen light field howitzers, and the majority of the grenadiers, and was only two battalions strong.

"Because of the enemy's mind-staggering use of men and materiel, and because of the ceaseless fire and the enemy aircraft's continuous attacks in successive waves, the combat strength of our troops is constantly sinking. On July 11, the 3rd Parachute Rifle Division counted a present strength of only thirty-five percent and the battle group of the 353rd Infantry Division, deployed at the 2d Parachute Corps, an infantry fighting strength of about 180 men" (KTB).

During breakfast, a discussion about the situation. The question was asked: "What do the people think who view the situation so completely differently?" Rommel replied, "One should not act according to wishful dreams, but soberly according to reality." Another question: "Do we actually have a constitution?" Speidel: "No, the old one has been sus-

217

pended; the new one does not yet exist. We are living under a system of despotism, in the crudest sense of the word." Rommel: "Sauckel has sent me his book on labor action. Very interesting. Next to him and above him again is Göring. It is common practice now that next to the old authority the party puts its new men. District magistrate, district party leader, etc."

The discussion then turned to the rule of mediocrity. Rommel: "The high leaders of the Hitler Youth were waiting to fill these new posts. They did not go to the front but made incredible demands." Tempelhoff related that once he had been liaison to the Hitler Youth regional leadership. The head man had received him in a huge hall, at least as large as Mussolini's, decorated with large oil paintings and beautiful rugs.

During the morning a major from OKW arrived, who had spent a few days on the front and had witnessed the battle for Caen. He was fully convinced that with the existing ratio of forces and materiel nothing could have been done. The bombing attacks had actually not caused too many losses, but had destroyed all roads through the town and delayed the advance of the tanks by half a day. Then two hours of barrage fire had completely smashed part of the front. All guns of an 88mm battery, which had destroyed every approaching tank, were put out of action. Resistance could just not continue where there was nothing to resist with. A special difficulty was that the upper and middle commanders down to some regimental commanders had recognized the situation and could no longer inspire their men's confidence. (Interesting that this coolheaded man from the general staff considered such values!)

The young officers and the men in the front lines did not yet view the situation in this way. This, however, could change any day now. He was of the opinion that only a political solution was still feasible and stated that he would so express himself ("I wonder!" [PAV]). I told him that this was the view one met everywhere because everyone, wholly independent of the others, reflected on the situation in about the same way. Even the troops were already beginning to ask: "How can we still win the war?"

The major was first to confer with Speidel, then Kluge, and finally return to OKW. I asked Rommel when we could expect Jodl's visit. Rommel replied that "they have forbidden me to ask anybody for a visit; Kluge will have to do this." Kluge was expected for a meeting in the evening.

At noon we talked about the role of organization in modern warfare. The tactical Luftwaffe has to be an organic part of the army, otherwise one cannot operate.

The divisions are bleeding white. So far our losses have been 80,000 men, almost 2,000 of them officers. A withdrawal on the left flank had now been permitted from the top leadership, which caused amazement, since until now the word had always been: "Hold on, hold on."

At 1400 I drove to Paris in a small half-open car. We saw several German fighter planes; even on the front they were a bit more apparent. The operations officer of Navy Group West informed me about the newly used small assault craft and their prospects. It became evident that despite some fine results, they were only weapons of opportunity. Then I read the war diary from Cherbourg, which unfortunately contained almost exclusively radio messages and reports and neither situation reports nor their analyses. At the command quarters of Security Area West I met with Homeyer. The arrival of fully loaded barges went well, but all berths were blocked because the unloading was still too slow. General Habicht of the navy fortress engineers had gone there to help. I read the battle reports of three security craft which had been under repair in a shipyard below Caen. During the first day of the Invasion, they had gotten to the bridge over the Orne near Benouville, but turned back when they found that it was already in British possession. This bridge was of the utmost importance for the supplies to the British bridgehead east of the Orne which had no road connections with the landing beaches. Fully committed, our boats could have destroyed the bridge but they had not been informed of the situation. Later attempts to reach the bridge failed, as did a try by an assault task force consisting of crew members and engineers to blow the bridge up. The navy men reached the bridge unnoticed. Those who carried the explosives, however, had lost contact. All together, a classical example of insufficient teamwork between the different branches of the Wehrmacht.

Under some antiaircraft fire I returned to La Roche-Guyon where the commander in chief was standing in the courtyard. Kluge had just left. I reported to Rommel on the assault craft. I then talked with Tempelhoff, who was pleased with the result of Kluge's visit and remarked that the two field marshals now agreed on the important points.

July 13. Quiet on the British front but deployments continue. Heavy attacks and ground gains by the Americans near and west of Saint-Lô (KTB, abbreviated).

At breakfast Rommel once more rejected the fried egg and ate only bread with little butter and some jam. News from the eastern front remained unpleasant. We discussed that Army Group G had released so many men that it had only a few left. Rommel remarked: "Poor people have no problems." On the eastern front, they had resumed the practice of forming battalions with soldiers returning from furlough and sending them into battle. The answer to my question as to where these men would get heavy weapons was: "They will just have to do without them." The result was an enormous loss of men, since the troops were not coordinated and, moreover, poorly equipped. Rommel related how a year ago they had proudly told him at OKW how pleased they were that the eastern front no longer received replacements. There they would have to help themselves with their own means, but for that a lot of new divisions were set up. Talking about the chain of command from above which meddled into the smallest details, the commander in chief remarked that he at times felt like a small civil servant and not like an army commander. "A pity that such a man is forced by such reasons to maneuver so carefully that he cannot fully realize his abilities" (PAV). After Rommel had left, Freiberg told me that the health of many officers, primarily those in the middle command echelons, could no longer hold out.

At 1000 a boatswain's mate came, in charge of a supply barge containing 200 tons of ammunition which he had docked a bit below La Roche-Guyon. His whole crew consisted of himself, a machinist, and a French pilot—a bit scanty. He moved almost exclusively at night and at dusk while keeping as close as possible to the trees on the riverbank. During daylight he waited, well camouflaged. It was a pleasure to see how well he had understood his assignment and how he tackled the difficulties by himself. He had come to me to ask my help in getting lubricating oil. His barge had not been used for a whole year and, because of a block in the oil lines, had suffered at first several oil fires. This had exhausted his oil reserves. We helped him and in addition gave him Michelin maps (originally intended for automobiles but of such good quality that they could also be used for river navigation), something to smoke, and something to read.

During dinner Tempelhoff talked about his visit to the front east of Caen. During little air and artillery activity, he had been able to go as far as the Colombelles factory. A new and very unpleasant weapon was the thermite bomb or something similar, containers launched by a mortar which radiated intense heat with the objective of bringing the infantry out of their holes. The British were very sensitive to our tanks and ran immediately when they appeared. Moreover they only went forward with their own tanks. The breakthroughs had been made possible by the incredibly strong artillery which crushed everything in its path. The British tanks withdrew as soon as they were fired on.

After dinner I showed the commander sketches of bombardment positions and reported on assault craft and U-boats. I could not report much that was pleasant, since little was available and the U-boats were not being used in the manner that had originally been promised. Navy Group West was not happy about this either and especially regretted that no reinforcements whatsoever came via the North Sea. Rommel would like to have known what the naval Supreme Commander (Dönitz) thought about the situation; however, his views were not known to me.

An evening walk up the hill followed the discussion.

With Kluge, matters now went very well. Taking a stand right from the start had been effective. When Kluge had first come to France his assignments had been completely different, but now he had informed himself about the true situation in Normandy. Those at the high command had been of the opinion that Rommel and Rundstedt were constantly at each other's throats and that Rommel did not obey.

Rommel then discussed the fact that General Bamler (who, while a prisoner of the Russians, had joined the National Committee) had remarked on Russian radio that we no longer had any command to speak of since everything was ordered from above. Bamler had apparently been very frank, which did not help us at all and only made our existence more difficult.

Rommel again described himself as merely an administrator. Before making a decision he now always inquired first at the OKW, so that later on they could not put the blame on him as they usually tried to do. "It is imperative that in this situation OKW will be held to its responsibility. These people on top are completely coldhearted." Then he said approximately the following: "The difficulty of the situation is that we have to offer the utmost resistance but, on the other hand, we are convinced that it is more important to prevent the invasion of the Russians than that of the British and Americans. Our misfortune has always been in overestimating our capabilities. A front like that in Russia requires large reserves and soberly planned operations." Last year at Führer Headquarters he had already had the impression that success could not be achieved with that kind of leadership.

The Field Marshal suffered greatly under the pressure that burdened all of us. Repeatedly he asked: "How will things look four weeks from now? Will the worst be over?" He was convinced that the front could not hold much longer and that a political decision had to come. On July 14, he planned to report this to those on top (PAV). I said that back in 1918 and at Scapa Flow nobody had believed that things would improve again. We agreed that one could be satisfied with very little, if only one was together with one's family. He thought the primary task would be secure food for all and build housing. One would have to attempt to continue social measures for the workers despite the country's poverty. Doctor Ley was, of course, a god in the workers' opinions. But well-trained managers should be able to accomplish the same. Of utmost importance would be to prevent a rift among the people. Unfortunately such a split did already show due to a leaning towards the Anglo-Americans or towards the Russians. One would have to try to exploit the natural differences between the Allies.

It would be a great service if Hitler on his own volition would do what the situation demanded. But according to all his statements, this was unlikely. Yet, what would follow after the fight for the last house? Great difficulties could be expected from the *Sicherheitsdienst*, the SS, and the Party functionaries. One would have to be watchful. The victors would probably want to have many people extradited. This could not be prevented in those cases where real guilt existed. In all events, Germany had not extradited the so-called "war criminals" after 1918. It demonstrated what could be achieved even in a situation of apparent powerlessness. The young SS men would have to be transferred to other Wehrmacht units as quickly as possible.

Rommel wondered what measures his letter would bring. He remarked that he did not care if they dismissed or killed him. Then, he added, that they would not do it. The military leaders in responsible positions should express their opinions openly. Unfortunately those around Hitler had not done so.

Once again he spoke out strongly against the commission investigating the fall of Cherbourg. In Berchtesgaden he had confronted Keitel with the matter. Rundstedt had been present and had nodded in agreement. Rommel had asserted that such measures served no purpose, made the troops insecure, and shocked those who on their own initiative would make decisions and achieve something. The end result would be that everybody just sat around and waited for the orders from above. Schlieben had done well.

July 14. French national holiday.

On the British front, artillery and reconnaissance activity only. On the American front, no unified attack, severe fighting for the hills east and northeast of Saint-Lô. Our own disengagement movement along the Sèvres–Lessay line has been successful without much pressure from the enemy (KTB, abbreviated).

Montgomery had commented favorably on the resistance of the German forces and, cautiously, on the end of the war. Rommel remarked: "We never get such praise from our high command." He drove to the 2d Parachute Rifle Corps where he met Lieutenant General (SS) Hausser, and was back at La Roche-Guyon around 2300.

The river transport on the Seine functioned well and affected the supplies for the right flank favorably, despite slow unloading and the insufficient communications. In the afternoon I drove a bit upstream to the Protvillez lock. It was guarded by naval personnel and two light antiaircraft guns stood ready for action; the position for a third one under construction. Against a large attack this was, of course, not enough protection. Obviously pleased, the men told me that many loaded barges had passed the lock during the last few days.

Moving a heavy railroad battery up to the front had taken four weeks! At the front the units were greatly mixed up. They suffered heavy casualties and their bearing was varied. In the evening I was at Speidel's and read the short report that would be sent to the OKW. It ended with the sentence: "I ask you to draw the political conclusions." But after some consideration the word "political" was deleted.

July 15. All quiet on the British front. The American grand-scale attack for the capture of Saint-Lô has essentially been repulsed, one area of penetration. The fighting is still in full force (KTB).

At noon we talked about secrecy. Details concerning Rommel and some of his close associates had found their way into the enemy press, as had descriptions of tapestries and rugs which the Organisation Todt had wanted to send the Field Marshal for his command post. That Rommel had rejected the offer was, of course, not mentioned. Apparently an unpublished propaganda (information) unit report had contained the information and had gotten into the wrong hands. The enemy also knew about some commanders and about other details. Some of it seemed to come from tapped telephone conversation. Some cynics remarked that the enemy would not attack our staff quarters since it was more profitable to listen in on our telephone calls. I did not hide my opinion that the army used the telephone too much which, of course, did not change entrenched habits.

In the enemy's account, one of our younger officers had been mentioned in a rather unflattering way. For a while we referred to him as *Depp Nr.1* (Simpleton No. 1) which, however, did not disturb him in the least. The Luftwaffe liaison officer could only answer the question about the status of the promised 1,500 fighter planes by saying that the Luftwaffe could just balance its losses. Therefore we would have to make do with the 500 missions a day. Nevertheless one occasionally saw some German planes in the air.

At 1530 Rommel and I left for the sector east and south of Caen. He believed the trip important since he expected a large-scale British attack with a general thrust to the south in that area around July 17 or 18, and wanted to discuss the situation with the commanders beforehand. In an assault boat we crossed the Seine and using side roads drove in a large open car with good road-handling via Vernon and Louviers to Pont-Audemer. Here Rommel remembered that in this vicinity a partisan area existed reaching to the west where several cars had already been destroyed.

Therefore we drove farther south via Cormeilles–Blangy through an especially pretty park-like countryside with small castles and manor houses to Dozulé to the command post of the 346th Infantry Division where the conference took place in a garden. The troops were now very well camouflaged everywhere. Our visit surprised them a bit, but they felt quite confident about the situation. The division reported a shortage of 800 men, which was bearable. With anger, they reported the heavy traffic west of Riva Bella where daily approximately 1,000 trucks were unloaded. Almost no fire was directed into this sector. They asked if a navy officer could not be provided for observation. They were surprised to hear that one was already there. The complete artillery including the mortars were now unified under the command of the panzer corps artillery commander and only fired against points of concentration according to the principle: "If the enemy pounds on our troops, our artillery will have to do likewise." Supplies of certain arms and especially of ammunition were urgently needed.

We continued on side roads and partly on main roads to Argonzes to the command post of the 16th Luftwaffe Field Division. The total population was apparently still living there. In the village we saw such idyllic scenes as residents working in their gardens and soldiers walking with girls and a light horse-drawn wagon filled with cheerful young soldiers. All this was underlined by the distant rumble of the artillery and occasional antiaircraft fire nearby.

The operations officer was well informed and reported very clearly until the commanding officer arrived. The division had been caught north of Caen during reorganization; had received a carpet bombing of 2,500 tons, which caused heavy damage and prevented the reserves from getting through. All antitank guns were out of action, the officer casualties were heavy; otherwise only 800 men were lost. In plain language, the division had not been equal to the strain since, as a Luftwaffe field division, it had had no combat experience and had temporarily disintegrated to a considerable degree. It had, however, regrouped south of Caen. It was characteristic that the division was better equipped for antitank defense than the "normal" 346th Infantry Division, that is with twenty-five antitank rocket launchers for each battalion, while the 346th Infantry Division had only six. During the last days they had pushed back the British near Colombelles with the aid of some Tiger tanks.

Our drive continued to the 21st Panzer Division. The staff was sitting in tents in an orchard, a few hundred meters distant from a village. The residents were enjoying a quiet Saturday afternoon; a father cut his young son's hair with concentrated care.

General Feuchtinger reported first on the tactical arrangement and supply situation of his division. It was pleasant to hear that for once somebody was sufficiently equipped with ammunition. Rommel then discussed with him his action on invasion day. According to Rommel's view, the division had been placed back too far, which had been contrary to his orders. The division commander stated that Panzer Group West had ordered this. Rommel countered with the statement that he had ordered the division into the Caen sector in order to defend the area against an airborne enemy and in order to eliminate this enemy at once. Feuchtinger cited an order from April that had assigned him to an area farther back. Obviously this had been a first general directive. But, during his many visits, the Field Marshal had consistently explained his principal tenets and had told Feuchtinger that he would have to move up front. Feuchtinger admitted that this would have made more sense and would also have been more expedient. The dispute between Rommel and Feuchtinger was conducted completely objectively and with almost scientific detachment.

It was news to me that the 21st Panzer Division at first was to attack and clean up east of the Orne, but then was ordered by 84th Army Corps to the west bank, which cost half a day. Towards evening 300 to 400 enemy gliders carrying supplies had landed on each bank of the river. The division had destroyed a lot of them, but not enough.

We were each given a glass of apple juice and then inspected the captured Sherman tank with its very long 7.62cm gun. Beside it stood a captured antitank gun of the same caliber, a nice and simple gun. Antitank guns with conical barrels were now in existence, an interesting novelty. We received copies of a fallen British reserve officer's diary, written for his wife with touching tenderness. The propaganda company did not get a copy.

In the meantime it was too late to drive to 86th Corps. Returning quickly to La Roche-Guyon via Saint-Pierre-sur-Dives we sighted several enemy airplanes, as we had during the morning, mostly rather distant but once almost directly overhead. We did not stop the car, only reduced the speed a bit. The drive continued via Conches through which the Field Marshal had passed several times lately. He was therefore known to the local citizens, which seemed a bit careless.

Rommel was in a good mood and told wonderful stories from his school years. Once his whole class had played hooky, skipping the afternoon's religious lessons in order to go to the fair. Afterwards for some mysterious reason nothing happened to the Catholics while the Protestants were to be locked up for two hours in the school's detention room. Rommel was afraid to tell his father, the school's principal. After lengthy negotiation, the boys achieved that as compensation for the Catholics' lack of punishment the sentence of detention was changed into staying after class for an equal amount of time. They were to serve the two hours on Saturday afternoon under the caretaker's supervision. The boys then negotiated with the caretaker on the premise that fifteen minutes in the detention room equaled two hours of staying after class. A beer-money collection to which each boy contributed fifty pfennigs helped strengthen the argument. The caretaker accepted it. They served the fifteen minutes immediately after class on Saturday afternoon, inspecting the school's detention room. Nobody found out about the episode.

Then the discussion became more serious. It dealt with life, how it would be in the event of a sudden peace or armistice and the absurdity of continuing an aimless war. Rommel once more talked about the laborers and the farmers whose standards of living should not suffer. Then he went on and remarked that it would be better to continue as a Western dominion instead of letting Germany be destroyed completely. He then talked about the still existing strength of our political position between our adversaries. Over and over he put the question: "When will a decision come?"

A lot of trucks were on the road. Some lay burned-out on the roadside. On the whole, however, the supply transport functioned well. We arrived at La Roche-Guyon around 2200 with the fall of darkness and ate quickly.

July 16. Little combat activity on the British front. Large-scale attack to be expected; a penetration cannot be prevented, but our own forces are placed in echelons which should prevent the breakthrough. Local combat on the American front (KTB, abbreviated).

During the night we had an air alert because of an air attack in the vicinity; I did not hear a sound. At breakfast the first topic discussed was the firing of ship artillery at land targets, which had already made a disagreeable impression on the troops fired upon at the Black Sea. The people on land quite understandably did not care if they were shelled by an old or by a modern ship. Particularly at the Black Sea it would have been especially promising to concentrate the Luftwaffe forces against the Russian fleet with the aim of completely eliminating it. The Luftwaffe's representative countered with the argument that the infantry had often not taken full advantage of the Luftwaffe's bombing attacks. This incensed Rommel, who said that the aviators had always grossly overrated the effects of their bombs. The Stukas achieved nothing whatsoever. The figures in question were so negligible that the actual effect on the objective had been ridiculous. Kesselring had demanded of him that he storm Bir Hacheim with panzers after it had been bombed. He, Rommel, had rejected this demand due to the many mines present and had done it with the infantry alone. On other occasions the Luftwaffe had bombed something without regard to other weapons. A realistic unified command organization of the Wehrmacht was necessary and this applied to the army quartermaster too. I interjected that in order for the army quartermaster to know what the other branches of the service needed, the quartermaster staffs would have to be trained to serve with an overall armed forces view. Rommel remarked that this also applied to military hospitals and that autonomous navy hospitals were superfluous. I disagreed and told of my own experience with hospitals in the rear area, where although the medical care was good the psychological attention left much to be desired. I also pointed out that there were illnesses common to ships' crews just as there were typical flyers' sicknesses. It was better for the different branches of the service to have their own hospitals in addition to centralized medical depots.*

Rommel went to watch the unloadings; then he visited Panzer Group West and the 86th Army Corps. This was the first time after the Invasion that he drove through the heavily damaged Lisieux.

An officer from the general of the engineers came during the morning to inquire about the supply of cement. It turned out that quite a lot was available in the vicinity a little north of Mantes, but that there were no trucks for the transport. And we had so many barges! We could have transported the cement to its destination weeks and months ago.

Towards evening Speidel invited me to his place to listen to a Brahms concert on the radio. When Rommel returned he heard the final movement. He told about difficulties with the 2d SS Panzer Corps' command, which lacked calm and perspective. On the whole the SS was quite differently trained and at times did not follow orders given by army officers, which resulted in constant friction. At the unloading stations, work still proceeded too slowly. Over 3,000 tons had, however, already been unloaded, including 800 tons of fuel. Fuel became the point of concentration. The number of casualties had now reached 100,000 for which only 6,000 replacements had arrived. In Germany, fifteen blocking divisions were in the process of being formed; ensigns fresh from cadet school were used as platoon and company commanders. Lattmann had just finished reading the sentence: "A government which faces ruin must cover up."

July 17. Isolated attacks at different places; grand-scale attack at Saint-Lô. During the previous night, fog in the Bay of the Seine had prevented the motor torpedo boats from attacking, while the Luftwaffe could attack only during the first half of the night.

During breakfast, the Field Marshal related that Keitel had boasted of having demotorized a part of the army after the winter of 1941–42. We now suffered the consequences of such action, since divisions using horse-carriages had no chance against a fully motorized enemy. Moreover the divisions here were only partly mobile.

During the morning, Seventh Army lodged a complaint about the withdrawal from Saint-Malo of crews from sunken vehicles and because some

---

*The Bundeswehr had Bundeswehr hospitals and Bundeswehr medical depots.

navy offices had apparently been pulled out of Saint-Nazaire. It turned out that the information had not been verified and that the navy liaison officer at the army command had not been consulted. Moreover he seemed to have been shelved for good.

A barge with 200 tons of food supplies destined for Rouen had been unloaded by mistake at one of the unloading stations. Later the barge was reloaded. No wonder that things there did not progress as they could and should. The navy liaison officer telephoned in utter despair.

The Field Marshal drove via Falaise to the 277th and 276th Infantry Divisions and found that they had not been sufficiently supported by the 2d SS Panzer Corps behind them, since it had been too far back. Subsequently he visited the 1st SS Panzer Corps command post where he received news of an enemy attack at Saint-Lô. This caused him to quickly return to headquarters. The sky was completely clear, and the enemy's aircraft very active. The driver of Rommel's car used secondary roads until Livarot and entered the main road before Vimoutiers. It was there that two low-flying planes caught the car and started to attack.

The attempt to get around the next curve at high speed failed. A 20mm bullet hit the driver, Daniel, in the left shoulder, causing him to lose control of the car which skidded and came to a halt across the road. Rommel was thrown out of the car and lay unconscious. Captain Lang who sat in the right rear of the car escaped unscathed. Major Neuhaus, sitting behind the driver, received a 20mm hit on his pistol holster, escaping with contusions to the lower part of his body.

Rommel was taken to the Luftwaffe hospital at Bernay. At headquarters Speidel called us together and informed us of the accident. The diagnosis came in the evening: a fracture of the base of the skull, three additional fractures of the skull, splinters in the face, disabled for a long time. Major (Army) Behr and Dr. Scheunig, our physician, drove to Bernay immediately.

July 18. Grand-scale attacks near Caen and Saint-Lô. The 12th SS Panzer Division had been moved to the Lisieux area because OKW feared a landing between the Orne and the Seine. The division was now called back to Caen with the corresponding loss of time and fuel. Behr returned and reported that the Field Marshal had recognized and greeted him at once, but that he was very weak. Despite his condition he wanted to be returned to headquarters, but had to lie in bed for at least three weeks. Not even an operation could save the life of the driver, Daniel.

July 19. The British grand-scale attack near Caen has been stopped. A counterthrust of the 1st SS Panzer Division at dawn destroyed many British tanks. Severe fighting with the Americans immediately in front of Saint-Lô.

Early in the morning I drove to Navy Group West where I talked with the chief of staff. The motor torpedo boats no longer get through; moreover, at night, traffic no longer moved. The one-man torpedoes had shown fine early results. For unknown reasons, Navy High Command had cancelled their next commitment of the torpedoes. Even equipped with snorkels, the U-boats had only limited prospects for success. I read the report of a U-boat captain who unintentionally had gotten into Spithead roadstead but was able to return. Unfortunately he did not sight a worthwhile target. A completely incredible venture!

At the command quarters of Security Area West I learned that the navy had built twenty Seine ferries at small shipyards. I briefly took a look at an exhibition of navy pictures and returned to La Roche-Guyon, because in the evening Speidel wanted to take me to Bernay to see Rommel. Unfortunately this visit had to be cancelled since Field Marshal von Kluge had decided to move to La Roche-Guyon at that time. He had rejected Rommel's replacement and since he could not find a suitable general decided to command Army Group B himself.

Brisk air activity; immediately after dinner bombs fell on Mantes and the earth shook. When a large low-flying bomber formation approached our headquarters we preferred to go downstairs and seek shelter.

Homeyer came; he had moored two boats in the vicinity and had come to tow off three barges that had run aground. Two of them were already free, the third one had gotten into a side arm of the river because some friendly Frenchmen had changed the traffic signs. In addition, the water level had fallen because a weir was no longer quite watertight after bombs had fallen nearby.

Homeyer got something to eat and was equipped with some bottles of wine for his men and himself. I drove with him to his mooring place and then on his boat to the lock at Mericourt. It was a quiet, warm evening; along the river the countryside was peaceful and lovely. We went alongside one of the recently freed barges. The navy crew, clad in field gray, had to take the unloaded fuel barrels back on board, not an easy thing to do without the aid of lift apparatus. But they managed.

Already 10,000 tons of materiel for the invasion front had been passed through the lock at Mericourt. On the other side of the river, Hatzinger and a driver appeared with one of our cars, driving through a meadow close to the lock. On the way back the car soon got stuck in the deep tire furrows. A young Frenchman and his girl watched with sympathy our attempts to get the car clear. The young man finally put his girl down on the grass and although he was wearing a good Sunday suit helped us in a forceful and friendly manner. But even that did not bring any success. Finally Hatzinger and I left the driver and the car and started to walk home after distributing our last cigarettes between him and the Frenchman. After walking for several kilometers the car picked us up. With the help of the Frenchman and an automobile jack, the driver had been able to get it clear. We had a flat tire later which we repaired while masses of planes (our own) droned overhead.

July 20. At Caen the front is quiet once more. The Americans have entered Saint-Lô. Field Marshal von Kluge drove to the front to confer with the commanders in chief and the corps commanders. Shortly before lunch Speidel called together our usual group of luncheon participants and told us, a bit embarrassed, that the new commander in chief wanted to have only the chief of staff, the operations officer, and the aides present at his meals. He, Speidel, had proposed the participation of the senior officers as deputies for the generals; however, this had been rejected in principle and would only occur from time to time. From now on we would have to eat with the younger officers at the officers' club in the village. During those times when the new commander in chief would not be here, he, Speidel, would eat with us, if we didn't mind. I replied that we would think it over, which made everybody laugh and ended this matter so unpleasant for Speidel.

By chance I found out that the funeral for driver Daniel was to take place that afternoon. I quickly changed and arrived just in time. Daniel had been a calm and pleasant man and a good driver, valued by all of us. A Catholic priest, Colonel Freiberg, and Major Jamin spoke with great warmth and affection. From the cemetery, the village Bennecourt and the valley of the Seine looked so peaceful and reassuring.

The director of the Navy Bureau of Personnel called me from the Navy High Command near Eberswalde to inform me that I was about to be transferred to the Navy High Command. He did not mention the day's events.

After my return I was called to the river where a barge was sinking. At least I was able to help the head of the group who kept it afloat with my car. The boat on which I had traveled the day before had bent its shaft on stones in the river.

The first dinner in exile was very funny. Naturally the younger gentlemen did not hold back with their mockery and we tried to defend ourselves as well as we could. Afterwards when I was sitting in my room reading, Speidel dropped in and in a few words told me of the attempt on Hitler's life, under the impression that it had been successful. Of the events in Paris and La Roche-Guyon nothing became known to me on that evening—not that at Paris General von Stülpnagel, the military commander, had had the whole *Sicherheitsdienst* arrested nor that at La Roche-Guyon Speidel and Stülpnagel unsuccessfully tried to persuade Field Marshal von Kluge into the rebellion. After the attempt on Hitler's life had failed, Kluge saw no way for success. He ordered the release of the *Sicherheitsdienst* and replaced Stülpnagel with Blumentritt.

I heard Hitler's 0100 speech by chance in the briefing room. It partly explained the situation to me. During the following days the events, the connections, and the consequences became more lucid, but only much later did I get a clear picture of the situation. In a purely theoretical way Rommel had discussed much with me, but he had only cautiously hinted at his concrete plans.

In our talks we had fully agreed that to end the war a political solution was imperative and that with Hitler in power this was unthinkable. But I must say quite openly that my ideas had not progressed to tyrannicide, despite the obvious historical examples. For most of us, our insight into the horror of the time was not yet deep enough to draw the ultimate conclusions.

In my opinion, Rommel was the only man in Germany strong enough to bring about a change in the situation, even after the revelation that Hitler was still alive. Rommel alone had the name, the energy, and the political intuition which together were necessary to assert himself against the demon Hitler. I believe that he would have certainly mastered the situation in the west and probably in the Reich if on July 20 he had been able to act as commander in chief of Army Group B. I think it possible that the offer of an armistice proposal to the Allies as planned by him would have been accepted despite the request for unconditional surrender declared by Roosevelt in 1943. The moment in time for an armistice was favorable after the heavy British losses at Caen, where the unsuccessful breakthrough attempt had cost as many British lives as they had estimated it would cost them to get to Berlin.

Proof can be given neither to one or the other side. It is certain, however, that the 20mm shell which fatally injured Rommel's driver, Daniel, greatly influenced the course of the war and the fate of Europe.

July 21. Under the circumstances, Rommel's condition was satisfactory. In Bernay, however, he heard too much of the noises of the front-bound traffic and became restless, for the situation at the front occupied his thoughts all the time. An early transfer was desirable.

July 22. Shortly after 0900 in hazy weather and under a low cloud cover Speidel drove with me on the direct road to Bernay. Fortunately the transport columns took welcome advantage of the weather. Many refugees were on the road.

When we entered Rommel's room, in spite of his physician's orders, he sat up at once to show us how well he was. His left eye was still shut, his face cut up from the crash. He confessed that he had gotten up during the first nights and that this morning he had tried to shave himself—all things which he had been forbidden to do. At a place so closely located to the front and as busy as Bernay, it seemed impossible for a man as headstrong as Rommel to get the medically ordered required rest. The situation on the front worried him greatly. He had not been told everything, but it was inevitable that he had fitted the pieces together. We appealed to him to be sensible, but were not convinced that it would be effective. We told him emphatically that above all he had to take care of himself, not for the war, since it was lost, but for the postwar reconstruction.

Then we drove on to Panzer Group West whose well-camouflaged command post we reached on sinuous roads. We found only Gause, who treated us to fried eggs and brandy. The situation was not discussed much since it was well-known and could not be changed.

Continuing our trip we met General Eberbach, who impressively described the fierceness of the fighting. During the night the infantry had bypassed one of the villages lost the previous day and recaptured it from the north.

Our next stop was Sepp Dietrich's staff quarters, which we found after some difficulty. He also treated us to fried eggs and brandy. General Bittrich, the commanding general of the 2d Panzer Corps, dropped in. Both Bittrich and Dietrich reviled, in the strongest language, the inept leadership and the interference from those on top. They believed that the breakdown of many things in Germany was due to sabotage. We subsequently drove to the chief of staff and the operations officer, who sat in a well-camouflaged command wagon nearby. Everybody was interested in Rommel's condition. This was clearly not a matter of politeness but of genuine concern.

On our return trip we drove in front of firing batteries and later through a completely destroyed Lisieux. We passed through Louviers where, in an almost open area, we met the tanks and assault guns of the 116th Panzer Division, which only now had been moved up from the Somme.

At 1900 we were back at La Roche-Guyon and at 1930 our three generals and I were invited to dinner with Field Marshal von Kluge, together with General Oberg, commander of the SS and of the police in France. I happened to sit to Kluge's left, who impressed me as agile, intelligent and stimulating, and who conversed with me very amicably. Sure enough he asked me at once why the navy deployed the coastal artillery forward. He smiled when I defended it with the well-known reasons of direct aiming, unhampered observation, and better hits, and remarked that I was just like the rest of the navy.

That Oberg had been arrested on July 20 by General von Stülpnagel I heard only afterwards, which perhaps was no handicap. The tension of the last few days was not noticeable; many innocuous stories were told. Dinner was simple and brief so that the staff members could make the second show of the cave movies at 2130. The picture was harmless and silly, and made the whole house laugh—a necessary diversion.

July 23 (Sunday). Generally quiet on the front. Early, at 0500, an ambulance moved the Field Marshal from Bernay to the hospital at Le Vésinet east of Saint-Germain on the right bank of the Seine. The drive took three and a half hours. Shortly after 0900 he asked when I would arrive for a visit. However, I did not go before the early afternoon because Rommel had to undergo a thorough examination. First I spoke with Professor Esch, the chief physician from the University of Leipzig. The doctor's prognosis was very satisfactory, thanks to Rommel's tough nature. But the move had tired him somewhat. It was my job to divert his thoughts a bit and unobtrusively to calm him down. We talked for awhile and then I read to him from the book *Wochenende auf Schloss Denbeck* (Weekend at Denbeck Castle), the most appropriate book I had been able to find. It did not interest him greatly, but had a soothing effect on him. Later he spoke about the situation and his urgent wish to get out of the hospital soon to talk with Hitler personally. I remained for over an hour and had the impression that it had been quite good for him.

During dinner there was, of course, a lively debate about the latest events and general indignation about Dr. Ley's speech against the officer corps. It became known that on his way to Führer Headquarters, Stülpnagel had unsuccessfully attempted suicide. The order came to salute in the German manner (Hitler salute). Rieve called and asked if he could see me. We arranged a meeting for the following morning.

July 24. On secondary roads which in places were very pretty, I drove in a Citroen, with a mediocre driver and much smell of gasoline, to Rouen. Along the way I inspected ferry landings and unloading stations. In Rouen the Hitler salute was already being used. The talk with Rieve led to no essentially new results, but was pleasant for both of us. He kept in good touch with General Kuntzen.

After an early lunch I returned and took along a general staff administrative officer on his way via Paris to Saint-Malo. Back in 1938 the two of us had attended a gymnastics course for senior gentlemen. I continued to drive through to Le Vésinet and came just at the right time since, after a mediocre night, the Field Marshal had slept a bit longer. His medical treatment had just ended. I read him the last part of *Schloss Denbeck*; later we talked about the situation and other things. He endeavored to get away as soon as possible but gradually convinced himself that it could not be as fast as he wished. He saw the solution only in peace with the Western Allies, to make it possible to defend ourselves with full strength against the other side, i.e., the Russians.

On leaving I spoke with his nurse, an older lady who made an excellent impression on me. She was touched by her famous patient's modesty.

July 25. The start of the grand-scale attack by the Americans to break out of the beachhead. From its right flank, Seventh Army released the 2d Panzer Division and, together with 116th Panzer Division, moved them to the sector south of Caen where Army Group B expected the next attack to take place. The sector vacated by the 2d Panzer Division was filled by the 326th Infantry Division, coming from the Pas de Calais without major combat experience.

I briefly went to see Speidel and then tried to find something suitable for reading to Rommel. Unfortunately no German edition of a Hornblower story could be found. The graphic description of professional and human problems would have pleased the Field Marshal. Finally I took *Tunnel* by Kellermann, and some other books. Rommel felt much better; he was more lively than during the preceding days. He recounted in detail how he had received his *Pour la Mérite* only after lodging a complaint.

Yet with his company he had stormed Monte Matajur, for which feat the decoration had been offered, and in addition had taken prisoner a whole Italian division. The starting point for our discussion was the bond commanding officers had with their troops. During the First World War the commanders of battalions and regiments were usually in the rear area suffering few casualties, which the lieutenants took a little amiss. This situation was better in the navy since everybody, including the fleet commander in chief, had to be on shipboard.

Rommel then briefly reflected on the Russian campaign, its failures that had caused the present situation, and about Stülpnagel. I could not tell him anything he did not already know. Again he stated that he wanted to speak to Hitler personally to express his opinion (peace in the West), because somebody had to tell him. Although he had always sent his reports directly to the OKW, he had never known if they had been passed on to Hitler. After discussion of some personal matters we talked once more about a commander's bond with his troops and educating children to independence. Just when I was about to read to Rommel, the physician came for his visit. Afterwards I spoke with him. He was satisfied; but it was doubtful if the left eye would ever be normal again. Evidently Rommel was concerned about it.

On our return trip we took cover temporarily, since large formations of Lightnings were in the air. The target seemed to be Mantes because the railroad to that point was back in running order.

During dinner everybody inquired about Rommel's health. Soon the air alert sounded and a deep hum filled the air. Most of the officers went outside to watch the formations of planes passing overhead, the rest continued with their dinner. We all had become very indifferent.

At 2000 I went to see the castle's owner to convey Rommel's regards, and to inform him of Rommel's condition. I also encouraged him to remain at La Roche-Guyon.

A teletype message from Berlin informed me that I was to start my assignment at Berlin on August 1.

July 26. The major American attack developed its fullest power. Our tanks evidently stood too far distant from the infantry. Rommel had always insisted that they be placed in such a way that they could intervene immediately.

It was very hot and sultry. In the afternoon I went to visit Rommel, who had a headache and was restless. We talked about the situation; then he spoke about his family, and finally I read to him from *Tunnel*, the technical problems of which interested him.

Driving back we once more found ourselves under air battles, and waited under a tree for them to end. During dinner I was besieged by several men who had not been allowed to see Rommel. "Our group of dinner companions is pretty much disintegrating; it becomes very apparent what the Field Marshal, despite his quiet manner and occasional one-sidedness, had meant for it" (PAV).

July 27. A difficult situation had developed at Seventh Army and von Kluge drove there to investigate. Meise was transferred to fortify Königsberg. Rainy, then sunny once more. The expected low pressure zone pushed finally through; low cloud ceiling and poor visibility were highly welcomed. In the afternoon I drove with our doctor to Paris via the Autobahn.

At Navy Group West I found only the chief of staff present. Admiral Krancke had gone to the Navy High Command to get a better command organization. The orders for the small assault weapons came from the neighborhood of Lubeck; those for the U-boats from somewhere else. Navy Group West did not even receive the combat reports. Of nine U-boats which had entered the Bay of the Seine, six had apparently made it back. Navy Group West wanted to have control over at least the small assault weapons, since the splitting up of command made an effective leadership increasingly difficult. Furthermore, Navy Group West was much concerned about the 80,000 navy men stationed on the French west and south coasts and the harbor destruction, which in certain situations and areas were undesirable from a European point of view.

Then I visited the Field Marshal, who was very chipper. He seated himself at the side of his bed to eat his dessert and with good aim killed a fly with his slipper. He first talked about Africa and then spoke about Goebbels and finally about concentrations of artillery which the British and the Russians always formed. He had done the same at Caen, especially employing mortars and successfully so. Back in November 1942 he had proposed at Führer Headquarters to evacuate northern Africa, after Göring claimed all space on air transport for Stalingrad. Hitler's reply had been: "You propose just what in 1941–42 the generals proposed in Russia. They also wanted me to retreat to the German border. I did not allow it and was proven correct. Neither will I do it in Africa, because I have to consider the political consequences." Rommel clearly repeated that it would be better to concentrate and organize the available forces for the defense of the Italian islands, rather than to lose them in Africa. Hitler asked him how many men he still had left. "70,000," Rommel replied. "With how many did you start the offensive?" Rommel: "With 80,000–90,000." Hitler: "Well, then you haven't lost all that many." Rommel: "No, but almost all the weapons." Of his seventy 88mm anti-aircraft guns, the British had destroyed fifty at El Alamein alone. Hitler: "How many rifles do you lack?" Rommel: "15,000–20,000. The supply trains have none at all." Hitler: "It will be ordered that 6,000 rifles be sent over by plane at once." Rommel: "This won't do much good against the tanks." Hitler: "After all, in Russia they were able to hold." Rommel: "That was different, in Russia one can seek cover. In Africa, however, one is shot at from a great distance." Hitler: "How long can you hold out?" Rommel: "Only until the British attack." The discussion continued in this manner for a while. The final result was the order to hold on the spot.

During dinner we spoke about secrecy and agreed that in the navy it worked well; even in discussions, teletype conversations were unknown to some general staff officers. The matter of evacuation from the Channel Islands was discussed next. I requested the navy personnel office to prolong my stay for a few days at least until the beginning of August when Rommel would be transported back to Germany. They were ungracious; I spoke my mind, and then it was alright.

July 28. Seventh Army was apparently in a state of confusion. I reported to Field Marshal von Kluge on the evacuation of the divisions stationed on the Channel Islands. Without enemy disturbance it would take sixty hours for the men and an additional sixty hours for the equipment, some more time for the horses. In view of the enemy's air and sea superiority it was hopeless. Back in 1941 there had already been agreement that a considerable part of the forces, especially the tanks, would better have been placed at the base of the Cotentin Peninsula, and that the islands would become of value only after the completion of the airfields when the Luftwaffe would use them as operational bases.

While I still was with Kluge a call arrived from Seventh Army saying that it intended to transfer the fighting troops from the Cotentin Peninsula's west coast to the southeast. Kluge intervened with extreme severity, used strong and harsh language with Lieutenant General (SS) Hausser and attempted to change the decision to retreat into an effort to hold on the coast and fill the gap with the 116th Panzer Division.

In the afternoon I drove to Rommel for reading and discussion. Before I saw him, Professor Esch explained to me the very complicated multiple fracture and the healing process. While I read to Rommel, he once more killed a fly whereupon I reproached him. The physician had told him he should only move very slowly and carefully. Rommel laughed and said: "That's exactly what I did."

I took dinner at the Commanding Officers' Club together with General Ellfeldt, who was to take command of the 84th Army Corps, and Lieutenant Colonel von Gersdorf, the Seventh Army's future chief of the general staff. While saying goodby Kluge told them: "Be extremely tough." Kluge complained about Seventh Army's decision, which he had received a half a day too late.

"Kluge is a completely different type than Rommel, even more factual, crystal clear, personally just as courageous, but he lacks Rommel's warmth and respect for other humans" (PAV).

July 29. The situation seems a bit less tense. Drove with Speidel in the afternoon to Paris. Rommel was in a good mood. For close to one and a half hours he entertained me with stories of his "phantom division," the 7th Panzer Division, which he had taken command of in February of 1940 without being a tank expert. He intensified the training, since it did not satisfy his standards and changed several commanders. During the war game in preparation for the western campaign, he started crossing the Maas River on the second evening. General Hoth rejected this as impossible; however it did take place. When Rommel had moved most of his division to the enemy riverbank, Hoth ordered him to release basic elements to the neighboring division which was not nearly so far. That's when Kluge intervened, giving him a free hand for the breakthrough to Avesnes.

I didn't get to read to Rommel at all. On the drive back, the clouds hung low and it rained heavily.

July 30 (Sunday). Von Kluge was at the front. In the afternoon I drove to Rommel who once more was very chipper. He insisted that he leave the coming Thursday. A bit of a rift had developed between him and the doctor since he did not follow the latter's instructions. No simple case, for, with his restlessness, remaining at the hospital did not do much good either. By now the British had reported on his injuries, in several accounts, all of them distorted. His mental capacities were completely intact; the left eyelid moved a bit, an encouraging improvement.

I read to him from Colin Ross and from *Tunnel*. Then we again talked about the situation. For the first time he expressed the idea that despite everything he was glad things had happened as they had. I had reflected likewise, although I would have opted for a broken arm rather than a complicated skull fracture. In any case, the awkward situation—full responsibility without full freedom of action—was ended for him.

Shortly after 1800 I returned to La Roche-Guyon. The sky had cleared; we watched air combats, one plane being shot down, and several large bomber formations.

July 31. During the night the Americans had taken Avranches, which looked disagreeably like a breakthrough. Kluge was still at Seventh Army.

During the morning I spent some time with Speidel; at noon Assistant Government Secretary Michel and Speidel's brother-in-law shared our one-pot stew for lunch. They talked interestingly about German politics in France, which had suffered from a lack of any clear-cut objective and had not taken fullest advantage of the available possibilities. Even now many Frenchmen were convinced of an ultimate German victory; industry worked at sixty-five percent of peacetime capacity, exports to Germany had been larger in June than in May.

In the afternoon I drove to the hospital and arrived at the moment when Professor Esch together with a physician from the general staff were about to enter Rommel's room in order to persuade him to postpone the transfer to Germany. I warned them, but they knew better, with the result that within a few minutes he berated them strongly. He was a Field Marshal and knew precisely what he could endure; he would take full responsibility for himself. Then, however, he became more peaceful, and an agreement was reached setting the date for the move at Monday, August 7. Afterwards he told me that he still wanted the move to take place on Thursday, August 3, because of the developing situation. From a purely medical point of view, the long rest made sense, but, of course, Rommel did not take any rest. He paced about the room, sat upright for too long, put on his new uniform, got a handsome pair of boots out of the closet to show them to me and promptly put one of them on. Our discussion followed the usual pattern. I read to him from *Splissen und Knoten* (Splices and Knots). The navy stories amused him.

Subsequently I drove to the command quarters of Security Area West where I met Rieve, who wanted to talk about the situation. We were invited to dinner at which Kranzbühler was present too. The idea of an attempt to exploit the situation politically was partly rejected, but nobody came up with another solution. No complete agreement existed as to whether one should go with the west or with the east. Our men had a much better instinct in this regard. The drivers wondered in earnest why everybody did not go to the east while ending the war in the west.

Shortly after 2230 I was back at La Roche-Guyon and went to see Speidel to inform him of Rommel's condition. We then talked about Rommel's transfer to Germany, the situation, Assistant Government Secretary Michel, Europe, music, concerts, our parents—especially my father, the Russian naval war 1914–17, the not-always-uncomplicated Navy Group West, and ended our talk shortly after midnight.

August 1. The definition of a front no longer applied to the western sector. Armored enemy scout cars had broken through at several points and operated in the rear area. With Speidel, I read Kluge's comment to Rommel's letter of July 15. Kluge said approximately the following:

> I can report that until now the front has held due to the remarkable bravery of the troops and the sheer determination of those in command, especially in the lower echelons, although losing ground daily. Despite our greatest efforts, the moment is near when this overexerted front will break. And once the enemy is in the open country, an effective command will hardly be feasible in view of the limited mobility of our troops. As commander responsible for this front, I feel it my duty to point out these conclusions to you, my Führer, while there is still time.

I arrived with the firm determination to enforce the order to hold under all circumstances. I have, however, recognized that in view of the enemy's vast superiority, expecially in the air, this is impossible. My final words during the commanders' briefing south of Caen were: "We will hold, and when no auxiliary means can fundamentally improve our situation, we will die on the battlefield with dignity."

In the afternoon I drove to Rommel. He was still asleep since during the morning he had had a two-hour visit from a propaganda man. The doctor was glad that Speidel had succeeded in postponing the departure until the beginning of the following week. After the preceding split, this had been a diplomatic masterpiece. Rommel looked well, the blue marks around his eye and the swelling were almost gone, although his left eyebrow was still somewhat flattened. For the first time his pulse and blood pressure were much better, and he no longer had a temperature; all signs of a normal healing process.

I had brought along the 352d Infantry Division's combat report, describing the unfortunate marches of the reinforced 915th Grenadier Regiment (Battle Group Meyer). On June 6 the regiment had stood in reserve about twenty kilometers off the coast—much too far in the rear. The 84th Army Corps had first sent it to the west and then back to the east. Finally, towards evening, in a state of disrepair, it had met the enemy not far from its original point of departure.

We talked about the situation. Rommel could not understand Jodl. Due to the constant pressure, Warlimont was now to arrive here. Then I read some funny stories to him.

In La Roche-Guyon was Rieve, who had just come from a meeting at Navy Group West but could report nothing new about the situation. The latest wisdom remained resistance to the last man, which did not solve the problem of the nation's survival. If necessary, the navy group was to move, but not the staff of Security Area West, the admirals on the south coast and the Bay of Biscay.

Speidel was pretty exhausted, not surprising considering the activity and the burden. For relaxation, we played some table tennis and went for a walk in the park.

August 2. "The Americans already touring about in Brittany" (PAV). Speidel drove to a conference with Kluge, Sperrle and Krancke. In the afternoon I brought Rommel some reports on the airborne landings of June 6. His physical condition was good; he had reconciled himself to the later departure. We spoke about the usual subjects, then I read to him for a while.

Major Neuhaus, who, during Rommel's accident, had been seated behind the driver, came for a visit. Ten days after the accident it had been ascertained that the detonation of the 20mm shell on his pistol holster had caused a fracture of his pelvic bone.

August 3. Rommel's "auto accident" was officially made public. He was outraged that the strafer's part in the whole incident was not admitted. Evidently, with a Field Marshal this was not possible.

My departure for Berlin was fixed for August 5.

On August 4 the Americans enlarged their breakthrough and pressed en masse into France. Their advance could now only be delayed, but not stopped.

In the morning I said my farewells at Navy Group West and at the command quarters of Security Area West, and in the afternoon reported for the last time to Rommel at the hospital. He spoke with me very affectionately and gave me a copy of his official evaluation of my services. Field Marshal von Kluge was at the front. This enabled our old dining group to exchange our subdued farewells seated at our accustomed dining place, the oval table in the castle. The commander in chief returned unexpectedly early around 2100 and we departed so he could eat dinner. Soon, however, he had us collected again and acted as cordial and highly entertaining host.

On August 5 Hatzinger and I departed via Boulogne, Utrecht, Wilhelmshaven—all places where I had some business to attend to—for Berlin. At Berlin I was assigned for training to the Bureau of Warship Construction, so I could take charge of it on November 1. On August 8, Rommel was moved to his home at Herrlingen, near Ulm, on schedule. We remained in touch by letter.

The Allies had planned to break out of an enlarged beachhead along the line Cabourg–Domfront–Avranches twenty days after their landing. After the British got bogged down near Caen, the Americans achieved a successful breakthrough on the fifty-fifth day after the Invasion. If Hitler could not decide to make the politically correct decision and make peace, then, from a military point of view, it was best to fight a delaying action and to inflict as much damage as possible on the enemy in order to gain time for the formation of a new defensive line beyond the Seine and the Somme Rivers down to the Swiss border. This later happened with fewer forces along the German border in one continuous front longer than the one from the mouth of the Somme to the Swiss border.

Hitler, however, refused to see the handwriting on the wall and attempted, by an operation of the concentrated panzer forces hurled at Avranches, to cut through the American divisions' connections with their unloading stations on the coast. His attempt to reverse fate ended in the encirclement of the Germans at Falaise, in the loss of the bulk of the heavy equipment, and in large numbers of Germans being taken prisoner. Field Marshal von Kluge, who had done his utmost to avert complete catastrophe for the panzer army, committed suicide since, as an incidental accessory to the July 20 attempt on Hitler's life, he could be certain of the dictator's revenge.

The fighting power of the German army in France was broken, the remnants retreated to the east incurring more heavy casualties of men, weapons, and equipment along the way. That the enemy unexpectedly stopped at the German border instead of rushing without delay into the barely defended country was partly due to supply difficulties and partly

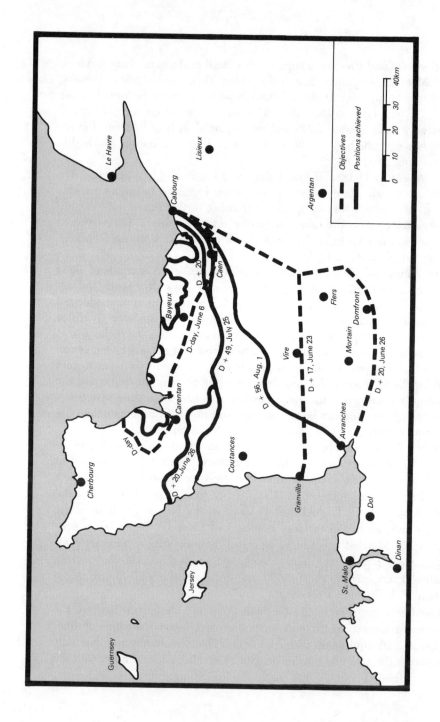

Situation until the breakthrough at Avranches. The Allies' heavy loss of time was noteworthy.

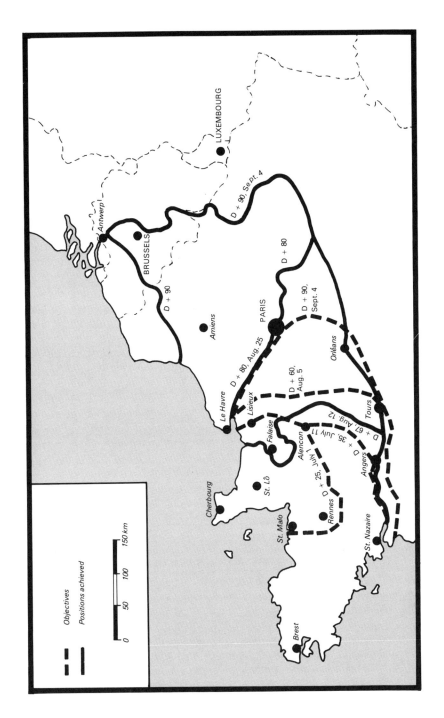

Situation after the breakthrough at Avranches, D-day + 90. The Allies make up for lost time.

to the respect he had gained for the German forces during the hard battles fought in the beachheads, and especially the stubborn resistance during the battles for Caen. The time gained by the brave troops under Rommel's leadership, however, was lost again, as was France, as a bargaining pawn for peace.

Rommel's Death

*H*itler and his attendants still refused to draw the conclusions from the hard facts. Consequently, at the armament conferences in Berlin, we worked on construction plans reaching far into the year 1946. In connection with this, I had the opportunity, in October 1944, to participate in discussions at the large engine works in Stuttgart and Augsberg.

Late in the afternoon of October 11, 1944, we had finished in Stuttgart and drove in a Mercedes fueled by wood gas via Ulm to Augsberg. The impatient driver, accustomed to more horsepower, was not on friendly terms with this economic type of engine fuel, a circumstance which, in view of the many ascending hills, was quite detrimental. The car lost power halfway up the first hill and we had to stop to refill the woodburner. Then we made tolerable progress and, without much difficulty, found Herrlingen, which is situated only a few kilometers off the Autobahn. Before we could take the last hill, the car went on strike once more. I took my suitcase and walked the rest of the way. It took the others three and a half hours to make the seventy kilometers to Augsberg.

Rommel was extraordinarily pleased to see me, much more so than I had expected. He had been concerned about us since, during the afternoon, strafers had appeared over the Autobahn, and was relieved that everything had gone well. Despite the difficulties of rationing, Frau Rommel had managed to create a festive meal around some roast venison and had set a lovely table.

245

After dinner Rommel and I retired to his study. Over a glass of champagne we talked until after midnight. He did not look as well as I had hoped he would after two months of rest. He complained about headaches and a lack of energy. Professor Esch had told me several times that it would take at least six months for a full recovery. The left eyelid was back to normal; the eyesight, however, was still worse than before.

On the whole he was in a good mood. He took it good-naturedly that effective October 15, inactive field marshals no longer had the privilege of a car and that his house lacked protective guards. I did not make notes on our talks about the situation and its development, but I remember well that he was disturbed about Speidel's recent arrest and that he told me that because of it he had written a letter to Hitler. On the whole he had few illusions. This became evident in one of his remarks, which I understood completely only several days later. He told me that the OKW had called (I believe it was Keitel) and asked him to come to Berlin for a conference. He had declined with the explanation that his physician had forbidden him to work for the time being and that he did not feel strong enough. Rommel then added: "I know that I would not arrive there alive." I took the remark as referring to his state of health and replied that I hoped it wasn't that bad. He said some distracting words and changed the subject. Unquestionably the meaning of the remark was that on his way to Berlin he would be murdered in an "accident," since Hitler could not let it come to proceedings against him.

Before breakfast the following morning (October 12) we walked up and down the terrace of the house. It was foggy at first, but then it cleared into a beautiful fall day. Since Rommel took me to Augsburg in his car, I did not need to call for the wood-burning Mercedes. An air raid alert delayed our departure. We could hear bombing not too far away. Then it was like the old days. Captain Aldinger, Rommel's aide, sat next to the driver, navigated, and watched the air situation; Rommel, in uniform and with his interim-marshal's baton, sat in the back with me. He enjoyed the opportunity to get out of Herrlingen for once. We had a good conversation during the one hour drive to Augsburg. We said goodby in front of the Augsburg–Nürnberg *Maschinenfabrik* (MAN), not knowing that it would be forever.

On October 14, I was back at Berlin. The following afternoon—it was a Sunday—I got a call from Hatzinger, whom, of course, I had told in great detail of my visit to Rommel. Completely bewildered he asked me if I had heard the news about Rommel's death on the radio. The consequences of his accident had been given as cause for his death. Deeply affected, I lay awake at night and brooded about the fate which had hit us so very hard.

The particular circumstances of Rommel's death became known to me only later. I will mention them briefly. In the morning of October 14, Generals Burgdorf and Maisel arrived at Herrlingen. The OKW had earlier announced their visit. In private, Burgdorf told him that the officers arrested after July 20 had mentioned Rommel as the army's future commander in chief, or even as the head of the state. Hitler had given him the choice to stand trial before a people's court or to take poison. Should he choose the latter, nothing would happen to his wife and son.

After this revelation, Rommel, stony-faced, went to his wife and told her: "I shall be dead in a quarter of an hour." She tried to persuade him to stand trial before a people's court, but he rejected it. He did this most likely in the conviction that he "would not arrive there alive," as he himself had said. He expected that he would be murdered on his way to Berlin possibly under the guise of an accident, since the proceedings before a people's court could not be kept secret and Hitler could not afford to have them become known to the people. To save his wife and son, whom he loved dearly, Rommel decided on the poison. After a brief farewell, he left the house and with the generals drove away in a car driven by an SS man.

Shortly afterward his dead body was taken to the military hospital at Ulm. They gave the reasons for his death as coronary sclerosis. On his face was an expression of boundless contempt.

In nauseating hypocrisy, Hitler ordered a state funeral for the murdered Field Marshal. The Navy High Command sent me as the navy's representative. During the night of October 17–18, a special train took those attending from Berlin to Ulm. Before the state ceremonies commenced at 1300, I walked with an acquaintance through the town that teemed with people. Despite all secrecy, every house displayed flags at half staff.

In the city hall I met Gause, Tempelhoff, and Aldinger. Shortly before the ceremony, four generals relieved the four young officers who had held the death watch at the coffin. Colonel Freiberg took from Captain Lang the pillow displaying Rommel's decorations. Frau Rommel arrived with her son and so did Rommel's two brothers, Baron von Neurath, State Party Leader Murr, Field Marshal Ritter von Leeb, and General Ruoff. Field Marshal von Rundstedt gave the memorial speech. Although curiously impersonal and somewhat restrained, it was a good speech to those who did not know what was played. Just how much Rundstedt knew I never found out.

I had the distinct feeling that something was wrong. After the ceremony the coffin was lifted onto a motorized gun-mount and driven through town to the crematory situated on a hill outside Ulm. The streets were lined with National Socialist Girls Associations representatives and Hitler Youth; all the people shared in the mourning. In one of the crematory's anterooms I had a chance to take Aldinger aside and, making certain that nobody heard us, asked him: "What is actually the matter here?" Tears rushed to his eyes and he said: "On Saturday they came." Then his voice broke, but I knew enough.

In the crematory's chapel, State Party Leader Murr spoke first, promising to take care of Frau Rommel and her son. The war reporter, Baron von Esebeck, followed. With his warmth and profundity, this excellent speech was finally a worthy tribute to Rommel. Esebeck also was the first who mentioned the strafing attack as the cause of Rommel's injuries. So far everybody else had carefully circumvented it. A comrade from Rommel's regiment in the First World War, who had earlier accompanied Frau Rommel, gave a fine and personal speech as well. A large number of wreaths were laid down, contrary to the instructions which allowed only Hitler's. Three salvos were fired and the music played the song of the good comrade while the coffin slowly disappeared.

Following the ceremony, Rommel's private staff assembled at a house in Herrlingen. From there we went around 1700 to Frau Rommel, where Frau Speidel was also present, to repeat our personal condolences. She invited us for a cup of coffee and we tried to console her by talking of our veneration for the Field Marshal and the good cohesion of the staff thanks to him, and by relating a number of small incidents.

On our way back to Berlin in the special train it was clear to me that with Rommel, Hitler had eliminated the only man who possessed enough respect inside Germany as well as outside to end the war. With savage cruelty, the dictator had shown how little he cared about the future of his people.

Ernst Jünger, who had been close to the men of July 20 in France and who knew Rommel through Speidel, later expressed in his book *Strahlungen* (Rays) his opinion that the Field Marshal was the only man who could have opposed Hitler with any prospect of success. In his introduction, Jünger mentions that his *Friedensschrift* (peace essay) had been read by Rommel before the latter drafted his July 15 ultimatum, and writes: "The blow that felled Rommel on the Livarot Road on July 17 deprived our plan of the only man strong enough to bear the terrible weight of war and civil war simultaneously—the only man with enough naiveté to counter the frightful simplicity of those he was to attack. It was a clear omen." And, on July 21, 1944: "Add to this Rommel's accident of July 17, which broke the only pillar that could have made such a venture feasible."

"Naive," springing from the word "nativus," in this connection has the meaning of innate candor, the clear vision for what is essential and of value, and the courage to act in accordance with one's conscience. This sounds simple, but is nevertheless very rare. Greatness is often very simple; Rommel was a great man, if the concept of human greatness is at all valid. In an unequalled way he embodied the modern general. He knew his craft of military operations superbly. This by itself does not mean very much because every officer should learn this who has a certain gift for it. But passing military exams and receiving good final examination diplomas from the military academy do not always make military leaders of quality. Certificates are only proof of a certain knowledge which requires the addition of essential talents and properties in order to make a leading personality.

Indispensable among these talents is a sense for the situation, which Rommel possessed markedly. During our inspection tours, he showed an almost uncanny ability to detect the weakest point in the sector we happened to visit. He used this talent on the enemy during the French campaign in 1940, as well as in Africa. In Normandy he urged the move of the frequently mentioned two panzer divisions, the antiaircraft corps, and the launcher brigade into those sectors where they would have been placed correctly.

In addition to a sense for the situation, Rommel had a strong feeling for the human element, a characteristic that is frequently missing or, if it can be done at all, difficult to learn. Rommel had instant rapport with the troops, faster than with many staffs. The men evidently felt that in him they had a man who understood them superbly, and who did not only think in terms of flags on a situation map. He demanded much, but never the impossible. He was especially proud that he had achieved his great military successes in Africa with a relatively small number of casualties. Once, when we discussed impossible orders given by the OKW, he said: "With my orders I have never sent anyone to his certain death."

Rommel did not belong to those commanders for whom only the best qualified officers are just good enough to serve on their staffs and as commanders, but had the ability to generate high achievements from average people. Occasionally he would get rough, but if this happened there was good reason for it. He never bore a grudge; once the thunder had passed, the air was once more clear. He understood how to express his thoughts in a clear, uncomplicated fashion to both the officers and the men.

A further essential part of his ability as a general was his comprehensive understanding of technology. This was lacking in many otherwise well-educated military leaders in both world wars, although it is indispensable in our times. He was greatly interested in all technological matters; immediately understood proposals, quickly assimilated them and often came up with improvements of his own.

He had natural dignity and knew how to act impressively when it was necessary. But he never pushed himself into the spotlight, neither during social occasions nor during discussions, and made no demands for his person. He possessed a quiet sense of humor and was an enemy of all obscenity. The picture of his personality was rounded out by a good sense for political interrelations, by a strong sense of responsibility, and by the courage to stand up for his convictions.

Rommel's thinking was logical and clear, which helped him to free himself of one-sided pictures of experience. In France and North Africa he had proven his ability for mobile warfare. Nothing would have been more natural than for him to base his plan for the defense of northwestern Europe on that particular talent. But while studying the situation in Denmark, he already realized that it differed vastly from the conditions that had existed during the times of his great successes. He knew the power of air supremacy from his own bitter experience, and he clearly saw how insufficient our resources were in some respects. Despite this, he in no way despaired, but developed a plan instead which "integrated," to use a modern expression, the very diverse resources of the different branches of the Wehrmacht and the service branches. In the meaning of the tenets of Gestalt, he created a synthesis which was much more than the sum of its single components. This ability to integrate and coordinate made him a great military leader in the fullest sense of the word, a leader who knows how to conduct in concert all instruments of battle, in contrast to the specialist whose special virtuosity prevents him from recognizing the totality of the task.

It was fatal for Rommel and for Germany that he was denied the freedom of action needed to integrate available resources as demanded by his plan. This was due to Hitler's belief in the method of "divide et impera" until the final collapse, the resulting bad organization of the command structure, the constant meddling in internal affairs by the OKW, and the lack of understanding by many agencies. Although he had only limited power of command when the storm broke, Rommel was, without doubt, the central figure in the defense of the west. He had been given the assignment and he possessed the experience and the fame. After the other commanders had presented their doubts and the OKW had decided in principle for Rommel, it could have been expected that they would have cooperated loyally with Rommel's plan. This, however, was not the case.

A comparison with the cold war situation seems pertinent. Now, too, the intentions and strengths of the aggressive enemy are no secret and there is no doubt about what would happen to us if they were to reach their objective. It is just as evident today as it was then that all forces have to be integrated to make the defense effective. But today also, individual plans are pursued and advocated regardless of their ability to fit into an overall plan, thereby giving the enemy the advantage, so that the whole must suffer damage. The individual citizen's responsibility for all is actually greater in the political sector than it is in the purely military sector, since the latter runs on a system of orders while a western style democracy does not. Because of this, an indispensable component must be the inner command, the duty to integrate one's own endeavors into what is good for the whole.

By no means should the goodwill of the individual be denied. The events in Normandy have shown, however, with alarming clarity, what happens if during the confrontation with a dangerous enemy the individual does not become an integral part of the general front and cooperate with the overall plan.

Rommel's fate was filled with deep tragedy. His unique successes in North Africa were denied the final culmination because OKW did not recognize the importance of the Mediterranean and failed to form a point of concentration there. During his duty at the Führer Headquarters in summer of 1943, Rommel had to play the part of a mute actor since Hitler did not give him the chance to be effective, evidently out of mistrust. Complaining about this treatment, Rommel once said that he would have felt capable of putting the 1943 Russian campaign on a realistic footing under the condition of complete freedom of action without any meddling from OKW and any inflexible orders to rigidly hold fast. In any case, his plans for the defense against invasion were suited to limit the initial success of the enemy severely. If they had been followed, it would be possible—with luck—to beat off the attack completely. I have the impression, without being able to prove it, that Rommel was determined after winning the invasion battle to act for peace by having Hitler arrested and put before a German court of law. Rommel never strove for absolute power, but emphasized repeatedly how he detested the dictatorship's violation of the law and his deep conviction that justice and freedom of opinion should be the basis for the state.

He was forced to fight the battle according to two diametrically opposed plans, and he did his best to delay the inevitable defeat as long as possible to gain time for reflection and political action. All the while he coolheadedly and in a superior manner played a dual role, that of the military leader who attempted with all the means at his disposal to delay the enemy for as long as possible, and that of the man who felt a responsibility to his nation and waited for the moment of liberating action. The later claim by some that he held back troops for political reasons is untrue. The events and the testimonies from Rundstedt, Blumentritt, and others unequivocally contradict such assertions. He kept an especially well-trained unit in the vicinity of his headquarters before the Invasion; afterward he emphatically used all available forces in fighting it. The battles around Caen are the best proof.

The hardest blow was his injury immediately before July 20. There can be no doubt that a Rommel in full possession of his faculties would have given a different course to the events in France and also in Germany. When he acted, he did so swiftly, deliberately and forcefully. He was the man whom the troops knew and venerated, and who knew how to communicate with them. The army in France knew of the hopeless situation on the invasion front and would have followed him on the road to peace. It was already very late for the attempt to negotiate for anything better than an unconditional surrender. It is possible, however, that the shock of the heavy losses and the prospect of a quick, great success would have persuaded the politician Churchill at least not to reject the negotiations completely. The Yalta conference was still in the future.

We do not know what would have happened. But we know that Rommel's revolt against the recklessness and barbarism which Hitler personified, no matter what the outcome would have been, would have sufficed to shake the system of tyranny severely and would have spared the German people much misery.

And finally we know that a successful Rommel would have used all his abilities for the moral and material reconstruction of Germany and Europe. Fate willed it differently. Renouncing Hitler cost Rommel his life. With his deeds and the greatest sacrifice a man can bring, he assured a place for himself among the great of his people. He has become an example, especially for the difficult situation of today, by showing ways to plan and to act, not willfully and in the clouds but soberly in accordance with reality, by integrating and employing all available faculties and means, and by acting with forethought and determination for justice and peace.

Index

Abetz, Ambassador, 162
Adinkerque, 118
Africa, 1, 37, 190–91, 196, 197, 203, 250
  anecdotes about, 50–51, 237–38
  casualties in, 238, 249
  landings in, 6, 16
  OKW and, 51, 146, 251
Agde, 75
Aigues-Mortes, 148
Air force, German. *See* Luftwaffe
Aland islands, 5
Alderney Island, 66
Aldinger, Captain, 246, 247, 248
Ameland, 166
Amiens, 141
Angers, 36, 109, 128
Antwerp, 40, 117, 121, 127
Argonzes, 224
Army, German (general), 206
  and command structure, 3, 17–18, 36–37, 43–44, 124, 204, 208, 214, 218
  responsibilities of, 35–36
    See also Panzer operations

Arromanches, 174
Aschmann, Captain, 132
Atlantic Wall, 33–34, 126, 203
Aubagne, 150
Auberville, 79
Augsberg, 245, 246
Aulock, Colonel, 95
Ault, 130–31, 168
Avignon, 74, 151
Avranches, 240, 243

Badoglio, Pietro, 1
Bagnoles-sur-Orne, 97
Bamler, General, 221
Bastico, General, 146
Beachhead, defined, 16
Beauvais, 127, 152
Behr, Major, 102, 157, 168, 229
Belgian gates, 71
Belgium, 3, 25, 26, 88, 113–14, 132
Belle-Ile-en-Terre, 94
Benodet, 110–11
Berchtesgaden, 108, 191, 202, 204, 222
Berck-sur-Mer, 58

Bergelt, Captain, 110
Berlin, 7–8, 243, 245, 246
Bernay, 229, 230, 233
Bernd, Assistant Secretary, 168
Best, Reichs Commissioner Dr., 14
Biarritz, 146
Bir Hacheim, 227
Bir Temrad, 51
Bismarck, 30
Bittrich, General, 233
Blanc, Commander von, 110–11
Blaskowitz, General, 28, 43, 75–76,
    146, 152, 154, 155
Blumentritt, General, 70, 72, 91,
    164, 197
  on inspection trips, 79, 80, 82
  and panzer operations, 82, 121,
    126, 128
  Sauckel and, 53
  as Stülpnagel replacement, 232
  and women civilians, 135
Bolbec, 55, 104, 136–37, 214
Boltenstern, General von, 62
Boulogne, 38, 58, 86, 101–2, 131,
    188
Breda, 117
Breskens, 132
Brest, 27, 36, 58, 80, 81, 111, 127
Breuning, Rear Admiral, 29
Bristol, 162
Brügge, 41
"Brüsseler Zeitung," 141
Brussels, 88, 113–14
Buhle, General, 167
Buoys, explosive, 22
Burgdorf, General, 247
Burrough, Admiral, 176
Busch, Field Marshal, 204
Buxtehude, 87–88

Cabourg, 54, 139, 191
Cadzant, 40

Caen, 66, 93, 120, 155, 224–25, 231
  battles at, 185, 199–215, 225, 229,
    230, 232, 237, 243, 244, 252
  OKW and, 181, 218
Calais, 58, 71, 100–1, 118, 157
Camargue, 74
Carentan, 156, 158, 183, 184, 185
Carpiquet, 208
Cayeux-sur-Mer, 57, 160
Cézembre, 61
Chalon- sur-Saône, 151
Channel Islands, 65, 66, 156, 201,
    238
Cherbourg, 26, 58, 68, 174, 212
  batteries for, 35, 156
  battle at, 181–97, 199, 200, 201,
    202, 206, 222
  Hitler and, 153, 188, 189
  mines off, 69, 152
  war diary from, 197, 219
China, 6
Christiansen, General, 115
Churchill, Winston, xiii, 252
Coburg, Prince Josias von, 49, 112
Commander in chief approach, 124,
    204
Concarneau, 40
Concrete, reinforced, 106–7, 122
Cotentin Peninsula, 26, 28, 66, 152,
    153, 155
  battles on, 174, 181–97, 199, 200,
    201, 202, 206, 222, 238
  inspections of, 68, 93, 96–97, 156,
    159, 162–63
Courselles, 159
Crécy, 159
Crimea, 129, 209
Cross Channel Attack (U.S. Army),
    xiii, 178
Cuxhaven, 9, 88
Czech hedgehogs, 13–14, 70, 101–2,
    150–51

Daniel (Rommel's driver), 229, 231, 233
Danzig, Bay of, 3
Dardanelles, 5
Das Reich, 208
Deauville, 54
De Beer, 117
Den Helder, 86, 115
Denmark, 11–23, 70, 127, 250
Diem, General, 112, 152, 167, 210
Dieppe, 6, 17, 56, 126, 168
Diestel, Major General, 104
Dietl, General, 202
Dietrich, Lieutenant General Sepp, 168, 173, 182, 186, 192, 233
Dinard, 94
Dollmann, General, 59, 63, 76, 82, 163, 188
    death of, 201, 204
Dönitz, Grand Admiral Karl, 81, 90–91, 152, 159, 221
Dordrecht, 117
Douarnenez, Bay of, 81, 111
Dozulé, 224
Dunkirk, 30, 58, 131, 147
Duropane, 2, 72

Eberbach, General, 203, 205, 233
Eighty-fivers, 3
Eisenhower, General Dwight D., xiii, 176, 177, 204
El Alamein, 16, 197, 203, 238
Elboeuf, 195, 210, 213
Ellfeldt, Major General, 71, 239
El Mechili, 51
"Elsass," 207
Engel, Rear Admiral, 87
English Channel Islands, 65, 66, 156, 201, 238
Erigné, 109–10
Ertel (war correspondent), 130
Esbjerg, 12, 13, 14
Esch, Professor, 234, 239, 240, 246

Esebeck, Baron von, 130, 248
Etretat, 103, 215
Evry, 90

Falaise, 158, 164, 243
Falkenhausen, General von, 114
Falley, Major General, 162
Fanö, 13
Farnbacher, General, 79, 127, 188
Fécamp, 55, 138
Feldherr Psychologos (Hesse), 50
Feuchtinger, General, 158, 225
Finland, 5
Flanders, 5
Fontainebleau, 25, 47, 48–51, 99
Food
    during Invasion, 213, 215, 219
    Rommel and, 31, 49, 213, 219
Förste, Admiral, 86, 87, 114, 115
Fort de la Roule, 68
Fougères, 96
Frederikshavn, 14
Freiberg, Colonel, 49, 135, 220, 231, 247
Frethune, 157
Friedel, Major, 130
Friedrichshafen, 103–4
Frisius, Rear Admiral, 30, 71, 118, 147
Führer Directive 40, 34–35, 36, 124
Führer Directive 51, 4, 7, 90
Funk, Baron von, 186

Gaillon, 167
Ganzenmüller, State Secretary, 153, 166
Gause, Major General, 2, 4, 7, 59, 121
    in Africa, 50–51, 133
    and Geyer, 63
    on inspection trips, 12, 37, 79, 80, 82, 88, 92, 94, 120
    in Italy, 2, 72

and panzer operations, 91, 109,
  119, 127, 233
  at Rommel's funeral, 247
  at table, 49, 50–51
  telephone arrangements by, 90,
    105, 122, 128
  transfer of, 129, 130, 133–34, 190
Gehrcke, General, 47, 49, 152
Gersdorf, Colonel von, 239
Geyer, General H., 63–64, 120
Geyr von Schweppenburg, General,
    28, 155, 173, 180, 182
  article by, 179
  bombing of headquarters of, 174,
    182
  replacement of, 203
  with Rommel, 44, 64, 105, 126,
    184, 190
  with Speidel, 143
Gilsa, General Baron von, 40, 132
Gironde, 76
Gneisenau, 30
Gone with the Wind, 193, 197
Göring, Hermann, 50, 126, 184, 191,
    218
  and Luftwaffe, 33, 175, 237
Goslar Jägers, 48, 140
Goulven, Bay of, 81
Grab obstacles, 175
Grandcamp, 156
Greif, Lieutenant Colonel, 187
Grube, Rear Admiral Engineer, 189
Guderian, General H., 78, 79,
    143–44, 168, 179, 200, 202
Guernsey, 156
Guingamp, 60, 111–12
Gümbel, Major General, 54
Gumprich, Captain, 39

Habicht, Brigadier General, 107–8,
    219
Hammermann, First Lieutenant, 49,
    51

Hannecken, General von, 11, 14
Hanstholm, 14, 21–22
Hardelot-Plage, 57, 70
Hart, Liddell, 180
Hatzinger, Leading Seaman, 41, 69,
    109, 230–31, 243, 246
Hausser, Lieutenant General, 68,
    190, 201, 223, 238
Heckel, Colonel, 168
Heim, Fleet Surgeon Dr., 108, 186
Helgoland Bight, 8–9, 86, 88
Hennecke, Rear Admiral, 67, 68–69,
    156, 188
Herrlingen, 23, 243, 245–46, 247, 248
Hesse, Colonel, 50
Hilfsvölker, 49
Hitler, Adolf, 92, 168, 172, 196, 202,
    222, 245
  and Africa, 203, 237–38
  and American breakthrough, 243
  and Atlantic Wall, 126
  attempts to kill, 232, 243
  birthday of, 133
  and Cherbourg, 153, 188, 189
  and equipment, 128, 161, 169, 175
  and Italy, 148
  on landing possibilities, 26, 27, 142
  and panzer operations, 44–45, 109,
    119, 128, 172, 173, 179, 180
  and parachute divisions, 142, 210
  PAV on, 143, 190
  replacements by, 129, 183, 201,
    203–4
  Rommel with, 108–9, 172, 189–90,
    197, 202, 203, 204, 251
  and Rommel's death, 246, 247, 248,
    251, 252–53
  and Rommel's quarters, 47
  and Rommel's wounding, 234, 236
  trip of, during Invasion, 191
Hitler salute, 235
Hitler Youth, 32, 119, 159, 184, 218
Hoffmann, Rear Admiral, 72

Höffner, Colonel, 70
Holland (general), 3, 25, 26, 58,
　114–18
Homeyer, Lieutenant Commander
　and Seine transport, 188, 192, 193,
　195, 210, 214, 219, 230
Honfleur, 54, 139
Hook of Holland, 58, 116
Horses, 213, 228
Horst, Dr., 171
Hospitals, military, 227–28
Hoth, General, 239
Houlgate, 155
Hoyer, Mr., 106–7, 134
Hube, General, 137, 140
Hunting, 48–49, 140
Hyères, 151

IJmuiden, 58, 115–16, 117
Infanterie greift an (Rommel), 50, 82
Ingersoll, Ralph, 215
Invasion 1944 (Speidel), xiii, 173
"Irish Defence," 179
Isigny, 156
Italy, 3–4, 15, 45–46, 72, 125, 147
　Allied landings in, 1–2, 4, 6, 60
　Hitler and, 148
　reconstruction in, 209
　Rommel in, 1–2, 4, 7

Jakob, General, 100, 167
Jamin, Major, 231
Japanese, 6
Jersey, 156
Jobourg Peninsula, 200, 201, 202,
　203
Jodl, General Alfred, 45, 77, 159,
　201, 218, 242
　and panzer operations, 58, 119
　staff of, 72, 119, 191
Jünger, Ernst, 50, 171, 172, 194, 248
Jutland, 12, 14, 19–21, 22
Jüttner, SS Lieutenant General, 146

Kähler, Rear Admiral, 111
Kaliebe, General, 148
Kanzler, General, 135
Kaufmann, State Party Leader, 164,
　166
Keil, Lieutenant Colonel, 201, 202
Keitel, General Wilhelm, 191, 222,
　228, 246
Kesselring, Field Marshal Albert,
　1–2, 148, 227
Kharkov, 197
Kleikamp, Vice Admiral, 47, 86, 91,
　114, 115, 117
Kleist, Field Marshal Ewald von, 129
Kloess, Lieutenant Commander, 85
Kluge, Field Marshal von, 218, 234,
　237, 238, 239, 241
　at front, 231, 239, 240, 243
　and Hitler, 232, 241, 243
　La Roche-Guyon move of, 230
　Rommel with, 205, 206, 207, 210,
　219, 221
Koch, Lutz, 130, 165
Königsberg, 237
Krähe, Colonel, 49
Kramer, Major General, 169
Krancke, Admiral, 29, 72, 152, 237
　defense ideas of, 38, 142–43,
　161–62, 189, 194
　with Rommel, 38, 90, 120, 155,
　187
Kranzbühler, 240
Kronborg Castle, 15
KTB *(Kriegstagebuch der
　Heeresgruppe B)*, xiv, 28–29,
　44–45, 77, 127, 128, 133
　on artillery, 54, 77
　battle notes in, 182-227 *passim*
　and Belgian defenses, 41
　and Boulogne, 101, 102
　and Caen sector, 66, 185, 200,
　203, 205, 210, 211, 212, 213
　and Cherbourg, 152, 153, 156, 191,

192, 193, 194, 197, 200, 201, 202
and command structure, 44, 77, 168, 208
and Denmark troops, 20
and foreshore barriers, 120
and Jobourg Peninsula, 200, 201, 202, 203
and Kuntzen's corps, 102-3
on La Cité, 61
on landing conditions, 32, 66
and Luftwaffe, 101, 152
and Nantes, 128
and navy, 34–35, 101, 152
and Netherlands defenses, 65, 114, 130, 141, 152, 154
and panzer operations, 32, 59, 78, 80, 82, 91, 119, 121, 134, 197, 208, 212, 217
and Saint-Lô area, 189, 202, 203, 205, 213, 219, 223
and Seine transport, 212
and Sète, 148
and women civilians, 135
Kuntzen, General, 54, 102, 120, 207, 214, 235

La Baule, 110, 128
La Cité, 61
Landing methods, 5–6, 13–14, 15–17
Lang, Captain, 49, 112, 187, 203, 206, 229, 247
Langemarck, 21
La Roche-Guyon, 79, 99–100, 133, 212, 236
La Rochelle, 59, 76, 147
Lattmann, Colonel, 49, 113, 157, 167, 193, 212, 228
Lautenschlager, Captain R., 76
Leeb, Ritter von, 168, 247
Le Havre, 58, 207, 209, 213, 215
    air attacks on, 129, 136, 186, 188, 189, 204

batteries for, 35, 55, 103, 136, 171
    shipyards at, 85–86
Le Mans, 59, 62–63
Leningrad, 22
Leutze, General, 103
Le Vésinet, 234, 235
Ley, Doctor Robert, 222, 235
Lightning barriers, 142–43
Lisieux, 228, 229, 234
List, Colonel, 171, 172
Lorient, 58, 80, 127
Louviers, 234
Ludendorff, General Erich, 63
Luftwaffe (general)
    and command structure, 3, 17–18, 101, 121, 200, 218
    weakness of, 16, 143, 152, 175, 187, 195, 208

MacArthur, General Douglas, 124, 204
Macholtz, General, 160
Maisel, General, 247
Manstein, Field Marshal von, 129
Mantes, 141, 152, 153, 167, 230
Marcks, General, 65, 67, 93, 120, 155–56, 157, 173
    death of, 184, 188
    on landing possibilities, 66, 156
Marcouf, 67, 157
Meindl, General, 163, 188, 211, 212
Meise, Major General, 47, 49, 56, 59, 63, 90
    on inspection trips, 70, 71, 73, 79, 81, 92, 102, 113, 152, 167
    at La Roche-Guyon, 130, 140, 165, 184, 203
    transfer of, 237
Mericourt lock, 230–31
Michahelles, Admiral, 76, 146, 147
Michel, Assistant Secretary, 165, 240
Mine Research Command, 20
Mines

coastal A, 20, 29, 95, 172, 175, 176
flat land, 70, 92, 95, 128–29
ground, 38, 176
with lead cap fuse, 69
nutcracker, 129, 134, 160
offshore, 127
surface A, 95
timed, 38–39
Westwall, 19–20
Mirow, Rear Admiral, 110
Monet, Claude, 202
Mont Canisy, 139
Monte Matajur, 236
Montgomery, General Bernard Law,
xiii, 197, 199, 203, 215, 223
Montpellier, 148
Montreuil, 31, 160
Mont-Saint-Michel, 62, 68, 94, 95–96
Monts d'Arrée, 82
Morgat, 81
Morsalines, 157
Mountbatten, Admiral Louis, 204
Murr, State Party Leader, 247, 248
Mussolini, Benito, 1, 148

Nantes, 59, 128, 145
National Socialist Political Officer
(NSFO), 50, 200, 202
Navy, German (general)
and command structure, 2–3,
17–18, 36–37, 86, 105–6, 204,
208, 214, 237
responsibilities of, 35, 36, 89–90
Ruge position in, 2, 106, 142, 152,
162, 231
Netherlands (general), 3, 25, 26, 58,
114–18
Nettuno, 60, 125
Neuhaus, Major, 229, 242
Neumann, Major General, 41
Neurath, Baron Constantin von, 183,
247

Nimitz, Admiral Chester William,
204
Norway, 6
Nostang, 39–40
Notholt, Reserve Lieutenant
Commander, 40
NSFO (National Socialist Political
Officer), 50, 200, 202

Oberg, General, 234
Obstfelder, General, 190
Octeville, 126–27
Oesel, 5, 6
OKM (Oberkommando der
Kriegsmarine), 23, 106
OKW (Oberkommando der
Wehrmacht), 2, 47, 85, 96, 177,
190, 249
and Africa, 51, 146, 251
and army responsibilities, 35–36
and Atlantic Wall, 126, 203
attack expectations of, 25, 26, 34,
44–45, 65, 100, 125, 153,
157–58, 183, 191, 209, 229
and battery supplies, 39, 113, 163,
220
and Caen area, 181, 211–12, 218
and Cherbourg, 184, 186–87, 193,
195, 197
and command structure, 43–44, 53,
119, 121, 124, 155, 221, 251–52
and Denmark, 15, 23
and Geyr, 203
and Holland, 86, 119, 126
naval officers in, 3
and panzer operations, 63, 80, 82,
91, 119, 124, 126, 134, 153, 155,
172, 173, 195, 205
and political solutions, 223
and power ratio, 16, 21, 148, 218
and Rommel's death, 246, 247
and Rommel's headquarters, 99
and Russia, 113, 195, 197, 205

and Saint-Lô, 206
and Saint-Malo, 201
and telephone use, 123–24, 161
Olshausen, Lieutenant Colonel, 49,
    200
Operation Neptune, 14, 175, 176, 179
Oppeln-Bronikowski, Colonel von,
    158, 173
Organisation Todt, 11, 115, 223
    work of, 81, 93, 126, 156, 158, 162
Ostbourg, 41
Ostende, 5, 58
Ostkämpfer, 105

Panzer operations, 32–33, 44, 62,
    177–80, 182, 196, 217
    in Africa, 16
    in Caen sector, 173, 178, 199–200,
    202, 208, 209, 210, 211, 212,
    225–26, 229
    and Denmark, 15
    Guderian and, 78, 144, 179
    Hitler and, 44–45, 109, 119, 128,
    172, 173, 179, 180
    OKW and, 63, 80, 82, 91, 119,
    124, 126, 134, 153, 155, 172,
    173, 195, 205
    in Saint-Lô area, 202, 213
    transfers of, 58–59, 63, 109, 121,
    126, 134, 172–74, 229
Paris
    navy command in, 29, 36, 208,
    219, 237
    Sicherheitsdienst arrested in, 232
PAV *(persönliche Aufzeichnungen des
    Verfassers)*, xiv
    battle notes in, 172, 181, 188, 193,
    194, 242
    on command structure, 191–92,
    220
    on dinner companions, 237
    on Dollmann, 82
    on Hitler, 143, 190

on Kluge, 239
on La Cité, 61
on navy, 190
on panzer operations, 142
on political solutions, 218, 222
on Rommel, 132, 138, 220
Peltz, General, 88
Pemsel, Brigadier General, 59, 62–63
Perpignan, 147
Petain, Marshal Philippe, 80, 163,
    164
Peters, Captain, 40, 88, 109
    at headquarters, 120, 122, 128,
    133, 142, 164
    in Paris, 88, 135, 143
Petersen, Lieutenant General, 74,
    147
Pfeiffer, Consul-General, 171, 172
Pickert, General, 166
Podewils (war correspondent), 130
Poland, 3
Polenz, Lieutenant Commander, 150
Politics
    Rommel and, 114, 138, 182,
    183–84, 199, 221–22, 227
    and war solution, 114, 182, 183–84,
    191, 199, 218, 221–22, 223, 227,
    232
Pompadour, Madame Jeanne, 25
Pontoise, 208
Port Louis, 80–81
Port-Vendres, 147
Pour la Mérite, Rommel's, 104, 235
Prater, Lieutenant, 192
Priller, Lieutenant Colonel, 41
Protvillez lock, 223

Queissner, Lieutenant Colonel, 37,
    49, 72
Quiberon, 80, 128
Quineville, 67
Quintin, 163

Raeder, Grand Admiral Erich, 22, 147
Rays (Jünger), 248
Reichert, Major General, 54, 92, 139
Reinhardt, Major General, 114, 117
Reischauer, Lieutenant, 72
Rennes, 62, 142, 144
"Report of the Defense Readiness of the Artois," 39
Rheinmetall, 158
Ribbentrop, Joachim von, 183
Richter, Major General, 92
Rieve, Vice Admiral, 29, 55, 106, 207, 240
  in La Roche-Guyon, 165, 242
  in Rouen, 29, 135–36, 191, 214, 235
Riva Bella, 93, 156, 167
Rodin, Auguste, 50
Rommel, Field Marshal Erwin (personal), 4, 7, 49–51, 124, 139–40, 141–42
  death of, 246–47
  and food, 31, 49, 213, 219
  in Friedrichshafen, 103–4
  greatness of, 50, 122–23, 249
  at home, 245–46, 247
  and human life, 51, 249
  military brilliance of, 51, 249–50
  and politics, 114, 138, 182, 183–84, 199, 221–22, 227
  school years of, 226
  staff relations of, 50, 51, 250
  on suicide, 196, 207
  wounded, 229, 233, 234, 235, 236–38, 239–40, 241–43, 246, 249
Rommel, Frau, 245, 247, 248
Roosevelt, Franklin D., 232
Rösing, Captain, 76–77
Ross, Colin, 74, 240
Rotterdam, 116
Rouen, 36, 86, 120, 206

Rieve in, 29, 135–36, 191, 214, 235
Royan, 76, 146, 147
Rundstedt, Field Marshal Karl von, 77, 80, 164–65, 185, 187
  and command structure, 43–44, 77, 200, 221
  dismissal of, 204, 205, 209
  on landing possibilities, 27
  and panzer operations, 32, 91, 127
  Rommel with, 25, 37, 45, 120, 155, 164–65, 169, 183, 189, 197, 222
  at Rommel's funeral, 247–48
Ruoff, General, 247
Russia, 1, 45–46, 197, 203, 221–22
  and Americans, 183, 194–95
  Behr in, 102
  Geyer in, 63
  Marcks in, 65
  OKW and, 113, 195, 197, 205
  panzer operations in, 44, 174
  Rommel's opinions on, 183, 213, 221–22, 235, 236, 251–52
  Speidel in, 130
Rust, Minister of Education, 71

Saint-Adresse, 55
Saint-Lô, 68
  battle over, 189, 202, 203, 205, 206, 213, 219, 223, 228, 229, 230, 231
  Marcks at, 67, 157
Saint-Lunaire, 61
Saint-Malo, 58, 61, 63, 95, 111–12, 201, 228–29
Saint-Nazaire, 6, 36, 58, 79–80, 120, 128, 229
Saint-Pierre-du-Vauvray, 210
Saint-Vaast, 68
Saint-Valéry-en-Caux, 55–56, 138
Salmuth, General von
  and panzer divisions, 32
  with Rommel, 29, 41, 57, 71, 133, 160, 165

Sangatte, 157

"Sarah," 132

Sauckel, State Party Leader Fritz, 53, 97, 115, 218

Scharnhorst, 30

Schelde
  Allies and, 27–28, 124–25, 129, 162
  defenses at, 40, 117
  OKW and, 25, 124–25

Scheunig, Dr., 229

Scheveningen, 116

Schiermonnikoog, 166

Schirach, Baldur von, 71

Schirlitz, Vice-Admiral, 59, 109–10, 147

Schlieben, General von, 192, 222

Schmundt, Major General, 90, 207

Schneckenburger, Lieutenant, 57

Schneider, General, 168

Schramm, Ritter von, 171

Schuerlen, Vice-Admiral, 8–9

Schulte-Mönting, Rear Admiral, 147, 148

Sealion, Operation, 3, 6, 26, 34, 99

Seams, 36

Sebastopol, 209

Seiffert, Major General, 131

Seine, 30, 102, 105, 175
  landing possibilities in Bay of, 26, 27–28, 38, 66, 129
  mining of Bay of, 27–28, 29, 120–21, 129, 143, 174, 177
  transport on, 188, 192, 193, 195, 209, 210–11, 212, 213–14, 219, 223, 230

Sengwarden, 86

Sète, 75, 147

Sicherheitsdienst (SS Security Service), 127, 130, 165, 232
  Rommel on, 184, 196, 222

Sicily, 2, 4, 6

Silkeborg, 11

Sinnhuber, General, 70, 130–31, 161

Skagen, 14

Skagerrak, 19, 21–22, 23

Snag-line, 20

Sodenstern, General von, 43, 74, 151

Soissons, 189

Somme
  defenses of, 29, 159, 184
  landing possibilities on, 25, 27, 124, 125, 129

Sörensen, Captain, 163

Southwick Park, 176–77

Speidel, Major General Dr. Hans, 133, 154, 161, 187, 205, 240, 242
  arrest of, 246
  and attack (first), 169, 172
  background of, 129–30
  and British prisoners, 165
  conferences of, 141, 143, 152, 211, 218, 239
  and Hitler, 182, 189, 190, 202, 204, 217–18, 232
  on inspection trips, 131, 213–15
  Invasion 1944, xiii, 173
  and Jünger, 171, 172, 194, 248
  and Kluge's eating companions, 231
  and La Roche-Guyon owners, 212
  leisure with, 171–72, 182, 186, 192, 194, 202, 228, 241, 242
  and political solutions, 214, 223
  and Rommel wounded, 229, 230, 233, 235, 241

Sperrle, Field Marshal Hugo, 37, 77, 143, 155, 195

SS, 12th division. *See* Hitler Youth

SS Security Service. *See Sicherheitsdienst*

Stahlegwitter (Jünger), 50

Stalingrad, 15, 237

Staubwasser, Lieutenant Colonel, 49, 202

Stolberg-Stolberg, Brigadier General Count, 61

Stöphasius, Captain, 86
Strahlungen (Jünger), 248
Strand, 180
Straube, General, 60, 94, 111, 127
Struggle for Europe (Wilmot), 14
Student, Lieutenant General, 166
Stukas, 15, 227
Stülpnagel, General von, 43, 152, 211, 232, 234, 235, 236
Stuttgart, 245

TBR *(Tagesberichte Rommels)*, xiv
  on attacks, 157, 169, 192
  on Dollmann, 76
  and Ganzenmüller, 153
  and Hitler, 169
  on inspections, 67, 93, 116, 131, 132, 155
  on Jodl, 45
  on landing possibilities, 26, 155, 169
  on Netherlands, 91, 116
  on panzer operations, 63, 64, 126
Telephone use, 123, 161, 223–24
Tempelhoff, Colonel von, 59, 133, 202
  and Caen sector, 220
  and Hitler Youth, 218
  and Kluge's visit, 219
  to Netherlands, 113
  promotion of, 168
  with Rommel, 37, 49, 90, 108, 113, 121, 218
  at Rommel's funeral, 247
Thomale, General, 200
Tigerfibel (Guderian), 78, 144
Tilly-sur-Seulles, 185, 191, 194, 197, 213
Tirpitz, 30
Tobruk, 50, 51, 197
Top Secret (Ingersoll), 215
Toulon, 72
Tourcoing, 32, 41, 71

Tourlaville, 69
Tours, 127
Treport, 57, 125
Tresckow, Rear Admiral von, 55, 85, 103, 215
Trouville-sur-Mer, 54
Tunisia, 4, 15, 181
Turkish, 207
Turrets, 19, 107–8, 122

U-boats, 1, 35, 163, 221, 237
  capability of, 23, 29, 76–77, 194, 208–9, 230
Ulm, 247
Utah, 28
Utrecht, 86, 114

Val André, 95, 163
Vernon, 153, 167
Villa Mond, 94, 95
Vlissingen, 58, 132
Volksliste, 3, 9
Voss, Rear Admiral, 72

Wagner, General, 59, 159
Wahle, General, 116
Walcheren, 40–41, 129
Wandervogel (German Youth Association), 184
War correspondents, 130
Warlimont, Lieutenant General, 44, 72, 80, 82, 91, 119, 242
Weapons au surprise, 192
Weather service, 176–77
Wehrmacht. *See* Army, German; Luftwaffe; Navy, German; OKW
Westwall, 19
Wetzel, Captain, 69
Wever, Vice Admiral, 72, 150
Willesen, Herr, 166, 208
William the Conqueror, 54
Wilmot, Chester, xiii, 14
Wimmer, General, 100, 115

266

Winter, Rear Admiral, 47–48
Wolff, Lieutenant General, 11
Wühlisch, General Reinhard, 91
Wurmbach, Admiral, 11, 70

Youth Movement, 71

Yport, 103

Zeebrügge, 5, 129
Ziervogel, Lieutenant Colonel, 191